Magick for the Elemental Witch

Magick for the Elemental Witch

from the
Copper Cauldron Series

Deanna Anderson

an imprint of Andborough Publishing, LLC

New Gaia Press
www.NewGaia.com
760991 San Antonio, TX 78245
USA

Magick for the Elemental Witch
Copyright© 2010 Deanna Anderson
First printing August 2010

ISBN -978-0-9823971-8-3

All Rights Reserved: Except for fair use in book reviews, no part of this publication may be reproduced or transmitted in any form or by any means, electronic or mechanical, including photocopying, recording, or any information storage and retrieval system or technologies now known or later developed or invented, without permission in writing from the publisher.

Disclaimer and/or Legal Notices: While all attempts have been made to verify information in this publication, the publisher does not assume any responsibility for errors, inaccuracies or omissions.

This publication is not intended for use as a source of legal or medical advice. The purchaser or reader of this publication assumes responsibility for the use of these materials the information herein. The author and publisher assumes no responsibility or liability whatsoever on the behalf of the purchaser or reader.

New Gaia Press is an imprint of Andborough Publishing, LLC
www.Andborough.com

Printed in the United States of America

Dedication

To Cat and Maya: one for being my muse and the other for being my self-appointed book promoter, respectively. I wouldn't be where I am at without the support of both of you, although I suspect you do it for the free books (just kidding). As always, this book goes out to my family: my mom, Del; my husband, Bill; and my daughters Kalista and Shanna and to my brother Dave who gives me great religious and spiritual sparring sessions; and also my niece Danielle who shares similar beliefs. Jenn, you know every book I write will be dedicated to you but I don't want to make you cry like in the last dedication, so just remember "catch ya on the flip side." I also want to thank Gaia's Wisdom Coven and its leaders, Mike and Stephanie, for helping me to further my studies and to all of the members who never complain about my shameless self-promotions or for using my book as a reference in class.

I also want to thank my new-found friend G.L. Giles for all of her support as a fellow author.

content

Dedication	v
Forward	viii
The Four Classic Elements	1
Magick for the Earth Witch	30
Magick for thr Sea Witch	90
Magick for the Air Witch	146
Magick for the Fire Witch	189
Magick for the Spiritist Witch	239
The Author	294
Bibliography	295

Forward

When I sat down to write a second book for the Copper Cauldron series I knew wanted it to focus on the elements to give people a wider sense of what they are and how they can be used in both mundane and magickal lives. This book started off as "Magick for the Sea Witch" with the idea that I would write four separate books, one for each of the elements. But then it would have been a "series within a series" and I wasn't sure I wanted to do that. After debating on just how to do a book of the elements I finally realized that since all of them work together in ritual they could all work together in a book. Therefore, a book about sea witchery became a book about elemental witchery.

I also tossed around the title quite a bit and asked a few friends for some advice on what the title should be. My working title was "elemental witch" but I didn't know if that accurately captured what I was trying to convey or not. After many months of speculation I finally decided to stop fretting over it and looked up the meaning of "elemental" in the dictionary: 1) basic and essential, 2) relating to or caused by powerful natural forces, and 3) relating to the elements of earth, air, fire and water that were once thought to be the basic units of matter (dictionary.com). Based on those definitions, yes, "Magick for the Elemental Witch" is exactly what I want to say.

The spells in each section are focused primarily on that element or have that element as a primary focus or "ingredient." If attempting to write spells remember to predominantly use whatever element fits with that intent. For example, money or job would be earth (materialistic) and love would be air or water (free-flowing, uninhibited).

If using anything from this book, like with all magick, take what works and use it in a way that fits with personal practices or beliefs. If feeling more drawn to earth magick and want to practice more exclusively with earth components or correspondence, so be it, just remember that power and energy increases when all the elements are present. In fact, when calling quarters, it is essential to call all of the elements so it is useful to become familiar with the attributes and correspondences of each one. Also, keep in mind, that this is a reference book to aid readers in understanding the elements. Many components in it are just brief references, such as gemstones or fairy magick, and if interested in any of the things mentioned I suggest doing further research with books or internet sites to get various viewpoints and additional information.

Before we begin, let me clear up a few definitions of words or terms that I have come across that are important. I want no misconceptions about what the message or meaning is that is being implied with these terms when I use them.

Ceremonial Magick: I kept coming up with this phrase a lot, both on the internet and in reference books. In Wikipedia articles it was identified separately from Wicca, even though Wiccans do ceremonial magick. According to its definition, Ceremonial Magick is "a broad term used to encompass a wide variety of long, elaborate, and complex magical rituals." So, it is a broad term encompassing many different paths. It is often seen as an extension of ritualistic magick and generally synonymous with the Hermetic Order of the Golden Dawn, which was a basis for Wicca. Throughout the text you may see references to Ceremonial Magick and to Wicca both. I do this to show the similarities and differences between the two, I also do this with other cultures and religions as well. However, it will be noted that Wicca is mentioned more than other pagan paths. This is for three reasons: 1) Wicca is the fastest growing pagan religion, one of the more organized of the pagan paths, and is recognized by the US government as a religion; 2) I started my path based on Wicca, as perhaps many others have, before branching off; 3) it is one of the most common of the pagan religions.

Neo-Pagan/Pagan: I might use these terms interchangeably, because to me they mean the same thing. Neo-pagan means 'new-pagan' and even though our paths or beliefs are based on ancient or even archaic paths and belief systems, we are all new-pagans in the sense that we are new to practicing it either as an individual or as a society. Neo-pagan is not meant in disrespect or to mean that a person is a 'newbie' or a 'fluffy bunny' (those who think magick is like Hollywood magick) or of any less value in the pagan world. To me it simply separates pagans today from pagans of the past.

Mythology/Folklore: It has always bothered me that ancient paths, beliefs and polytheism are referred to as 'mythology' and monotheistic faiths are theology. One implies it is a false tale and one implies it is truth. However, the word folklore can mean both legends and traditional stories or customs that have been passed down through the generations in a community, and this is the sense in which I use the term. In no way do I try to imply that anything labeled as folklore is false or any less valid then pretentious religious texts. Mythology is the study of myths which identifies a group of stories belonging to a society or culture that talk about their ancestors, heroes, gods, history and other supernatural beings. Like folklore, this definition does not imply the stories are false. In the book 'Christo-paganism' by Joyce and River Higginbotham there is an excellent explanation that says "pagans use the word 'mythology' to refer to the religious story that informs and guides a faith's tradition. While some may use this word to mean fictional, superstitious or silly, pagans do not."

Pentagram/Pentacle: These words both can convey different meanings to people depending on who is hearing it and who is saying it. A pentagram if often associated with the Devil or evil by non-pagans, and because of this misnomer many pagans have gotten away from using the term, preferring instead the word pentacle. Some say that a pentagram is the star and the pentacle has the circle around it or even that a pentagram is the star with the point down and pentacle is the point up (this is an error since the point down is known as an inverted pentagram). In reality, neither word implies that there is a circle around the star or which way the point goes. Pentagram means a five-pointed shape much like a pentagon is a five-sided shape and pentacle is a synonym for pentagram. I use pentagram and pentacle interchangeably; to me they mean the same thing.

Superstition: Often what we refer to as superstitions are really just little snippets of bygone magick. They were people's ways of making sense of their world and attempting to control it. Many of the superstitions do not really have any scientific or metaphysical logic behind them, but there are just as many that do have basis in reality and can be used in magick or daily life. Weather, herbal lore and home remedies are the most common that hold scientific or metaphysical merit and that can still be used today. To rephrase the common cliché "one's mans trash is another man's treasure" we can say that "one man's superstitions are another man's beliefs."

In this book, and in my previous one "Magick for the Kitchen Witch," my readers will have noticed a fair amount of Islamic, Jewish, Catholic or Christian references. This might be disturbing to some who consider themselves strictly on a pagan path, but it shouldn't cause alarm. These monotheistic religions make their way into my writings for a few reasons: 1) many people are combining both Christianity and Paganism into a belief system known as Christo-Pagan. I am still leaning how it works but I do know a few ladies who make it work very well; 2) many people are coming to paganism from a Christian background and I hope this eases the transition; 3) The more I research religions the more I discover they have a lot of similarities. Sure, there are vast differences but there are also enough similarities that I like to showcase them in the hopes that people will realize we're not all so very different.

I am forming a belief that all religions came from one central point at the beginning of creation and the first hominids. Pre-historic people did not have a concept of gods or magick like we do today, but they probably held reverence for the basic survival items; they probably had the first concept of earth, air, fire and water but didn't realize it. Early man's survival existed only in shelter, food, water and procreating; the very acts of creating fire, making clothing, herbal medicines or planting crops would have been a form of magick to them. Today, those items are common occurrences that anyone can do. What seemed like magick then is simple science and common sense now. Perhaps in another hundred years we will have discovered the science behind magick, just like the ancients discovered the science behind their magick, and the spells we perform now will have become common occurrences that anyone can perform.

In each section there are two tools listed that represents the element. I chose the tools based on being readily available, their multiple uses and their flexibility. For example, bells can be found in any store and a chalice can be anything from a paper cup to a fancy goblet. There many more tools out there and each set varies from path to path, but the ones listed here will give an idea of how tools are used in magickal correspondence.

There might be some confusion, as well, to the pentagram and candle showing up as a tool in two areas. Pentagram is a tool of all the elements as well as of earth and candle is of fire and all of the elements. So, both pentagram and candle appear in the first book The Four Classic Elements as tools representing all of the elements, and also appear again for use an another elemental tool. I debated on changing this but I feel that it should stay as is since they are both very excellent representations of the specific element and of the elements as a group. So, keep in mind that they can be used in either fashion and become familiar with what they mean when either representing an element or representing all of the elements.

Magick for the Elemental Witch

The Four Classic Elements
Section I

The Basic Elements

When speaking in magickal and alchemical terms, the elements are only four basic elements rather than the Periodic Table of Elements we memorized in high school science class (known as the Atomic elements). In neo-paganism, particularly of Greek, Roman or Celtic traditions, these four elements are: air, earth, fire, and water. These elements are a breakdown of the universe and the basis for survival. We need air to breathe; fire for warmth and cooking; earth for shelter; water to drink and bathe; and spirit is within us as our soul. In survivalist teachings the order of importance goes: shelter, fire, water, food; there is no air since that is generally not lacking in terms of survivalist situations. The elements, in more complex terms, also represent life in symbolic terms: water is representative of giving birth; fire cleanses, purifies and renews life; earth sustains us by providing our food; and air is the atmospheric conditions that create our weather.

All of these elements, while they give us life, can also be destroyers of life. To remember this keeps us humble in respect to the forces of nature, the universe and the elements. Air can destroy with high winds such as in tornadoes and hurricanes; fire or volcanoes devastate large regions; water floods and drowns; earth destroys and buries (earthquakes, cave-ins or mudslides). Give each element its due respect. As they give life, they can take it away.

In paganism there is also a fifth element called spirit, or the self. As this is not a tangible form of matter it is not always included in the classification of the Four Classical Elements but it is generally acknowledged and appears in many belief systems. It is harder to define and sometimes appears as a void, as ether, or as the soul. It is not always mentioned when calling the quarters as is the other four elements since it is usually considered to be represented by the practitioner doing the ritual or spell. It can also be represented in the form of the God and Goddess and often a statue, representation, or an offering (breads or grains) to that deity, is placed in the center of the altar. The spirit can also be considered the intent, or purpose of the ritual or spell.

These four basic elements (spirit excluded) are not a randomly created by pagans as a formula for spell casting or rituals, but rather they have ancient Greek origins and were derived by philosophers and alchemists. The four elements are the result of attempts to reduce all things in life to single substances; the whole of the universe compressed into a simple philosophy. To quote both Aladdin and Genie from Disney's animated movie "Aladdin" (1992) when the antagonist, Jafar, is turned into a genie and trapped in a lamp, "Phenomenal cosmic powers, itty bitty living space!" The Greek philosophers attempted to condense the cosmic powers of the universe into four itty bitty substances. This division of all elements is considered a part of Alchemy; a predecessor to chemistry and was the efforts to change base metals into gold, to discover a life-prolonging elixir for life and a universal solvent (to create life with).

Known as the 'archai' by pre-Socrates philosophers there were actually more than just the four elements (or forms of matter, in scientific terms). The exact number of elements that existed is unclear, but Empedocles of Acragus (495-435 BCE) simplified this by extracting only four of the archai as the roots for his studies and philosophies, these became the elements we see today and most commonly associated with Greek Philosophy.

In science class we probably learned about these elements but referred to them as solids (earth), liquids (water), gasses (air), and plasmas (fire). If we base our beliefs on basic science, water is the more important element because it can be all four forms with the ice being a solid, the steam being gas (air), boiling water is as hot as fire, and the liquid state. In Paganism, there is no differentiation between prominent elements, other than perhaps spirit, and all have equal value. Each of these elements also had qualities that if changed slightly, it changed the element. For example: air is dry, fire is hot and dry, earth is cold, and water is cold and wet. If water was turned hot enough it became steam, which is of the air element. If fire grew cold it became ash which is of the earth element.

Philosophers after Empedocles, such as Plato (427-347 BCE) and Aristotle (384-322 BCE) took his idea and created their own theories about the four elements as far as positioning in the physical planes, symbolism and geometric shapes. There is really too much to go into in this book and it is not relevant to Pagan practices, but if interested readers can learn more about Plato and Socrate's ideas and theories about the elements at Wikipedia (www.wikipedia.org) by typing in the element name and clicking a link labeled 'classic element.' Suffice it to say that the idea of four classic elements comes from BCE (Before Common Era) times and is thought to be the root of life.

Mainly used in ancient Greek medical and alchemical studies, these elements first came into practice with paganism as far back as 1888 with the advent of the Hermetic Order of the Golden Dawn system. This system is a magickal order of theology, spiritual development andone of the largest influences on 20th century Western Occultism including, but not limited to, Aleister Crowley's mysticism and Wicca. The concepts that Golden Dawn holds in magick and ritual centers on tradition, initiation and an hierarchy similar in format to those of Masonic lodges. This is due to founders William Robert Woodman, William Wynn Westcott and Samuel Liddell MacGregor-Mathors all having left the Free Masons to start the Golden Dawn order. Free Masonry is an ancient practice and many prominent figures have been Free Masons such as Ben Franklin, Thomas Jefferson and George Washington. Though the main belief by society is that it is a Christian-based organization the Free Masons hold no account of religious preference. Indeed, many of their rituals and customs seem very Christian and yet others seem very Pagan.

Wicca and Paganism are not the only paths to use the concept of elements but do seem to be the only ones that fluctuate between honoring spirit as an element or not. In other cultures or religious areas the fifth element is always represented equally in the form of Ether, Space, Void or some other immeasurable form. We see an exception in Chinese lore where there are five elements but all of them are physical forms with no representation of a spirit or a divine element.

Working with all of the elements either separately or combined can really lend a sense of 'old-world' or ancient power to magick and rituals. Exploring and working with each element separately helps one to get attuned to that element and to know it well, if it is an element that they feel a kinship to or it is of their birth sign it may even help a person explore their inner selves and learn more about themselves. When combining the elements it adds power to what a person is doing and gives a primal connection to the world, the universe and to life.

All of the elements work together in some fashion and just as we need them, they need each other. Fire needs earth (wood) and air in order to burn and water to extinguish it; water needs earth to hold it (metal or wood bowl, river and lake beds), fire to boil it, and air to move it; earth needs fire to replenish it (forest fires), water to nourish it, and air to move it; air needs all of the elements in order for it to be seen (it blows the trees, fires, or waves).

When I first started practicing I had devised my own "prayer" or chant to say prior to spell work or just as a form of silent prayer. I hadn't yet fully explored the elements or learned how to call quarters so my version went something like this: "I call upon the earth below me, the skies up above, the seas to the East and all of the things in between…"

Then I would continue on with my prayer or protection blessing. It worked for awhile and at the time I didn't even realize that I was calling upon elements, quarters or directions, I hadn't had a clear concept of these yet. My method was simply to choose the "seas to the east" because we had recently moved to the eastern coast and I feel drawn to the ocean. I also had heard the refrain "as above, so below" and growing up with a Christian concept of Heaven (skies) and Hell (under ground) I figured that asking for the skies and earth would take care of the things in between. Looking back now I realize that all four elements can be seen here if we tweak the concepts slightly: skies are air, earth is earth, the seas are water, and "everything in between" could be fire if we consider the scientific view of fire as plasma or the metaphysical view of it being life force.

The elements can be honored in simple ways such as spending time in or near the water (even just taking a bath); going for walks in the woods, gardening, walking barefoot outside; lighting candles or sitting by a toasty campfire or fireplace; sitting on a hilltop or spending time in the air (hot air balloons, flying, or even flying a kite). Take time to explore all of these things and get to know the elements you are working with and what they mean to you as a person and as a practitioner of magick. If standing outside while the sun is up and near a water source, a person is surrounded by all of the elements at once with the air all around, the water nearby, standing on the earth, and sun (fire) up above.

If a person doesn't already feel an affinity with an element, then try a few spells or rituals of each and see which one feels the most comfortable or has the strongest connection. Maybe a person is stable, secure, and grounded like the earth or is free, turbulent and uninhibited like air and water? Maybe they are passionate, fierce and lively like fire. Often, a person's birth sign's element is the one that they feel the strongest pull towards, but this does not have to be the rule. My sign is water and while I do feel a connection to the water (love being at the ocean, collecting lighthouses and fascinated by stories of pirates and ships) I also have a fear of drowning so other than shallow pools or baths I honor water from a distance. I grew up in a small farming community on a small farm (chickens, rabbits, ducks, dogs, cats and one stubborn goat) so I feel a deep connection to earth (playing in the dirt, nature walks, camping).

Also, while exploring these elements personal meanings can be created as long as it makes sense and can be incorporated into practices. For example, fire generally represents passion, energy, emotions but for someone living in colder climates or a fan of camping fire might mean comfort, warmth and life. Water is for dreaming, intuitiveness and creativity but to someone living on a houseboat or making their living with water it might mean home life and stability. The key to a spiritual life is to be consistent. If water means home and stability then it should mean that each and every time the element is worked with or called upon. Have fun creating personal symbols as well; there are standard symbols based on zodiacal, astronomical or alchemic studies that I will go into in each section, but personal symbols can be fun to create. On a long drive back home from visiting my brother a couple of years ago I came up with my own 'modern-day' symbols to represent the elements: a farm silo is earth (it holds grain); windmills are air; wishing wells are water and a lighthouse represents fire (the light is a beacon).

The elements are very important in life and in magickal practices because of the natural energy they give off. There is even a type of Psychic Vampire (known sometimes as a Psy-Vamp) that gets energy from the elements. Psy-Vamps are people who 'feed' off of energy and an Elemental Vamp will get their energy from the elements such as trees, running water, or the concentration of energy is the highest. An Elemental Vamp might be a person who is what we call the "outdoorsy" type and may feel energized from being around the elements or be a person who likes to do sports or extreme sports involving the elements (swimming, skiing, hiking, etc).

Each element is also thought to have an "elemental being" associated with it. The belief among Wiccan-based traditions is that the elementals are Guardians of the Watchtowers, which are the four corners of a ritual circle. The elemental creatures (sometimes referred to as 'elementals') personify the qualities of earth, air, water and fire. The four corners of the ritual circle may be derived from pre-Christian beliefs of both Greek and Egyptian in which there is one pillar in each of the four directional points that help to hold up the sky. The Aztec civilizations also believed that their world had four directional points and that their capitol was in the center.

The Four Classic Elements
Section II

Correspondences

The practice or belief in the elements is not restricted to just the Greek Philosophers but goes back centuries and spans a wide range of cultural and religious regions. They are seen more prominently in cultures of the western systems stemming from cultures such as the Middle Eastern, Egyptian, Greco-Roman, Druid and Hermetic orders, and modern occultism such as witchery and wizardry. I have tried to showcase as many as I can without over inundating the book with correspondences in order to give an impression of each element and have looked for a variety of both cultural and religious influence. There are many ways to interpret the elements and what they stand for and each practitioner should develop their own system that fits with their beliefs or practices, as long as it is consistent and that method used each and every time then it will work.

Druids/Celtic

Edward Williams (born 1747) was a prolific writer of Druidic studies and a Welsh antiquarian. He later changed his name to Iolo Morganwg's and eventually wrote his own system of Runic writing. In his version, we see a variation on the elements defining the universe. Unlike the four classic elements of Greek studies, Druidic orders are said to have only three elements:

Nwyfre (pronounced NOO-iv-ruh) is the source of life and consciousness, otherwise known as the "life force." It is represented in the skies or heavens and by the color blue.

Gwyar (GOO-yar) literally means blood in Welsh, and generally means flow or fluidity. It is the source of change, motion, growth and decay and is represented by running water.

Calas (CAH-lass) is solid and is the source of form, differentiation, manifestation and stability. It is represented by rocks or stones.

Druidic belief further states that everything within the known universe is comprised of three elements in some combination, with one element being more dominant in each area.

Curiously enough, if placed within the four classic element categories that we know today, the Druidic elements are only air, water and earth with no form of fire or spirit and in scientific terms we have a solid (Calas), liquid (Gwyar), and gas (Nwyfre) but no plasma. It seems that Nwyfre could be both air and fire if air is represented in the skies and heaven and fire is represented in the life force.

Chinese

The Chinese root elements are: wood, fire, earth, water, metal. Known as Wu Xing (loosely translated to mean five movements, five stages or five phases) the Chinese elements are used in everything from medicine to martial arts and are broken into correspondences much like the Greek four classic elements.

WU XING (Five Elements)

Element	Color	Direction	Season	Planet
Wood	Green	East	Spring	Jupiter
Fire	Red	South	Summer	Mars
Earth	Yellow	Center	every 3rd month	Saturn
Metal	White	West	Autumn	Venus
Water	Black/Blue	North	Winter	Mercury

The Wu Xing are represented with a five-pointed star inside of a pentagon (connect the five points of the star in a straight line and a pentagon forms). Starting at the top and moving clockwise is wood, fire, earth, metal, water. There is a neat mnemonic trick to remembering the order:

Wood feeds fire;

fire creates/produces earth (ash);

earth creates metal;

metal carries water (bucket, faucet or water condensing on metal);

water nourishes wood.

In reverse order it can be remembered as such:

Wood absorbs water;

water rusts metal;

metal breaks up earth;

earth smothers fire;

fire burns wood.

These five elements are all associated with the zodiac of the Chinese as well. Most people are familiar with the Chinese Zodiac where there are twelve animals each representing a full year within a 12-year cycle. For example, I was born in 1972 in the Year of the Rat. The next rat year is not until 1984 and the rat year prior to my birth was 1960. This is different then the Greek Zodiac that is commonly associated with birthdays and horoscopes where each of the twelve symbols represents approximately a 4 ½ week cycle.

Each animal is not associated exclusively with an element but rather each element is associated with a specific year, similar to the animals being associated with specific years. Using the previous example, my birth year is water so I was born under the sign of Rat-Water but someone born of the rat in another year might be a different element, such as Rat-Wood. If interested in learning more about Chinese astrology I recommend the book "Chinese Astrology: Ancient Secrets for Modern Life" by Sabrina Liao.

Japanese

In Japanese studies the elements are known as Godai and are represented as wind/air, water, fire, earth and the fifth element being a word that is best translated as 'void' but can be called sky or heaven; basically, it is the universe or space.

The Japanese element of earth is known as Chi (not to be confused with the life energy known as Ki, Qi or Chi) and is the solid or tangible objects of the world. Obviously, this includes things like dirt, vegetation and stones of the natural world but in people it also represents bones, muscles and tissues.

Fire, or Ka, is all of the energetic and moving things in the world. Predatory animals (thought to be fast and using great force) are of the fire element. In a person it is our body heat, metabolism and emotions. Lightning would also be under fire since it is heat, energy and moves quickly.

The Wind element, Fu, is anything that can grow or expand and like water it enjoys the freedom of movement. Imagine a kite on a string or a balloon that has been let loose that bounces freely of its own accord, sometimes sporadic and sometimes almost as in a choreographed dance, this is what Fu is. In our bodies it is, of course, respiratory function and also means keeping an open-mind and creativity.

Water, or Sui, is a fluidic and formless element. It flows freely and can take the shape of any vessel it fills. This makes concepts or people of the water element very adaptable. In humans it is our blood and body fluids but is also our emotions that ebb and flow like tides.

The Void, or Ku, is pure energy. It is an immeasurable, eternal concept that represents things beyond our everyday experience or mundane life. This would be where the magickal, supernatural and paranormal realities exist.

Hinduism, Buddhism and Tibetan

The Hindu, Buddhist and Tibetan belief systems follows closely with the Japanese elements: air/wind, water, fire, earth and ether/space (akasha). Known as The Tattva, the elements are symbolized by colors and geometrical shapes (similar modern pagans use of symbols and colors) and the word in Sanskrit means "principals, reality or truth." Tattva is a concept of reality that is perceived as a deity or having a life force. Various sects or regions of Hinduism have different numbers and types of Tattvas but for the purpose of this book I will focus only on those of earth, air, fire and water and will go into more of this within each element's section.

Tarot

Tarot cards are an age-old divination practice that is typically made up of 78 cards divided into the Major Arcana and the Minor Arcana. The Minor Arcana has suits similar to modern playing cards and are thought to have been the basis for them. Tarot cards have an Ace through a King similar to a playing deck but with the addition of a Page and a Knight.

The four suits of the Rider-Waite decks (most common of the Tarot decks) and any of the decks based on the Rider-Waite are as follows: swords (fire or air), pentacles (earth), wands (air or fire), and cups or chalices (water). Other sets of Tarot might have different names for the suits, it is up to each individual creator, but they are almost always still representative of the four elements.

Each of these suits has a personality fitting the element they are associated with and the zodiacal signs of that card and element. For example, if a court card (page, knight, queen or king) of pentacles is drawn it could mean a person who exhibits traits similar to either Taurus Virgo or Capricorn signs. In the book 'How to use Tarot Spreads' by Sylvia Abraham the correspondences of the suits are as follows:

Suit	Time	Season	Element	Other Names
Wands	weeks	spring	fire	clubs, staves
Cups	days	summer	water	chalice, hearts
Pentacles	years	winter	earth	coins, diamonds
Swords	months	fall	air	knives, spades

The Page in a Tarot deck is generally thought to be the basis for a Jack in a regular set of cards while the Knight seems to have been deleted from regular playing decks completely. The Joker is often thought to be the Fool card in a Tarot Deck; which seems to be the only remnant of the Major Arcana that we see in playing cards today. The Fool in Tarot has a place value of zero and the jokers in playing cards also have no point value but are usually used as a wild card or, in my family, as a replacement for a missing card. On the joker we would draw the number and suit of the missing card rather than buy a new deck; this worked as long as we had jokers.

The Major Arcana does not have an element attached to it, but my personal belief is that the Major Arcana is representative of Spirit since it is not made up of suits but of people or positions such as: the Fool, the Magician, Priest, Priestess, Empress, Emperor and so on. These cards are often used as a depiction of the person receiving the reading or a person who may have influence in events to come.

In a spread that I use called the "Universal Message" the suits and arcanas are separated and each one represents a different area of life: wands are the working life, swords the intellect, emotional state is the cups, the physical life is pentacles and the Major Arcana represents the spiritual life. To complete this spread, simply separate the cards into their suits, shuffle the decks and then lay the cards out in a pattern like the number five on dice: top row, wands and swords; middle row, Major Arcana; bottom row, cups and pentacles. Flip the top card of each deck and divine its meaning based on the type of deck, intuition or preferred tarot references sources.

East Asia

In parts of East Asia there is another concept of the elements that corresponds slightly with that of Chinese specific thoughts, but also adheres to its own set of ideas and dates back to the 2nd century. The elements are viewed as four guardians that watch over the four compass directions and are celestial emblems, or symbols, of the empire. Each creature corresponds to a virtue, color, season, element and direction. The tortoise is a warrior symbolic of the north, winter, the color black and the element of water. The white tiger is known as Kirin and is symbolic of west, the season of autumn, the color white and the element of metal. The Red Bird is a phoenix-like creature of the south, season of summer, color red and the element of fire. The dragon guards over the east, springtime, the color blue and the wood element. This is similar to a belief in Wicca that there are four guardians in each of the cardinal points and the reason for most calling of the quarters starting out at "I call upon the Element of Air, Guardian of the Watchtowers of the East…" and so on.

Dragon Magick

Dragon Magick is a form of Chaos Magick that revolves around the mythical beasts from a variety of cultures and lore. The aspects Wiccan-based pagans are familiar with are varied slightly in Dragon Magick as it is truly its own unique brand of paganism. If working with this type of magick there are dragons representing each element and still follow along the basis of earth, air, fire and water. The one exception is that of what Wiccan-based paganism views as spirit. In Dragon Magick this is known as Chaos which is defined as the beginning of creation. It is the force, or energy, that was used to remove everything else in the universe in order to make room for the four basic elements to begin life anew.

This could be viewed in a less universal and more global scale such as the Ice Age which caused the planet to 'start over;' the feared apocalypse of doomsayers, or the Final Judgment in Christian lore. In more personal settings, it can be the situation that causes a person to start over in their life such as heartbreak, a sudden move, or loss of a long-time job. Chaos, in this sense, basically wipes the slate clean in order to start things over. There is an excellent website referenced in the Bibliography titled "Fox Moon" with a link to Dragon Magick.

Scythia

Scythians were a people that inhabited an area known as Eurasia (landmasses now divided into Europe and Asia) from the 8th century BCE (Before Common Era) to the 2nd century AC (Common Era). The first Scythians were Targitaus and the river Goddess Borysthenes (a son and daughter of Zeus, respectively) that left Greece to inhabit their own region. Together, they had three sons: Lipoxais, Arpoxais and Colaxais. The sons ruled equally after Targitaus' death but during their reign a plough, yoke, sword and flask fell from the sky. All of the objects were made of gold and whenever Lipoxais or Arpoxais tried to get near the objects they were burned. Colaxais, however, was able to not only get near them but to pick them up and handle them without getting burned. Because of this, his two brothers ceded all royal power to him. These four items have become symbols of power and represent each of the elements.

The plough (American spelling, plow) represents earth because the ground is made ready for planting with a plow; this makes it a working tool as well as a tool actually used in dirt. Incidentally, this is also the name of the Big Dipper constellation in some countries since it looks like the archaic and old-fashioned plows used.

A flask was used to represent water as it is a vessel made for holding liquids. Today, flasks are generally thought of as the silver hip flasks carried in a pocket and filled with alcohol, but it can also be defined as any small, glass bottle with a long neck, often used in laboratory work. Many pagans already have such bottles to keep rose water, elixirs, or blessed water in and they can be purchased in craft stores.

In keeping with a farm-tool theme, the yoke (a wooden harness) represents air. The yoke, in the time of the ancient Greeks and Scythians, would have been a simple wooden frame that harnesses two draft animals, such as oxen or horses, to whatever item they are pulling like a wagon or plough. It doesn't sound like it relates to air, except maybe in that it acts as a bridge between the animal and the object and bridges are suspend in air. But, it is curious that centuries later when airplanes were invented the word 'yoke' became an aviation term for the handle of a steering mechanism for the plane's ailerons. Airplanes are definitely of the air element. Did the early Scythians have a bizarre knowledge of things to come, or did airplane manufactures pull the term from Ancient Scythians and their use of the yoke for the air element?

Fire is represented by an axe, an appropriate object since the blade is forged in fire by a blacksmith. While it is a working tool and used to chop wood, which would be of the earth, it is of the fire element because blacksmiths work fire and metals are forged in fire. Blacksmiths could actually represent either earth or fire since they work with fire and earth (metal) but they have been considered of the fire since Ancient Greek and Roman mythology times with the blacksmith Gods, such as Vulcan.

Ceremonial Magick

In the Golden Dawn system of beliefs each element is associated with a cardinal point of a pentagram and placed in the care of the Guardian Watchtowers and air is thought to be in the East. These 'watchtowers,' from the Enochian system of Magick, have spilled over into many pagan practices today of both eclectic and specific path followers.

Enochian is a term that is often applied to occult or angelic languages as recorded in the private journals of Dr. John Dee (1527-1608) and his seer Edward Kelley. Kelly was a spirit medium with capabilities of communicating with angels and spirits through the use of crystal balls. He worked with Dr. Dee in magickal investigations. Dee, an astronomer mathematician, astrologist, navigator, imperialist and occultist devoted his life to the study of alchemy, divination and Hermetic philosophy.

Through the workings of both Dee and Kelley this Enochian alphabet was devised, however in Dee's time he referred to it as "celestial speech" and claims it was used by Adam in paradise to name all things. It is so named Enochian because Dee emphasized that the Biblical patriarch Enoch was the last human, prior to Dee and Kelly, to know the language. Now used as a magickal alphabet it, and the teachings of the Enochian system, have found their way into Ceremonial Magick and the Hermetic belief system, of which the Golden Dawn derives its belief system.

Hermeticism is a set of philosophical and religious beliefs that is based primarily on the Hellenistic and Egyptian writings often attributed to Hermes Trismegistus who is a combined form of the Greek Hermes and Egyptian Thoth. The beliefs heavily influence western esoteric traditions and beliefs and was of great importance in the Renaissance era. Each of the points on the pentagram and the correspondences of the elements can be read about in each element's section.

The Four Classic Elements
Section III

Tools of the Elements

When writing this book I wanted tools for each element and while the four classic elements were easy to write tools for, having tools that represented spirit and all of the elements at once was not so easy. I have done my best and what I think are accurate portrayals of these concepts but keep in mind that there are other ideas out there and that all of magick is based on a motto of "take what works for you and use it." In that way, paganism is the ideal path because of its flexibility and allowance of incorporating other ideas and influences into practice.

Pentagram
The pentagram is a powerful tool seen in art work, jewelry and clothing and is often how pagans recognize each other as such. On an altar it might be seen as adornment on a tool or altar cloth in which it becomes just decoration and not representative of the elements, but if using it as a tool it becomes either earth or spirit. It is earth because it is considered a working tool (all working tools are of the earth since people work the earth when gardening, mining, etc.) and would be placed in the north. As spirit, it is placed in the center and now represents all the elements (the points) and the unity of them (the circle).

Pagans today use the pentagram with the point up which represents that the Spirit (or soul) comes before all material things (earth, air, fire, water). In the practice of Satanism use of the pentagram is with the point down, signifying materialism comes before the spirit. In ancient Christian times, the pentagram was used to indicate the five extremities of Christ (head, arms and legs) or the five wounds he received in his Crucifixion and can also represent the five sense of man (hearing, sight, touch, taste, and smell). In Ceremonial Magick the pentagram is used for protection or to invoke or banish spirits.

In Freemasonry there is a division for women called "Order of the Eastern Star" that uses the pentagram as its symbol. Traditionally, women cannot be Freemasons but this group was established in 1850 by Rob Morris and is open to both men and women. It is based on the teachings of the Bible but any monotheistic belief system is welcome. Their symbol is an inverted pentagram in a circle but with other symbols filling in each space between the points.

Even though Spirit is always represented with the same main point (whether it is upside down or right-side up) there appears to be no set order for the remaining elements around the other points. In the each section I will go over the order as seen in Ceremonial Magick and Wicca but any order can be used as long as the same order is used each time, consistency is the key. I usually go with and order of (starting at the top and working clockwise) spirit, earth, air, water, and fire just because it flows easily in speech that way for me and is easy to remember.

Candles

On an altar, a candle is usually used to represent fire or the God and Goddess, but it can be so much more than that: it a tool for spells, color correspondences, divination, ambience, a tool in rituals, and can also represent all of the elements.

Practitioners with limited means or space or just starting out can honor the elements with a simple object: one candle. Early occultists believed that the candle represented aspects of the human self with the flame representing the spirit, the wick is the mind or intellect and the wax is the body. In much this same manner, we can see the four elements represented in one candle with the smoke rising as air, the flame as fire, the melted wax as water, and the solid wax as earth. By lighting one solitary candle each element can be acknowledge if it is named and call upon for its power.

For those with a slightly bigger budget, go crazy and buy two candles in different colors to represent the God and the Goddess. Traditionally the God is seen as gold (sun) and the Goddess as silver (moon) but also a stereotypical pink and blue works well. A practitioner can even choose their own colors that represent the feminine and masculine to them. A black candle and a white candle can also be used because they are a of a yin-yang balance (a Taoist belief representing duality). Black is night, negative and darkness whereas a white candle is day, positive and light.

A final way to use candles to represent all four elements is to set up four candles in colors corresponding to the elements. For most neo-pagans today, those colors would be green for earth, blue for water, yellow for air and red or orange for fire. Prior to any magickal or mundane workings light a candle fitting intent by considering the components behind what is being done and how it fits into the elemental scheme of things (which will be learned in this book).

For example, if cleaning, light the blue candle for water since it is a cleansing element. Or, when cooking, light the earth candle because food comes from the earth. Fire could be lit to revitalize or energize someone or to create passion. Air could be lit when airing out a house, airing out grievances or simply for creativity. Additionally, a purple candle can be used to represent spirit or psychic work and, again, a gold or silver candle can represent the gods.

The Four Classic Elements
Section IV

Working with the Elements

In modern magickal practices, pagans will represent the four elements on an altar or during rituals (celebrations, rites, etc.). There are many different ways of doing this, but the most basic are: incense for air, chalice for water, a candle for fire, and salt for earth. There are many other methods to show the elements and each element has its own tool representing it on its own without the addition of other implements. Every practitioner should have their own idea of tools or items they can use to represent the elements and also know something of each element and its purpose.

Low Magick and High Magick

Using the elements is considered Low Magic because the person's energy and the energies of the elements are being used and not the powers of the divinity. A Low Magick spell is one of materialistic, selfish or base needs such as for a job, money, or love. The practitioner still has some control and direction over the spell. In Low Magick, the elements are called upon for their energies, the circle is cast, the ritual work done, and then a small repast of fellowship and dining (solitaire ritualists would eat a small snack) and then the elements and dismissed and the circle uncast. A Low Magick ritual might take a few minutes to a few hours depending on the number of people involved and the details of the ritual. It is up to the ritual leader or group to decide when to close the ritual.

High Magick is when the God and Goddess are called down to work the magick and is used for more serious or non-mundane intents such as Sabbats or blessings. In High Magick, the elements are called, the circle cast, the God and Goddess invited down and the ritual work completed, and then before leaving the circle the elements are forcibly dismissed so that only the God and Goddess remain. The elements have a life force of their own and will remain if not demanded to leave the circle. Then, the practitioners leave and no more is done with the ritual for the time being. Later on, the High Priest or ritual leader will go in the circle and when they feel the deities have left, they will close it.

An easier way to remember this is that in Low Magick means that the practitioner is doing the work and the God and Goddess are merely invited to the party. In High Magick the God and Goddess are the party and being asked to do the work.

Know the Elements

Another way to work with the elements is to be immersed in an element, as much as possible, and have the remaining elements nearby. For example, if needing the powers of water, take a bath and have the other three elements represented with a candle, incense, and a crystal. Or, if needing fire then sit by a fire place (or outdoor fire) and have a crystal, incense and a chalice of water nearby. The bath or fireplace becomes the primary element and more power is being drawn from it then the other three. This might explain why sitting in front of fireplaces is often considered romantic, the fire is primary and the couple is getting the passionate energy of the fire element. Or, why is it if we sit on the ground or work in the garden we feel connected to the earth? Because, we are close to that element and it is easy to receive the energy from it. Riding a rollercoaster or relaxing in a hot air balloon and we might feel free and uninhibited because air is the primary element and we are receiving its energy.

Observing the elements is also important. Know what is needed to make fire (spark, fuel, air) and watch a candle burn to learn all its idiosyncrasies. Watch a stream or waterfall and observe its actions and sounds, what does it mean to people and life around it? Hold rocks or dirt and observe all the little nuances with it or sit and listen to and feel the breeze blowing all around. Try to observe these elements like observing people or they way we might examine a new toy or gadget recently purchased. Examine each of the elements using all of the senses possible (fire can be examined in spicy foods and air can be tasted and smelled with one deep breath). Learning the elements in such a way helps a practitioner know how to represent them with the items they have on hand, this is especially useful when away from books or internet sources.

Indoor Space

For indoor spaces, most practitioners have an altar set up with the elements already represented on it. If not, there is an example of how to set up a basic alter later in this section. Within each practitioner's home there should be an altar, even if the most basic; play around with some of the altar ideas mentioned in this book and find what works. Altars can change with the Sabbats, seasons, intent or stay up year-round and be added to as needed. Permanent altars can adorn side tables, desks, or shelves or temporary altars can be created on a kitchen table, counter or any room of the house.

However, if an altar is not set up or a person is not near their personal altar the elements can still be focused on within any building by the items in it: cooking and heating appliances are of the fire element; faucets or water features are of the water element; air is always all around us or can be represented by a fan; and the earth is always underneath or is our food at lunchtime. Kitchen or break room areas are the best places for connecting with the elements since there are usually faucets, microwaves and food in them.

Outside Space

An outside space for altars can be just as important as the indoor space and one of my friends always has an outdoor altar that changes with the seasons. Add items that represent that season such as pinecones or pine boughs in winter, nuts or leaves in summer, and potted plants for spring. Change the altars at the equinoxes and solstices and if using all natural items, then can tossed back to the earth with a simple refrain of "from the earth we get to the earth we give."

Another way to have a sacred space outside is to place representations of the elements in the yard, preferably in their four directional correspondences. First, locate the spot in the yard or patio for the desired space and then mark the directional points. The easiest way to do this is stand with the right side to the setting sun (East) and stretch arms straight out. The nose now points north, the south is to the back, and the left arm points west while the right points east.

A simple way to mark each point is with stick or smooth stone that has been painted in the corresponding colors for the elements but a more advanced method is to place objects corresponding to the elements in each direction. For example, plants or a large stone for earth in the north; a bird bath, pond or fountain for water in west; wind chimes or weather vanes for air in the east and a fire pit in the southern point (a red dragon, tiki torches, or a lantern can also be used).

Elemental Cauldrons

A couple of years ago I found the website "The Inner Sanctum" which has some wonderful information on it. One of my favorite pages talks about elemental cauldrons that are excellent for cauldron or ritual work and represent each of the elements. They could be used to honor a specific element for spell or ritual work, or used on the solstice of equinox of their corresponding season and are an excellent way to add visual effect to the magick. So much of what we do is based on faith and the magick is unseen until the results occur later on. Using these methods will add the right touch to 'see' the magick and further empower the spells or cast aside any doubts of the results.

To make an air cauldron put dry ice in a glass bowl and place the bowl into a cauldron (use tongs, dry ice is harmful to the touch) and when ready, pour water from a chalice onto the dry ice. When water hits dry ice it causes a vapor to rise, resembling the vapors from cauldrons in Hollywood movies. The mist or vapor can be used for scrying in the same manner as smoke-scrying. The vapor is like steam (though not hot to the touch) and is of the air element. Air cauldrons can be used for divination, communication and initiations.

An earth cauldron can be achieved by placing salt, wax shavings, three herbs of choice, ivy leaves and some lighter fluid (to help it get started) in a fire or heat-proof container. Light it with a candle while chanting or visualizing the intent and let the smoke roll and drift for awhile before extinguishing by placing a lid over the cauldron.

Fire cauldrons require a layer of sand to be placed at the bottom of the cauldron and setting a lit charcoal disc on top of the sand. Sprinkle either salt peter or flash powder (Vesta powder, it can be purchased in metaphysical supply stores) onto the flame. They are flammable powders and will cause a sudden and short flash so do not look directly into the cauldron at the time. Flash bombs can also be made by filling a paper pocket, about the size of a thumbnail, with one of the powders and tying it with thread. Drop it onto the disc, again not looking directly at it, and listen to it pop. This is useful for group participation because as each person states their intent they can drop the flash bomb in as an affirmation.

Water cauldrons take a little more prep work but have a great visual effect if done right. Seven days before the ritual, place three equal quantities of herbs in a jar with 200-proof alcohol such as Everclear. Cap tightly and shake the jar will meditating on intent. Store the jar in a warm, dark place for seven days and shake it twice a day. Just prior to the ritual place a fireproof container into the cauldron and pour the mixture into it. Light it with a candle and be amazed at the beautiful blue flame that emerges as the alcohol burns. This cauldron is good for burning away hate, prejudices or negative self-images.

Seasonal Work

Each element corresponds to a season and but this can vary depending on the belief system or culture observed. In each section I will go into this more including the traditional correspondences (Wiccan-based) of general paganism. Regardless of which season is corresponding to which element, it should be consistent and used that way each time.

My family's correspondences are slightly different than traditional ones and are based on my daughter's observation of the elements and seasons. In my home, earth is autumn because it is our favorite season and we feel more connected to earth with the smells, sounds and sights of that season. Fire is winter for the simple reason that we need fire (heat) to keep warm. Air is spring because air breathes life into things and spring is a season of birth and re-birth. Water is summer because that is the time we visit beaches or pools to try and stay cool.

Rituals and Spell Work

In ritual and spell work all of the elements are called on but a practitioner can work with just one element if needing something from its energies. Working with a specific element can be done in its season, corresponding Sabbat, or whenever that energy is needed. For example, if needing the stabling influence of earth, summon it up by concentrating on all of its correspondences and what they mean.

Feel those qualities, visualizing them with clarity, and push that forth into the magick being done. Seasonal magick does not necessarily mean waiting until that season to call upon an element, but if it can possibly be done in that season it can add power to it. In this way, it is similar to moon magick, a spell can be done anytime but if it goes in accordance with the phase of the moon it lends more power to it.

Calling and Dismissing the Quarters

There are hundreds of different ways to call the quarters and, as stated earlier, the most common is to call upon the element and the guardian of the watchtower of that direction. These watchtowers are in each of the directions and are believed to keep an eye on the world's events. Calling the quarters simply means to call on the energies of the elements and is usually done prior to casting the circle which is usually done 'drawing' a circle with a wand or making a circle of salt.

These next ideas can be used in one of two ways: to either call the quarters or to make a circle, in which all of them can be used as each quarter is called or just one method can be chosen for casting a circle. The order in which the elements are called depends on the Sabbat or the purpose of the ritual. For example a sun Sabbat would call upon fire first or a spell or a house blessing would call upon earth first. The remaining elements are then always called in a deosil (clockwise or sun wise) direction. To uncast the circle, start with the last element called and go in reverse, or widdershins (counter-clockwise). Each verse can be stated either before walking the circle or during it.

For the air element light incense and place it in a censer or incense burner that can be carried. Walk around the circle or move it around an altar space and recite the following verse:

> *I call upon air, element of the east that gives us breath;*
>
> *take our prayers up to the divinity of our path.*

The fire element can be called by lighting a candle and placing it in a spill-proof container (to keep wax from dripping or breezes blowing out the candle). Walk around the circle and recite:

> *I call upon fire, element of the south that gives us passion;*
>
> *may our magickal workings on this night grant us inspiration.*

The earth element is called on by placing salt or dirt into a bowl, or if there is already a prepared bowl of earth then just sprinkles a little in the center of the altar. Carry the bowl around the circle, sprinkling a little of the salt around in a circle, and recite:

> *I call upon earth, element of the north that gives us stability;*
>
> *protect us with your grounding force and fill us with humility.*

Water is called by pouring blessed water into a chalice or flicking a little towards the center of the circle. Then, pick up the bowl and carry it around the circle desoil flicking a little water as the circle is walked. Participants can also dip their fingers in the bowl and anoint their foreheads. Recite the verse:

> *I call upon water, element of the west that cleanses us;*
>
> *bless this circle, may it grant us inner sight with its caress.*

Dismissing the quarter is usually done by simply saying goodbye, thanking the element and then putting the words from the previous statements in past tense, of example dismissing water might be said as such:

> *I thank the water element of the west for cleansing us;*
>
> *for blessing this circle and for granting us with inner sight in its caress.*

These closures are usually more informal and less wordy than the calling of the quarters and might be as simple as "element of water, direction of west, we bid you goodbye." This closure, like the calling, is up to each individual person and how they want to do it. For anyone performing a solitaire ritual or if recited as a group incantation, all of the elements can be dismissed at once by reciting:

> *By all the powers of flame and air*

By all the powers of earth and Sea;
By all the powers invested in me;
As I will it, so mote it be.

Then each element is bid goodbye in the form of extinguishing candles and incense and pouring earth and water onto the ground (if outside) or just by leaving it on the altar to be cleaned up later (if indoors).

Personal rituals or spells involving 1-3 people usually take place at an altar rather than a large sacred space. The elements are then represented in four corners of the altar and each one can be called upon and either placed or lit (as in candles or incense) as it is called on. For large group rituals (four or more people) four small tables can be set up in the four directional points, each one representing the corresponding element.

In the group "Gaia's Wisdom", of which I am a member of, we all stand in a circle and four people are used to call the elements. Each one stands in front of a small end table that is in their quadrant. On the table are corresponding tools and representations of that element. We switch which element we call each time to let each member have a turn calling a quarter. One time, at a council meeting, we were discussing Samhain and someone suggested, in a moment of pure frivolity, that we wear a costume befitting the element we were calling. Our council meetings are usually filled with laughter and silliness, so we agreed that this was a great idea. I ended up with the air element and when I groaned about that (I wanted to dress as a mermaid) my friend leaned over and said, "you can dress as a windmill or a pinwheel." I dressed as a fairy.

Element Charm Bag

Charm Bags are wonderful portable spells and here is a great one to keep the elements nearby and also to remember to be humble in their presence.

Gather a piece of parchment paper; a black pen (or black ink and quill); a small feather for air; a pebble for earth; a seashell or piece of drift wood for water; and a bit of ash or a lava rock for fire. Place each of the objects into the charm bag except for the paper and writing implements. On the paper write the following verse:

Air gives me my breath but it will not blow me down;
Water refreshes me but in it I will not drown;
Earth gives me sustenance but it will not overcome me
Fire provides me warmth bit it will not consume me.

Fold or roll the paper up and place it into the charm bag and secure it. To convert this to a witch ladder tie the objects into the twine and either carry the ladder or hang it in the home.

This spell keeps us humble with the elements because it recognizes what they give to us (breath, warmth, and sustenance) but yet we will not let the elements destroy us either literally or figuratively. For example, in earth we are asking for it not to destroy us literally by mudslides, earthquakes, or other such disasters or even by over-eating since it also represents our food. Figuratively we are saying that we will not be so consumed but it (finding a job or home) that we other things such as family, friends, or just having fun and enjoying what we have.

Altars

Each section will go into how to represent the elements on an altar so I won't go into details here but will give examples of two different types of basic altars. Usually each element has an item placed in its directional quadrant to represent it. Altars can be done many different ways and many different cultures or religions have seen the use of altars including Christianity from the Old Testament, Judaism, and Catholicism.

Basic Altar

An altar has four directions, or quadrants, like a map. If an altar's directions can be aligned with true geographical directions it can make it more powerful but generally an altar is set up like a map which if held right-side up north is always at the top, south at the bottom, east on the right and west on the left. To remember which way the directions go I quote my friend when she reminds us, "Never Eat Soggy Waffles." Starting at the top of the map (or the back of the altar) move deosil around the map and recite the phrase. Each letter of the word is the same as the first letter of the direction, "North, East, South, West."

The elements are then placed in correspondence with earth in the north, fire in the south, water in the west and air in the east. To help remember this I came up with this little mnemonic trick:

Earth is north, the sound of 'erth' is at their end;

Water is west because a 'w' is where they begin;

Fire is in the south because it's hotter there;

And the letter 'A' is seen in both east and air.

These directional correspondences are based on traditional and Wiccan practices, but are not steadfast rule and can be adapted to fit a person's beliefs. If living closer to water on the eastern shores then on the western east might be water and west as air to correspond to geographical positioning. Earth might be in the south because the southern hemisphere or southern part of a region is where the person was born and raised.

After the elemental correspondences are placed in their directions usually something representing spirit is placed in the center. This can be in the form of an offering (small bit of food), personal charms, effigies, fetishes or god statuary. The god and goddess may also be invited to the altar in the form of a gold and silver candle. Tools are then placed with their corresponding elements and directions. Those are the basic items on an altar and everything else is just "fluff." I've been known to add corn dollies for a harvest Sabbat, seed packets for spring equinox, pine cones for the autumn equinox, and Santa statues for Yule/Christmas. For a money spell and to honor Goddess Fortuna (Roman Goddess of prosperity) I placed a wooden treasure chest with fake coins and a bunch of fake beaded necklaces, sort of like a pirate's treasure. None of these decorative components are necessary but it adds to the altar and further empowers it.

Pentagram Altar

A couple of years ago I was researching altars for a message board I maintained and this is where I learned that there are forms of altars in almost every religion and culture. Some are very complex, some temporary, and some permanent but one of the neatest diagrams I saw was for a Pentagram Altar. This altar differs in that the elements are placed according to the points of the pentagram and not their directional points. Spirit also has its own positioning at the top of the altar rather than in the center or not at all.

To set this up, first cleanse or bless an altar space. A round table works best since it is already in the circular shape around the star. Cheap round side tables can be purchased in most department stores or found at garage sales. Paint or wood-burn a circle and a star onto the table or cover it with a cloth that has a pentagram design on it.

In the center of the pentagram place a symbol of the intent (coin for money, heart for love, etc) or a representation of a deity then start at the top point and work around the points of the star in a deosil direction. Call on the elements in a similar fashion to a ritual or basic altar. At the top point of the star is the practitioner's symbol of spirit (a picture, a deity or an object of personal value) then each point will hold an object for that element such as salt, candle, incense, and water. Use this altar for all spells or ritual work in the same way a basic altar would be used and dismiss the elements in the direction of widdershins.

Magick for the Earth Witch
Section I

The Earth Elements

Earth is the foundation of all the elements, both literally and metaphysically, because it is a grounding force and means of stability in our lives. It is the physical realm where we live, work, play, rest and where we make our home. In a sense, earth is the mundane world. We may feel closest to this element because it is our hearth and home and without a shelter, without a place to call home, we feel lost and insecure. Nomadic tribes might be thought of as not having this stability since they do not have a physical address, no place to call home.

The Bedes tribe of Bangladesh, known as "river nomads," or "river gypsies" certainly could say this because their lives are spent on the rivers. When monsoon season is in full-swing and the lands flood this nomadic tribe has to pack up their meager tents and huts in order to take to the rivers and make a living through snake-charming, selling their wares, and non-traditional healing methods. Forced into a nomadic lifestyle because the citizens (home or land owners) of Bangladesh do not want them on their shores, the Bedes live a double-standard: ostracized for not having a physical address and can't get a physical address because they are ostracized.

However, land-based nomadic tribes such as the Roma or Himalayan nomads travel the land and go where the food or their herds go. There is no home-base, or if there is it is not one that they inhabit for twelve months of the year such as non-nomadic peoples, and it really should be said that they are more of the earth element than those of us with a permanent base since they see more of the earth than we might and they rely on it more for its natural resources or follow its cycles. Most people follow the cycles of the earth simply by changing the type of clothing for the weather or weatherizing homes and cars. But to truly know the earth element is to rely on, utilize, and know intimately each of its cycles and what they can bring to us.

This element is not just the planet or its cycles but also is considered anything in the natural world that is not made up of air, fire or water such as: animals, humans, trees, dirt, stones, sand, and plants. Because the earth element is of physical and tangible things it governs over all stone, knot and tree magick. Stone magick is any spells, ritual or divinations that require sand, pebbles or rocks as a component of it. Knot magick involves spells in which knots are literally tied into threads or strings to seal the magick, witch ladders are the most popular and powerful of the knot magick spells. Knot magick can also be used for air or sea spells when the knotted ropes are used as a way of sailors controlling the winds at sea (more on this in *Magick for the Sea Witch*). Tree magick primarily stems from Celtic traditions in which trees are believed to harbor spirits and have their own meaning, power and energy.

Physically, earth is important to us because it is our shelter, clothing, food and any material possessions. Spiritually, it is important to us because the physical need earth provides means for us a sense of stability, home, and solidity. It is also what keeps us in the 'real world' where we manage the day-to-day mundane events and rituals that get us through life. People who feel a kinship to earth are stable, grounded, have a real sense of belonging to their surroundings and take great value in the concept of 'being home.' They probably work with their hands and enjoy physical labor either as a profession or pastime. Earth people enjoy activities like camping, gardening, or anything concerning nature and its cycles. Think of the phrase 'down-to-earth' when considering whether someone else is an earth person.

As an earth person we may be someone who is like the sand, content to lay around mingling with many other particles similar to ourselves. Or, maybe an earth person is someone who is like a large boulder or mountain that stands up from the landscape and is distinguishable amongst all the other features. Maybe we are like a stone that changes slowly with time until one day we realize that we are a different person now, or we are like the rock that is is blown up by man, and we change suddenly with a prolific event. Maybe we are the rolling stone gathering no moss but preferring instead to bounce, plummet and roll through life experiencing new things all the time. Or, we are a solid stone that stays put, never moving but reveling in the stability of one spot. Maybe we are the small stone mingling with the rest of the small stones and going wherever we are led.

An earth person might also be the soils that provide nourishment and food to those who need it; they are the nurturing side of the element. Or, an earth person is the tree, the hut, the cave that provides shelter to anyone who needs it; providing security and stability so that others may feel safe. Perhaps an earth person is the grass and dirt that covers long-ago and hidden secrets, tragedies, or events and covers up the scars of the world. They are the protector and try to 'wipe the slate clean' so that others can start anew. Maybe, like the earth, they are a little of all of these things.

Magick for the Earth Witch
Section II

Correspondences

Traditional

Earth is a feminine element personified by Mother Nature or Gaia. It is represented by the colors green or brown, its elemental creatures are gnome, and on an altar it is represented in the north with salt, dirt, a plant or a rock. I once used snapdragons to represent earth on an altar I designed for Earth Day in April. There was no reason for choosing Snapdragons; they are just a plant I have always liked and they were on sale and, considering the altar was for Earth Day, I wanted a living plant in the north. Earth can also be represented by a cauldron or a pentagram because they are considered working tools.

Alchemy and Ancient Medical Practices

In Alchemy the symbol of earth is a downwards pointing triangle with a bisecting horizontal line. This triangular symbol has been adopted into modern pagan practices and is often seen on jewelry, decorations or art work. The alchemical mineral of earth is salt, which is another idea adopted by pagans as a representation of the element. Alchemists associate earth with the season of autumn, femininity and, in exact opposition of Wicca, it is located at the southern point of the compass instead of the northern.

Zodiac/Astrological

Anyone that has the Zodiac signs of Virgo, Taurus and Capricorn are of an earth sign and their positive personality traits tend to be calm, practical, hard working, wise, stable and patient. Negative personality traits might include being stubborn, possessive, jealous, nearsighted or harsh. In astronomical studies the planet Earth is represented by a circle with a line bisecting it both horizontally and vertically (like a + sign inside of a circle).

Greek and Roman Mythology

In the mythological tales of the Greeks, the planet Earth is represented by Gaia (one of the original Titans and our basis for Mother Nature) but also has been connected with other Greco-Roman Gods or Goddesses of fertility and crops such as Ceres, Proserpina, Persephone and Demeter. The Romans had a deep respect for the Earth as a planet and homeland with reverence to its cycles and growth. They have a Roman goddess named Terra Mater, which literally translates to Earth Mother, and is the Roman equivalent of Gaia who rules over earthquakes, farming, productivity, women, marriage and child birth (anything dealing with cycles).

Ancient Greco-Romans used a wheel to represent earth, which is also a symbol of the Roman Goddess Fortuna (Greek equivalent Tyche). The Wheel of Fortune is synonymous with Fortuna and known as 'the Rota Fortunae.' Using the wheel for earth is showing the cycles of the seasons and life. Goddess Fortuna represents luck and prosperity, qualities of the earth element, and may be the basis for the Lady Justice symbol seen in the American judicial system (Justicia is also believed to be a source of inspiration for Lady Justice and this goddess' name means 'justice.')

Hinduism

In Hindu belief systems, earth is known as Prithvi and associated with the mother goddess 'Prithvi Mata' (earth mother) with her counterpart being Dyas Pita (father sky). This is in contrast to modern-day beliefs stemming from a Greco-Roman ideology of pairing Mother Nature with that of Father Time (said to be the based on the Greek Titan Chronos). Father Time can be said to be of cycles, the past, the present, and the future. Between him and Gaia life is pretty much covered. However, in the Hindu beliefs the pairing of the earth mother and father sky encompasses only two areas unless considering the seas part of the earth as a planet and the sky as the whole of the universe and void.

Further symbolism in the Tattva is a yellow square as the geometric symbol and the lotus flower, a flower much prized in Hindu cultures, especially Chinese. An emperor was so enamored with this flower that he ordered all women to a ritual of foot-binding. This re-created the shape of their foot so that it was smaller and with four of the toes tucked under the foot, which made their foot resemble the shape of the lotus flower. Earth is so revered that rather than straight deity or god worship, certain regions or buildings might be considered sacred and given reverence to.

Ceremonial Magick

In Ceremonial Magick the elemental tool of earth is the pentacle, a concept carried into Wiccan, eclectic and solitary paths of paganism. Ceremonial Magick has more correspondences than many pagans may acknowledge or practice today with many of them in accordance with Christianity in that there are archangels and angels that rule over each element.

For the earth element, the archangel is Uriel who is named in the Acrophya of Hebrew traditions. The angel is Phorlakh, the ruler is Kerub (modern day word is 'cherub' and seen in Hebrew mythology as a sacred celestial being) and the king is Ghob (king of the elemental gnomes). Remember, Ceremonial Magick as defined in this book is a set of rituals and beliefs derived from the Hermetic Order of the Golden Dawn which was founded by Freemasons. This allows for the Christian concept of angels but in no way indicated that a pagan has to believe in angels or acknowledge them in their practices.

Earth is a passive element represented by the same symbol used for Taurus in the Greek Zodiac. In Ceremonial Magick's "Supreme Invoking Ritual of the Pentagram" it is represented on the lower left point. The invoking ritual of the pentagram is simply a ritual used to invoke energies prior to magickal workings and banish negative energies (when done in reverse). To learn how to do this ritual, visit the website: www.livingwithmagick.com/magick/sirp.php for instructions.

Wicca

In Wiccan practices, the element of earth is associated with north and the season of winter. Its colors are brown or green and can be represented by percussion instruments, animal fur, coins, a pentacle, milk, the heartbeat, jewelry, bones, or a staff. As with Ceremonial Magick its placement on the pentagram is the lower left point. The symbol used for it is the same as the alchemic symbol and the elemental creature is a gnome.

Other Symbolism

In Aztec cultures earth is seen as stability and security and is symbolized with a line drawing of the shelters used by the Aztec people. Their symbol looked similar to a child's line drawing of a house, a box for the house and triangle for the roof. The ancient Aztecs seem to have a grasp on the idea that shelter was one of the most important things required by man. Exposure to the elements greatly reduces a person's chance of survival from days or week to only a few hours.

Christian mythology is not without its use of the elements and a lot of this monotheistic belief has adopted various concepts of paganism in an effort to convert pagans. For Christians, earth is represented by a bull possibly because of the fertile and stabile qualities associated with the animal. When Ceremonial Magick was created, the Freemasons (of Christian beliefs) took this bull symbolism with them and adapted it to their new system.

Magick for the Earth Witch
Section III

Tools of Earth

Staffs (and similar objects)

Staffs, walking sticks, brooms and scythes are all considered the same tool magickally speaking in that they all serve the same purpose and relatively the same shape and length. There are some differences among them in regards to use, correspondence and gender but a pagan can use whichever of these tools fits with their lifestyle or beliefs.

Today these items are still common household objects and just owning one does not mean a person is pagan, but for those of us who are, they are a great way of having the magick "out in the open" without it really being seen or condemned by non-pagans.

The staff is an important tool in pagan practices as a symbol of protection. In older times it would have acted as a walking stick, and possibly a weapon. For modern practices it is used to cast or open a circle by symbolically drawing a circle with it. A staff, due to its phallic shape, also represents the male or the God.

Walking sticks have a mythology and superstition all of their own. These were a common item and could be used for a variety of mundane or magickal purposes. It should be cut from the wood from an Elder tree on All Soul's Day, hollowed out and stuffed with seven leaves of Vervain. If it is hung over an exterior door when not in use it further aids in good luck to the owner of the house.

A scythe is more accurately classified as a cutting tool and would correspond with a bolline (a working knife). Since bollines are typically placed in earth (remember, all tools that are for physical work correspond to earth) and because its resemblance to a staff, it can represent earth. It can also represent fire if all blade instruments correspond with 'being forged in fire' for a practitioner. Modern depictions of Father Time and the Grim Reaper are both seen with scythes or staffs and the Titan Chronus is often seen with the same tool.

A staff can be considered a larger extension of a wand and can be used in a similar manner, this is especially useful in large group rituals were a ritual leader will need a longer reach when casting circles or calling the elements. The use of brooms and staffs in modern pagan practices has continued, I'm sure, partly due to the novelty of it and from the stereotypical depictions of witches and wizards. But, more importantly, it comes from the respect that long ago these were common household objects and in a time where witchcraft was illegal these items could be owned (and secretly used for magick) without the user being condemned as a witch.

For women the broom is considered a staff because it is a working tool, and in a time when there were distinct lines of what was 'women's work' and what was 'men's work' it was generally females who cleaned with a broom. It is also said that the bristles of the broom were made with a plant of the same name which is a feminine plant. The handle of the broom is phallic shaped and represents the male. Therefore, the broom represented both male and female. It can be used to magickally sweep away debris and cleanse a space prior to rituals.

Brooms have a long list of lore and superstition that ranges from the practical to the bizarre. It is said an old broom should never be brought into a new house as it will bring all the old 'dirt' (magick, luck, etc) of the old house. If it is hung over a door it is said anyone entering with evil intent the broom will fall. Also, it is good luck to store a broom bristles up and if stored near the front door evil cannot enter because it will have to count every bristle, which will take all night and with the sunrise the evil will die or be banished.

Pentagram

The pentagram is considered a working tool and therefore it belongs with earth. However, as mentioned earlier, it can encompass all of the elements with each point representative of an element. When using it only for earth it should be placed in its corresponding directional quadrant.

When using a pentagram to represent one element it really should be just the symbol itself and not another elemental tool with the pentagram on it. I have a piece of wood that I wood-burned a pentagram into and some stores sell soapstone discs with pentagrams etched into them for this purpose. However, other tools with a design of a pentagram on them (such as an incense burner) can be used if that is all that is available but do not use that tool for any of the other elements. In the example of the incense burner, place it in the earth quadrant and do not use it for burning incense too. The burner is not the elemental tool, the pentagram on it is.

Magick for the Earth Witch
Section IV

Working with Earth

Earth is probably one of the easier elements to work with because it is something people do anyway, perhaps without realizing that they are. Simple acts such as gardening, cooking, taking a walk, or going camping are all ways to work with earth and a great way to connect with it and understand it as an element. Plants, dirt, stones and all types of natural foods are the items we commonly will be handling or working with and are easy to come by simply by going outside.

Indoor space

To work with earth indoors, try cooking a hearty meal from scratch and place intent into the meal such as good health, happiness or prosperity. As each ingredient is added remember their metaphysical purpose and envision those qualities being added to the food. When I make a roast or whole chicken for my family I always add whole peppercorns for flavoring but as I add them I also think about the grounding and protective qualities of pepper. I also have made it a tradition to add an odd number that is greater than the people dining. For example, my family is only four people so I add five peppercorns. If I had an uneven number, such as seven, I would go up to the next odd number, which would be nine. Odd numbers are sacred in pagan practices and also this aids in blessing any unseen family members, guests or deities who may also have come for a visit during our meal.

Serving dishes can be held prior to being served (use gloves if the dish is hot) and imbued with some extra magick by reciting a simple phrase:

Bless this food that I serve here and pass along its magick to all who share.

Or think of a specific intent the food can pass on and imbue it with those properties by envisioning it is bringing those qualities to all who dine on it. At first glance, this might seem like doing magick on someone without their knowledge but it is not. Spells of protection and blessings are always welcome and do not need a person's permission prior to being cast. Also, these little techniques are more like blessings rather than spells. They do not go against anyone's free will and are not with ill-intent, therefore safe to use.

Aside from cooking, just having plants in a home can lend a little magick to any space. In the kitchen plants can be dried and hung in braided ropes, like garlic or chilies, or small herb gardens can be grown to use in cooking or for spells. In other parts of the house or outside living plants can decorate the home. They are decorative and useful in a variety of ways in that a person can get seed or shoots to grow more, they have metaphysical properties and there is a ready supply of fresh plants for magick. Potting the soil and caring for the plant honors the earth element, places personal energy into the plant, and helps the environment by filtering out toxins that may be in the air.

Decorations of natural wood or stone statues and decorations can also adorn a home to connect a person with earth even when indoors. Decorative vases or bowls filled with colored and polished rocks make great centerpieces, especially if fake flowers stick out of them or a candle is set on top of the rocks, and a bunch of sticks or dried reeds can be bundled together with a pretty ribbon and hung on the wall.

Outdoor space

The most obvious connection to earth outside is a garden. There are a variety of garden styles that a person can plan such as a flower garden, herb garden, vegetable garden or any combination of the three. Plants or trees potted by the practitioner can also add magick outside and give a ready supply for magickal workings, or the plants already in existence can be used. Spend some time outside studying the plants and taking pictures. Later on, books or internet sources can be used to determine what the plant is and then its metaphysical properties can be searched. We have a Morning glory vine growing outside of our house and I was pleased to learn that even though every part of it is poisonous, just having it out there traps negativity and the vine can be used on poppets or in binding spells.

Working the land and caring for the garden is the best way to connect with the earth, but for those without a green thumb (like me) earth can be honored in other ways besides gardening.

Simply by sitting outside a person is involved in the earth element since it is the ground we walk on and, essentially, the entire planet. Create a serene sitting area outside that can be elaborate and expensive to a simple plank of wood on cinder blocks. My favorite bench in our backyard is a plank nailed to two stumps that we received for free by a crew digging up trees in the area.

Statues or ordinary rocks can also be placed outside, or for apartment dwellers with a small patio or balcony try adding a few plants and a couple of medium sized rocks and a chair. Rocks act as sentinels known as 'watcher stones.' They aid in guarding a home from evil and negativity. Typically they are placed at property corners but medium sized rocks can be placed on porches or balconies and serve the same purpose.

Rituals and Spell work

Rituals or spells focusing on earth might include acts such as burying an object in dirt, drawing symbols, planting seeds or writing words in the dirt, going for a walk, herb magic, or carving images out of wood or stone. To determine if a spell fits in with the earth element think of the terms 'home-based' or 'feet firmly rooted in the ground'. If the spell involves stability, grounding or anything related to the home or job it is of the earth. Spells involving natural items such as stones, leaves, nuts or twigs are also under the earth element. The earth element is enhanced by all kitchen magick, caves, forests, farms, and plant nurseries. It rules over spells of magnets, knot magick and binding. Types of spells that correspond to earth are witch bottles (also known as bottle spells), charm bags (also known as mojo, gris-gris or medicine bags) and witch ladders. Technically any spell or magickal workings not involving fire, air or water would be ruled by earth and this could include manmade items. For simplicities sake, in this book I will focus on spells or divination where the main ingredient or focus is a natural item.

Witch Ladders

Witch ladders are a form of knot magick that is devised by tying knots into twine. Natural materials should be used as much as possible such as wooden or glass beads, twine or hemp, and feathers. Knot magick also has a small place in Sea Witchery since knots were tied in cloth and used by sailors to unleash the winds needed for their sails.

In older times, witch ladders were contrived of forty knots (a common number that pops up in mythology and religion) but today, practitioners tend to make witch ladders in nine knots. The number nine is sacred because it is a triply trinity (or 3x3) as well as being an odd number. Witch ladders can be used as key chains, hung in windows or rearview mirrors, tied into long hair or a ponytail, or just carried in a pocket. To make one, concentrate on the tent and pick colored beads that fit that intent.

A few examples I have made are a money ladder (green beads for money and yellow for hope), a chakra balancing ladder (all seven chakra/rainbow colors), a spirituality or psychic connection ladder (purple for spirituality and blue for power) and a love ladder (red and pink). I alternated the beads and tied a knot in between each one; feathers were added at the bottom for decoration and extra enchantment. I used natural feathers, but colored feathers that match the beads can also be used.

Recite the following verse as each knot is tied:

By knot of one, this spell has begun

and by knot of two, I know my intent is true.

By knot of three, I can clearly see

that by knot of four, opportunity is at my door.

By knot of five, the magick is coming alive

And by knot of six, the magick is fixed.

By knot of seven, my wishes are sent to the heavens

And by knot of eight, it is in the hands of the Fates.

By knot of nine, I seal the magick in this twine.

Hang the ladder in the home or carry it in a purse or pocket and be confident that the knots have sealed in the magick. Once the desired outcome has been achieved the ladder can be untied (reusing the beads and discarding the twine) or the whole ladder can be buried. If making one for long-term use such as protection, spirituality or psychic intuitiveness it can be carried, used as a keychain or stored near magickal items for as long as necessary.

Altars

When standing at an altar or to call the quarters there are hand symbols that can be used to show reverence for the element. For earth, hold arms down, slightly out from the sides with fingers splayed out to resemble the roots of trees. This gives a person a greater connection to the element and puts one in the right frame of mind for working with or calling it.

For someone wanting to work exclusively with earth can have an "Earth Altar," which is an altar representing earth more predominantly than the other elements. The simplest way is to do this is to add an extra item representing the element in the coordinating quadrant. For example, if putting salt for earth then just add an extra bowl of salt or some other component of the element such as a plant, a rock or a pot of dirt. Another simple method is to simply color-scheme the altar by adding tools of the other elements that are also colored with browns and greens (a brown candle, a green chalice, etc).

For those feeling a little creative there is a more advanced way of doing an earth altar. Consider the four elements around the altar: earth, air, fire, water and then try to figure out how they can all be represented through an object that is both earth and fire such, as a lava rock. A feather is both air (birds fly) and earth (from an animal) or, even better, a flightless bird feather can be used because it's a grounded bird. Salt water is perfect for the water element because we already know salt is the mineral symbol of earth and it is in water. Additional ideas are to use a male gnome for the God and a female gnome for the Goddess, a small globe for a centerpiece; and a map (particularly a topographical map) as an altar cloth. Have fun with these new correspondences and be creative, remember that if the reasoning can be explained and has purpose, then it can be used in correspondence.

Magick for the Earth Witch
Section V

The Soils

Dirt is what we walk on, it's where we plant our gardens, we build our homes out of it and it is, essentially, the makeup of our planet. Granted, our planet is made up of the other elements as well (fire at the core, the seas and atmosphere) but earth materials (wood, rocks, soil) are predominant in our lives. Earth is seen in our mountains and valleys, our sand dunes and muddy bogs. It is a healing force (covers scars of the land or buries the deceased) and a destructive force (earthquakes and mud slides).

The best way to connect with the earth element is by playing in the dirt. Remember the joy of making mud pies or trying to dig to the other side of the world. Connecting with earth through its soils is important in understanding this element and is a wonderful way to meditate or relax. Working with the soils by gardening, sitting and playing in the dirt, going for walks, or sculpting with clays and mud connects a person to the element in a hands-on way.

Pick up a handful of dirt or sand and examine it; notice the particles of rocks, twigs, shells or other debris. Think about what the dirt has seen and who has walked on it. Imagine mountains or impressive rock structures that broke down to form these tiny grains. Perhaps a glacier passed through eons ago and left some of the dirt behind.

When working with dirt remember that just playing in it won't make anyone sick, however covering up wounds and washing hands afterwards are always great practices to follow. Also, dirt used in spells should be free of debris such as litter, twigs or bugs. The easiest way to do this is buy a sifter (like a flour sifter) and sift the dirt. But, use it only for sifting dirt, never try to wash it and use it in the kitchen later.

Because dirt is so prominent in basic life necessities it is no wonder that it is surrounded with superstitions and folklore. English lore tells us that dirt has luck-giving qualities and worrying too much about cleanliness risks cleaning the luck of the person or household away. Certainly, this was seen in medieval times when baths were taken maybe once a month, or less.

It is also said that bringing mud into the house is lucky; particularly if in the month of January as it is an auspicious month and events occurring on that day portend how the remaining year will play out. If a person is moving it is said to always leave a little dirt behind, preferably in the fireplace, so that the luck is not entirely swept away for the new owners.

Barren Ground

Barren Ground (where no grass grows) has superstitions of its own that are found world-wide and usually encompass local legends involving curses as the cause of the barren land. In the British Isles there is a spot where the drowned body of British Admiral Sir Cloudesley Shovell was temporarily laid to rest (Scilly Islands) after his fleet was destroyed in 1707. Admiral Shovell was a real person whose victories of him and his crew were unjustly honored by a simple navigational error that caused their deaths and destruction of the ships.

On the Summit of Dragon Hill of Berkeshire, where St. George legendarily slew the dragon, the ground is barren because the dragon's blood poisoned the ground and nothing can grow there. St. George, the patron saint of England, gained notoriety with his adventures and soldiering. In the book "Legend Aurea" (the Golden Legend) these events are recorded, and it is in this book that popularized the tale of him and the dragon. The origin of this legend is obscure with theories stating that it is about his assistance in persecuting Diocletian (a Roman emperor, who was referred to as "the dragon" in ancient texts) or is a Christianized version of the Greek legend of Perseus rescuing Andromeda from a sea monster.

Legends also abound regarding barren ground being the graves of notorious criminals or wrongly accused criminals. This is the case of the Montgomery Churchyard and the grave of John Davies, a plasterer from Wrexham in Wales, who was hung in 1821 for a crime he protested innocent to. He was accused of assault and robbery by William Jones from Welshpool, Wales who even produced 'witnesses' (the story is that Jones paid people to be his witnesses to a crime they never saw). Davies entered a plea of "not guilty" but a jury found him guilty he was sentenced to execution. Up until the moment of execution he proclaimed his innocence and prayed that if this was so, no grass should grow over his grave. In the churchyard there is a simple wooden cross marked "The Robber's Grave." More can be read about the legend at its website of the same name (see biblio).

Graveyard Dirt

In many cultures, society teaches that the dead are unclean, taboo, frightening and generally just not something to mess around with. Cultural beliefs on this have led to laws against graveyard desecration; however there are societies and tribes where the dead are revered and not feared. The use of graveyard dirt is just one way of connecting with the deceased and using what energies remain from them. While this concept fits more neatly with that of necromancy (communication with the deceased to predict or influence the future) or ancestral worship, it is also of the earth element because it literally involves dirt.

My personal disclaimer is that while this has not become a part of my practices, I include it here because I like to showcase a variety of customs and traditions. But, I also recommend that if adopting this practice, do not use graveyard dirt from an unknown source and this includes buying it from a metaphysical store. This can go against the advice of "never calling up what can't be controlled or banished." There is no telling what sort of person the dirt covered. Also, be wary of the laws of grave desecration; taking a small sample (what can be held in the hand) should be okay but shovels of dirt is clearly against the law and an insult to those buried there.

Working with the spirits of the deceased sounds a little like a horror movie plot, but ancestral worship is common in many areas and is really meant as a means of guidance. A common belief is that those who have passed are wiser than those of us remaining. As with all magickal workings, graveyard dirt can be used for good or bad; it all depends on the intent of the practitioner. Graveyard dirt can be used for spells ranging from drawing in love to binding someone (keeping them from harming someone).

There is a misconception that graveyard dirt is a code word for powdered mullein (an herb) or talc (like talcum powder) and while many herbs and plants have folkloric names graveyard dirt is just as it sounds: dirt from a grave or graveyard. The misconception might stem from the idea that mullein is called 'graveyard torches' (and also known as 'witch's candles') because it grows in well-spaced, dry, waste ground (like a graveyard) and if dipped in oil or lard the stalks will burn like torches or candles. The website "Lucky Mojo" has an excellent debate on this controversy that I recommend reading.

The use of graveyard dirt in magickal practices stems from African-American beliefs of Hoodoo and Obeah. Hoodoo is a set of religious beliefs that is the basis of Voodoo; a religion practiced in Caribbean countries, especially Haiti, as well as Caribbean or Haitian settled parts of America. It is a mixture of Roman Catholic rituals and animistic beliefs (that everything has a spirit). Hoodoo and Voodoo mainly involve magick to ward off the evil eye, communication with ancestors and augury (seeing meaning in patterns). Obeah is a religion involving witchcraft originally practiced in Africa and surviving today in parts of the Caribbean.

In both Hoodoo and Obeah, graveyard dirt is a very important magical element based on cultural beliefs surrounding the deceased and rituals of invocation (calling on higher powers). This form of magick is usually referred to as ancestral worship or veneration. There is also a link to beliefs in which the ancestor is an important key in how a practitioner relates to the spiritual world.

In Hoodoo the ritual of collecting graveyard dirt is referred to as 'buying' it since payment is expected. Nineteenth century folklore states that in the United States the usual payment is a silver dime, preferably one made of mercury, but for today's practitioners any token of gratitude may be used. The use of graveyard dirt by modern pagans probably comes from the influence of Hoodoo and Voodoo practices in America, but there are other belief systems that make use of graveyard dirt.

The Palo Mayombe is a mix of Congo magic (Cuban and Brazilian) and Catholicism. It is practiced most often among Cubans or Brazilians descended from central African slaves of Bantu heritage. Palo literally means 'stick' and is used due to the practice of using wooden sticks in preparation of altars. The Palo Mayombe also believe in the veneration of ancestor spirits as well as in natural earth powers and reveres all natural objects, especially sticks which are thought to be infused with special powers.

Altars are commonly referred to as 'nganga' or 'prenda' and often take the form of a consecrated vessel filled with sacred sticks, graveyard dirt, human remains and other sacred items. Some sources say the prenda is the vessel placed on the nganga, or altar, and others say that the vessel is considered the altar. Either way, the vessel or altar is believed to be inhabited by a 'meurto', or spirit of the dead, who acts as a guide for all religious activities.

Salts

Salt has always held prominence in superstitious lore and mythology. It was so highly prized in Ancient Rome that soldiers and workers were paid a 'salarium' (root word for 'salary') in the form of salt. Salt was also a common offering used to placate the Gods and considered especially lucky by sailors because of the salty waters they sailed on. The Aztecs had a salt goddess named Huixtochihuatl in which sacrifices, often in the form of people, were made to her in the month of June. Mina Koya is the salt Goddess of the Pueblo Indians and is revered in the autumn months. She has the power protect, preserve and cleanse, which is same qualities we give to salt in today's practices.

This simple household and magickal staple should be in everyone's home whether pagan or not. It has many uses from the mundane acts of cooking and cleaning to the metaphysical acts of protection. A lemon cut in half and dipped in salt works as an abrasive when cleaning; salt is used for seasoning, salt water is an antiseptic when gargled; a circle of salt around an object will cleanse it or when around a house protect it from evil; magickal or sacred items can be buried in salt (non-metal items, as salt can cause rust); and it adds empowerment to any spell. Salt is a multi-tool to have, economical and easily obtainable.

Edible Salts

Table salt, Epsom salts, rock salt and sea salt are all edible but Epsom and rock salts are not used to season foods; Epsom salts are used as an antiseptic when gargled and rock salt is used in making homemade ice cream. Regardless of which salt is used remember to keep magickal salts and food salts in separate containers (or rooms) to avoid cross-contamination. When I purchase kitchen herbs and spices I will either purchase two of each or I divide it into two separate containers. One container stays in the kitchen and one with magickal supplies.

In pagan practices, table and sea salt are the more common salts to use for cleansing, protection or to symbolize the earth element. Sea salt is considered healthier for the body and seems to be the preferred salt in many homes today, but table salt works just as well. Both are economical to purchase and can be found in bulk containers in grocery stores. Table salt is a finer grain and sea salt coarser, the preference is entirely up to each practitioner (I prefer sea salt because the larger grains make it easier to work with). When using table or sea salt in cooking or magick think of its qualities and as it is added to the food or used to draw a protective circle recite the verse:

Salt of the Earth; protect all in my hearth.

(Hearth, in this sense, means the home or area a person lives and not just the fireplace.)

Rock salt is usually used for homemade ice cream and not any other food additive or bath salt, it can be used in the same fashion as sea and table salts when it comes to magick. Epsom salts can also be used, just as economical and in coarse grains this type of salt works best for bath salts. Even plain, Epsom salts can be added to a bath or foot soak to aid in relieving tension. Follow the basic bath salt recipe below and add coloring or oils per choice or intent of the salt at the time:

Basic Bath Salt Recipe
3 parts Epsom salt

2 parts baking soda

1 part table salt

a few drops of essential oil

a few drops food coloring.

Add the dry ingredients together and mix well. Add essential oils and food coloring 1 drop at a time, stir, and then add more if desired. Add drops until the desired scent and color is achieved. Let the mixture air dry in a large bowl or tray to prevent clumping and store in an airtight container in a dry place. Add at least two tablespoons to bath water as the tub is filling up. Bath Salts can be added directly to the water, but if adding bits of dried herbs or flowers it is better to place it in a sachet bag (mesh or muslin bag) and place the bag into the tub so that the herbs don't clog the drain.

Black Salt

Black Salt is another great form of salt for all magickal purposes. It protects against negativity or evil, can be used in banishing negativity or evil spirits and entities, and can be used to represent earth on an altar. Black salt is not a natural color for salt, in fact most black salt sold in metaphysical stores has been dyed and the color can come off on skin or objects. Recently, I learned how to make black salt in a more natural method that does not require dyes. There is nothing wrong with dyed salt, but there is a better way to make it that is more empowering and is cheaper than buying it dyed.

To create a more natural and powerful black salt, dump out any chunky residue from a small cast iron cauldron (such as herbs and burned charcoal discs). Pour in some salt until the cauldron is about half-full. Sea salt is preferred since it is a larger grain than table salt but other salts will work. Using the pestle for a mortar and pestle kit, grind the salt as if grinding herbs in a mortar and pestle. The salt will start to take on the color of the cast iron as well as mix with the other residues, which creates a unique and magickal blend. Adding two or three drops of an essential oil (or base oil) will help to further enhance the black coloring. Salt can cause rust in metals, so make sure to wipe out the cauldron with a cloth and then oil the inside to help prevent rust. Let the black salt sit in a shallow pan or tray to dry out if oil was added, and then store in a dry and airtight container.

There is also a quaint spell called Sacred Salt Jar in this section that can be done with regular salt or black salt, it could even be done with sand if preferred. It is more powerful than plain salt in that it has had things added to it such as bits of herbs and plants, ash, waxy bits from candles, or any other random little bits of stuff.

Spells and Rituals

For basic spells sand, dirt or soil are imbued with the same qualities; there is no 'good dirt' versus 'bad dirt' for spell work, so go with what is available. Remember to always take small samples, especially if obtaining dirt or sand from public areas. On many beaches, or public parks it is illegal to take out even a bucketful of sand or dirt. But, gathering approximately a handful of soil or sand should be allowed' just never take more than one can be cupped in one hand.

Stability or Grounding Charm Bag

From my first book, "Magick for the Kitchen Witch," I borrow this charm bag spell (with some minor revisions) that is very simple because the only ingredient is dirt. This bag is to be made when the need to for stability or staying grounded arises. It can also be used if traveling and wanting to remain connected to home. While this spell does require the practitioner to cut fabric, there is no sewing involved. At my best I can sew on a button, so I will not subject others to sewing projects if I can help it. But, if someone is fortunate enough to have sewing skills, a permanent bag can be sewn and used more than once.

Cut a square piece of fabric at least six inches by six inches and place it in the center of an altar. Meditate or perform a simple self-blessing while sitting at the altar, then place a small handful of dirt or sand in the center of the fabric and visualize being grounded and stable or remaining connected to the home. Visualize the dirt as coming from the earth and that tiny fibers of roots are streaming out from the dirt to connect to the ground below. Imagine that the roots can grow through the floors or walls and deep into the ground; nothing stops these roots from burrowing deep into the ground, neither pavement nor concrete, neither wood nor plastic.

Once the roots have become firmly planted in the ground symbolically, hold the bag in the projective hand (right) and visualize the roots again but this time they are already firmly planted and very secure. Know that the bag is connecting to the earth and recite the following verse:

Sachet of earth, in whatever may cause me contention

Keep me grounded and aware of my earthly connection.

Bring up the sides of the fabric and tie a string around the bag. The color of the bag and string is not as important as the visualization in this spell, but colored bags can be used to correspond with the intent. To recharge the bag it can be placed on an altar, held in the hands as the roots are visualized again, or when finished with the bag scatter the dirt on the ground (never throw it away) and make a new bag with fresh dirt.

Earth Bottles for Moving

The following spell was also in my kitchen witch book and was two separate spells. But, for this book, I have revised them into one spell since they really go hand-in-hand. The first half is for moving out of a home and the other half is for moving into a new home. It can be separated again and just one half of the spell completed, but as a person will always be moving into a new home after exiting one, they should be done as one spell just keep in mind that the second half won't be completed until the move is.

Prior to moving out of a house, but after all the furniture has been removed fill a bottle with dirt from the yard. Leave the jar uncapped and walk around the entire house, getting into every room, into the yard and any out buildings on the property. Let the dirt absorb all of the memories (good and bad), special feelings, or emotions, that occurred in that house. All of the furniture and personal items should be removed as they carry their own energies and if the spell is done before hey are removed they can leave some of the memories behind with them. The object of this spell is to take all that emotional energy away from the house when moving.

Visualize the house slowly being purified and starting fresh for the new inhabitants, leaving nothing of personal essence behind. When the house is cleansed take the bottle outside, seal it and mark a protective symbol on the lid and recite:

Earthen jar that I have filled let my memories now be sealed.

Bury it in an uninhabited place and walk away, do not look back at the spot. This is not meant to repress those memories, but only to gather them all up and not leave residual energy behind.

Before moving into the new home, fill a small jar with dirt from the yard or surrounding area and seal it with a lid or cork, then draw a protective symbol on the jar. Hold it in the projective hand and visualize good times and memories waiting in the new house as well as the dirt acting as a protector as long as that house is inhabited. Recite the following verse:

Earthen jar that I have filled, protect this home and all within.

Place the jar near the main entrance to the home, in a prominent window or even near a gate to the property. If at any time the magick and protection feels like it is gone from the jar, scatter the dirt on the ground and repeat the spell.

The second half of this spell can also be done by itself as just a general protection spell. However, use sand or salt in the jar because it has more identifiable granules and will stop the evil spirits. The belief is that evil is addicted to counting and will have to stop at the door to count every grain in the bottle before they can enter the home. Clearly this will take all night in which the evil spirits will get caught by the dawn and either die or leave. Similar beliefs also exist in the form of placing newspaper print on the walls (a Gullah belief involving the Boo Hag), the seeds in a charm wand or rain stick, and with the belief that a broom near the door will confound spirits. Basically, anything that has an infinitesimal amount of objects to count (seeds, words, granules) will take all night and stop the evil. Objects should always be placed near the main entrance where evil is likely to enter.

Sacred Salt Jar

This bottle is very good for the beginner to use because it is flexible and each time a Sacred Salt Jar is made the ingredients will be different. It can also be added to constantly which changes its properties and keeps it continually empowered. The purpose is to create a sacred salt that can be used charge stones, to add into bath water, to consecrate objects, to sprinkle around the home or for any other purpose involving salt (except for human consumption).

This is one of the few bottle spells (also known as witch bottles) that can be given as a gift to someone as a 'starter salt.' Make a batch and give it to a friend and let them know it can be continuously added to. If a few friends all make their own batch of salt then they can be dividing into small portions and each person receives a share of their friends' salt. Combine the portions so that now each person has a very sacred salt empowered by their friends.

To make the salt start with a salt base (any of the previously mentioned forms of salt will work) and place it in a jar. Set the salt aside and for the next few weeks start collecting any small tidbits of natural items that can be found: herbs, flower petals, tiny crystals, small stones, ground nuts or seeds, ground incense or ash are a few examples (in my jar I even have bits of a hatched robin's egg my daughter and I found). A few drops of essential oil can also be added to the salt at any point in the process. As the items are gathered, grind them up as fine as possible and mix with the salt. Keep the jar near magickal workings and continually add to it and use it as needed.

Divination, Meditation, Scrying

To meditate with the earth sit down on the ground, feet and hands firmly planted, and imagine them growing roots deep into the earth. Feel the roots connecting with the past, the future, and with all the living things in the area as they dig deep into the soils. Continue to do this until a deep connection is felt and the mind can drift away into a peaceful daydream. Let the thoughts flow freely without dwelling on what they mean, but just acknowledging that they are there.

Meditate however long is comfortable and then start drawing the roots back into the body. Feel them becoming untangled from the ground and other roots and shrinking back into the hands and feet. Thank the earth for allowing the connection to it and go about magickal workings or the rest of the day. By doing this form of meditation a person will get acquainted with the element and learn basic mediation skills. Meditating is a wonderful way to cleanse the body and prepare the mind prior to any high magick, rituals, or divining.

Magick for the Earth Witch
Section VI

Rocks, Stones and Pebbles

While nothing more than large chunks of dirt, rocks are as important to the magickal worlds as they are to the mundane. They are solid and stable with interesting textures, colors and patterns; we collect them, decorate with them and use them in functional ways. They have withstood the trials of time and of the other elements such as fires, water and wind erosion. Imagine if we could tap into that sort of strength and sense of survival, or imagine if we, as humans, evolved to a point where we could not only feel the energies of rocks but also communicate with them as easily as the lovable character "Ludo" in Jim Henson's 1986 movie "The Labyrinth."

Stones are forever changing but at a process so slow that it is almost imperceptible and are essentially immortal, mountains and boulders may lose mass, but all that really happens is they break down into smaller rocks, sand and dust particles. The sand, soil and dirt we walk on are, in essence, small grains that have come from something greater. Never gone forever, only transformed into something infinitely measurable, what once was large and great has become a minuscule particle that helps to make up our universe. Stones in general have a lot of myths and folklores attributed to them. In ancient times, large stone structures were believed to be used as calendars or as sacred religious sites (Stonehenge). When placed near the edge of property lines, known as "watcher stones," they protect from evil. Some stones even have properties we cannot yet explain, such as the ringing rocks in Pennsylvania.

Rocks can be used in ordinary types, such as those found anywhere, or as gemstones. Gemstones are typically very popular in pagan practices, but I won't go into them a lot since there are many wonderful books already on the market. I also want to focus on ordinary rocks because they are easily obtained and are often ignored in pagan practices even though their energies are just as powerful. My eleven-year old daughter taught a class about gemstones in our group and she said, "Sometimes an ordinary rock is more powerful because of the personal meaning placed on it."

All rocks, whether purchased or found; gemstone or ordinary, should be cleansed and charged by the person using then. To cleanse, place the rock in a bowl of water and let it sit through a 24-hour cycle so that it gets the blessings of both sun and moon. They can also be buried outside in the dirt or a bowl of sand or salt. To charge rocks, hold in the projective hand (right) and think of what their intent or purpose will be: stability, divination, grounding, etc.

Gemstones

Gemstones, often known as semi-precious stones, are a large part of pagan practices and believed to hold their own magickal properties. These are not the precious stones that have been cut and faceted to adorn jewelry, but the raw or polished versions. Anyone working with gemstones could be said to be working with earth since they are rocks, however the stones each stand for a different element, usually based on color correspondence, such as a blue stone for water or a red stone for fire.

They can be set on altars to represent elemental qualities or altar intent, be worn as jewelry, used for elixirs, or placed in charm bags. There are many different gemstones out there and they all have their own properties and purpose both metaphysically and physically. Take some time to research on the internet or other book sources for a variety of gemstones and their uses. Gemstones also have an array of metaphysical and healing properties and can be worn or used to cure certain ailments.

Worry Stones

A common charm in a variety of religions and even among non-pagans, worry stones are smooth, flat, polished rocks with an ovoid or beveled indent on one end. The indent is usually thumb-sized and the idea is that to alleviate worries stress, hold the stone in one hand and rubbing the thumb in the indent. This custom appears to have originated in Ancient Greece but gained popularity in the 1970's with the 'peace-love' generation. Often seen as just a novelty now, worry stones actually have therapeutic value because the motion and texture is a sensory-stimulation sensation that is soothing. It is similar to a toe-tapper, hair-twirler or pencil-chewer who displays those behaviors when nervous, anxious or worried.

Purchasing a worry is like purchasing gemstones, there is no right or wrong stone but it all depends on the vibrations and feel a person gets from it. Pick up several stones and get a feel for one by holding it and rubbing the indent. Typically, stones will be purchased but if very observant when out on nature walks or camping, it is possible to find flat stones that have a naturally occurring indent. I have a few of these at home, and even a "worry shell" which is a flat piece of seashell that just so happens to have a slight indent on one end. Some worry stones are made using gemstones, as with using crystals; match the gemstone's properties to the problem at hand.

Holey Stones

This is a stone with a naturally occurring hole all the way through it and these powerful amulets go by many names: hag or witch stone, nightmare or dream stone, a pledge or wish stone, eye stone, Holy stone (or holey indicating it has a hole), fairy stone or Odin's stone (Nordic God). The hole must have occurred naturally through some type of and not drilled by man. It is a powerful talisman that can be carried, worn as a necklace, placed around one's home or property, and can be tied to a string for use as a pendulum.

When worn around the neck, carried in a pocket, nailed outside of a building's entrance or hidden inside the home it will ward off negativity, illness, evil, misfortunes, curses, hexes and diseases (which were believed to be caused by evil spirits rather than physical and physiological causes). If it is hung on a tree or outside building it is said to protect the area from natural disasters or negativity and when hung from a boat or car it is said to protect all the passengers. (Keep in mind that these are supplemental and in no way should a person engage in dangerous acts or toss all caution aside just because they have a stone in hand. No stone or any amount of magickal practices can replace common sense).

As a fairy stone it can be used to see spiritual, supernatural or paranormal realms if peering through the holes. To prevent nightmares, night terrors, or other nighttime attacks hang a stone by the bed or place one under the pillow. As a pledge stone they ensure honesty and insight by whomever is holding it or if worn as an amulet it will protect the person from betrayal and dishonesty. They have also been used by the wise women of the past for healing or in birthing. The hole represents the womb and these stones were often near a birthing bed, or worn by a woman in labor, to ease the pains; the bigger the hole in the stone, the easier the birth.

Any hole in a stone or tree that is big enough for a person to walk through is said to cure ailments and make people fertile. However, the downfall is that after walking through the hole the person is indebted to protect that rock or tree for the rest of their life. Their fates have become intertwined with it and should any mishap occur the same will happen to whoever has walked through its hole.

Cornerstones

The cornerstones of building foundations are very important for more than just the structure of the building, but also are an important cultural component of western architecture. A cornerstone is usually the first stone set in the construction of a masonry foundation and was so important symbolically that it often became a ceremonial stone engraved with images, the date of the structure, the architect's name, and culturally significant symbols. Time capsules have also been known to be placed near it a corner stone with an inscription on the stone indicating at what date it should be opened.

This perhaps comes from the tradition of churches and cathedrals placing relics of saints in near the cornerstones as a way to both honor the saint and bless the building. In ancient structures, the cornerstone was always in a northeast point as this was considered an auspicious position. This is such a prominent corner that in Freemasonry, an organization originating with stone masons, an entered apprentice is placed in the northeast corner of the room where the initiation is taking place in honor of the ancient customs.

In ancient Japan the practice of the Hitobashira (human pillar) was practiced. This was a ritual where maidens were buried alive under the cornerstones to ensure that the buildings were protected against disasters or enemy attacks. This is similar to Scandinavian cultures crushing their prisoners under the keels of the longboats as away to appease the Gods before a ship made its first sail.

In kinder and more modern times, ceremonies simply involved placing offerings of grain, wine or oil on or under the cornerstone. During his presidency, George Washington, a suspected Freemason, was even said to place corn kernels and oil on the cornerstone of a building as a way to bless it. These small rituals would bring good luck, prosperity and protection to the building and its inhabitants.

Tombstones or Gravestones

Tombstones, gravestones, grave markers or headstones, they all sound ominous due to their association with graveyards. These markers placed at the head of a burial site to commemorate those interred below may be derived from the belief that heavy rocks were placed on burial sites in order to keep the dead in the ground. Fear of the dead coming back to haunt us either in a spiritual form (ghost) or physical form (zombie or vampire) occupies not only ancient mythology and lore but also that of modern times.

Many superstitions surround ideas of how to keep these creatures of the night at bay. Similar to the collection of graveyard dirt, desecration of graves and cemeteries (while seemingly created for respect of the dead) probably arose from the fear that any mishaps would cause the dead to walk. This fear is so strong that one superstition states to simply point at a tombstone will cause the dead to grab onto the offending finger and not let go. Decorations are also added to the stones in the hop that the spirits will be pleased and stay where they are

Less scary superstitions involve such things as rainwater found on a tombstone will cure freckles (German lore) and the ancient Greco-Roman belief of placing coins with the deceased for payment across the River

Styx. Today, coins are often placed on the gravestones to ensure good luck and payment to the afterlife and as recent as Abraham Lincoln (American president, 1809-1865) this practice was still carried out. These superstitions can be transformed into a form of ancestor veneration by placing coins at the site of a loved one or the dew collected to be used in anointing or blessing magickal tools or spaces.

Spells and Rituals

Most stone magick comes in the form of charm bags or as talismans. They have energies of their own and are as old as time, so they have an eternal quality that lends importance and long-lasting abilities to any spell or ritual work. For most of the spells below (and also for divination) regular rocks or gemstones can be used.

Basic Charm Bags

Charm Bags are what I call "portable spells" and are meant to be worn or carried by the person using the magick. Any small trinkets such as charms, bones, roots, herbs or stones can be added to the bag. The bags are usually made of all-natural materials, but I know plenty of people who enjoy the mesh, drawstring bags available in craft supply stores because of the drawstring and for the choice of colors.

Color correspondence can play a large role in charm bags, for example a green bag is used for money or a red bag for love. Items in a charm bag can be in odd numbers such as three, five, seven or nine, but a general good rule of thumb is to keep them at five items. Too many items and their magick or energies start to counteract each other.

To make a charm bag of stones choose stones befitting the intent and as they are placed into a small bag reflect on each one and what it will do. I always make sure at least one stone is a clear quartz crystal because it enhances the other stones and binds them together. Carry the bag for as long as needed.

When tying a bag closed there is also the option of reciting a short verse as each knot is tied:

> *By the powers of the lord (tie the 1st knot),*
> *By the powers of the lady (tie the 2nd knot),*

By the powers that I hold (tie the 3rd knot),
And so it harms ye none, blessed be.

Once the need has been met, the bag and stones can be put away for future use. If the need has not been met and the bag doesn't seem to work set it on an altar for twenty-four hours to charge it. The purpose of a charm bag is often not necessarily to draw something towards us, but more to boost a person's emotional state by enabling the carrier to feel confident or be more receptive to what they want (love, success, etc.).

Roma (Gypsy) Putsi Amulet

The Roma culture, commonly referred to as 'Gypsy,' (a term which is often used in an offensive manner) is a mix of cultures and religions, and similar to Voo Doo they have a strong basis in Catholic beliefs that is mixed with the traditions of where they live. A nomadic people, they travel and pick up bits of information, spells, recipes, cultures and folk-lore from the cultures surrounding them. Their magick is very secretive and handed down through the generations by word-of-mouth so it can be very hard to gather magickal spells and rituals from this area. But every now and then some surface.

This is similar to the charm bag spells mentioned earlier but instead of being used as a talisman it is used more for directing the magick toward a specific need or wish. In a black pouch place a Holey Stone, a sea shell and a piece of paper with a spiral drawn on it. Then, wear the putsi around the neck go for a walk in the forest, beach or any place of nature

Pay attention to the surroundings, but also try to focus on a need, desire or wish. Look for natural objects and if something stands out (a rock or a seashell for example), pick it up with and hold it in the projective hand. Feel the vibrations of it. If it feels 'right' place it in the putsi while still focusing on the need or wish. Wear the amulet until the wish has come true or the need has passed. Go back to nature (it can be a different spot) and take the previously found object out, and bury it while saying a prayer of thanks to Saint Sara (patron saint of the Roma):

Saint Sara, patron of travelers and gypsies,
I thank you for your aid and guidance, blessed be.

Once the object is buried walk away and don't look back. The putsi can then continue to be worn for protection or it can be stored away with magickal supplies to be used again later.

Ward Stones

This is an excellent charm for children and a great way to introduce them to spells and the magickal world, but it's great for adults too. Spend some time in nature looking for smooth, flat rocks. On one rock paint the name of the person the stones are being used by (paint pens or permanent markers are easier to use then a paintbrush). On the other stone paint a picture of the person's favorite animal or cut out a picture from a magazine or clipart and adhere it with glue. Stones can be coated with clear varnish to ensure the longevity of the decorations. The Eye of Horus can also be drawn on one of the stones (an Egyptian eye that is believed to hold protective powers).

Whenever the need to feel their protective powers arises, or to stave of negativity, illness and any other ill-well hold one stone in each hand and clack them together, once for each line of the stanza below:

Once to call the Lady [or Goddess];

Once to call the Lord [or God];

Once to call the power these stones hold.

Visualize the fear, illness or negativity dissipating with each clack of the stones and disappearing completely on the last line. The process can be repeated two more times if needing that extra boost and with which repetition speak in a louder, more confidant voice. Try visualizing sparks, or flames coming from the rocks as they are struck together. Visualization is a powerful aid in boosting that confidence that the magick has worked.

Circle of Stones

Because of their natural properties, stones are good for blessing or cleansing items. Objects buried in dirt or small pebbles will be cleansed by the natural energies of the soils but for objects that are too big to be buried or of damage might occur, placing pebbles around the object is the perfect solution. Take a handful of high vibration stones (see Meditation in this section) of an odd number and place them around the object. Leave it overnight to get the blessings of sun and moon and then retrieve the object and either leave the stones to nature or place them with magickal supplies. To enhance the power of the stones protective symbols, such as runes or elemental symbols, can be drawn on with a permanent marker.

Small stone circles, like their larger scale cousins such as Stonehenge, are also great ways to map out scared outdoor space, a fire pit, ceremonial circles or labyrinths. Place stones in a circle large enough to accommodate the needs and visualize what their purpose is (protection, barriers, blessings). Symbols can be painted on the stones either for protection, a coded message or to show the directional points.

Pebbles of Protection

This is a simple protective charm that can be done anywhere there is running water. Reach down into the water and remove five small pebbles (about the size of dimes or pennies) and hold them in the projective hand, visualize a need for protection. Imagine each stone emitting its own protective white or blue light until the rays merge into one and create a protective circle or barrier. Carry the stones in a pocket or charm bag and charge them as needed by holding them and visualizing the light. To return the stones to the earth, place them back in running water.

This can also be done with just one pebble, it should be a slightly larger stone than the five pebbles above, but still small enough to fit comfortably in the palm. With it in hand, sit on the ground (to connect to earth) and meditate for ten to fifteen minutes. Then, start reciting the following verse:

> *Evil and negativity this rock will deny;*
>
> *Sending it harmlessly to earth and sky;*
>
> *Sending it towards the flames and seas*
>
> *and sending it all away from me.*

Carry the stone and hold in one hand anytime its powers are needed.

Divination, Meditation, Scrying

Stones for the purpose of divination are quite common and an age-old practice (the Futhark Rune stones are one example) and can be as simple as using two stones of opposing colors or an entire set of stones marked with symbols.

As always, with any divinatory method, keep in mind it is meant to be more of guide then a set-in-stone prediction (pardon the pun.) No future is pre-determined but can be varied depending on the paths we choose. There are always contributing factors to off-set a divination such as geographic conditions (magnetic, weather, or electrical interferences), the diviner or querent's mood, atmospheric conditions and other natural occurrences that can't be controlled. Never let go of common sense when deciding what to do about a divination's responses or answers.

Black and White Stones

Divination can involve interpreting symbols, signs, meanings, and 'yes and no' methods. The 'yes and no' method is the easiest to learn and interpret because there is no symbol meanings to learn and memorize; the answer is quite literally either yes or no. There are many ways to do this with stones and other methods can easily be created, but here are a few simple ones that I enjoy.

Place one black and one white stone in a container. Think of a question that can be answered in a 'yes or no' method (sometimes this might take creativity to rephrase a question in this manner, but the time it may take to focus on a question helps to make the intent more specific and secure). Once the question is formed, shake the container and then reach in blindly with the receptive hand and grab a stone. Or, toss the stones onto a flat surface like dice and gauge the answer depending on which stone is closest to the querant. A white stone is a positive answer and a black stone is a negative answer.

There is also another method involving four to eight stones with an equal number of black and white. Make sure it is of an equal number, having six black and two white stones will throw off the results, kind of like stacking a Tarot Deck. Place the stones on a flat surface and have the querant close their eyes. With one hand, jumble the stones around while concentrating on a question. Once they feel adequately mixed, the querant will grab one stone (without opening their eyes). After a stone has been grabbed the querant can open their eyes, a white stone is yes or that the outcome is positive and a black stone means no or that the outcome is negative.

Prophecy Pebbles

This is one of my favorite divination methods that I came across on the internet years ago. It requires only three to four rocks of either gemstones or found rocks. For my set I purchased polished river rocks from the craft section of a department store. Anything will work as long as four hues or distinctive markings can be found. I keep my prophecy pebbles in a small mesh pouch, and with the rocks only being the size of nickels or pennies they can be carried in a purse or pocket.

The pebbles all represent different aspects: a positive answer, a negative answer, and an indicator stone The fourth stone is optional, but if used it will represent 'maybe' and will be used in conjunction with the yes and no stones. Seashells can also be used, which makes this a perfect divination for Sea Witchery. The stones or shells need to be of enough color variation that it is easy to remember which stone represents yes, and so on. In my set I have a white stone for yes, a black for no, a gray for maybe and the indicator stone is smaller and red.

The site never talked about charging the pebbles but I charged them by holding each stone and imbuing it with energies of its purpose. For example, if charging the positive answer stone, hold it and think positive keywords: yes, positive, okay, yeah and so on. For the "maybe" pebble think of words like: maybe, so-so, could be, perhaps, it may happen, possibly, etc. The indicator stone does not need to be charged as it is only used as a marker of sorts.

Hold all of the stones in the projective hand and think of a 'yes and no' question, then shake them and onto a flat surface. Look at the stones and determine which one is closest to the indicator stone, use a piece of string, a stick or a ruler if they look to be a close match. The stone that is closest to the indicator stone is the answer; the closer the stones are to the indicator stone the more definitive the answer is. If the maybe stone comes between the indicator and the answer stone, then interpret it a 'maybe' but leaning more towards either yes or no (depending on what the answer stone is). If it is not between an answer stone and the indicator stone, then just cast it out of interpretation and go with whichever stone is closest to the indicator.

The Nine Stones

This divination technique is one that can be created and kept in a magickal box or taken along during travels. Gather nine stones of nine different colors. It may not be possible to find nine different colors naturally so use gemstones or paint rocks in the different colors. Instead of stones I used buttons when I created my set. Stones should be kept in a yellow sack made of natural cloth; drawstring bags work great because they can be tied off to keep the stones safe in between uses.

Whenever needing a sneak peek into the future, focus on a time period (tomorrow, next week, etc) or a general question and reach blindly into the sack to pull out one stone. Questions should not be asked in a specific format like a 'yes and no' even in a 'should I' format but need to be more generic like "what can I expect for today?" or "what do I need to be aware of next week?"

If familiar with color magick the interpretations may come easy, but let me recommend copying down the color interpretations and keeping it with the stones, it can be stored in the same bag. Each stone's color is representative of a particular emotion or aspect of life, but interpretations also need to be based on the querant's life situation, mood and emotions.

White—protection or positivity; the querent should surround themselves with protection, the outlook is positive, good things are coming, or it can simply mean 'yes.'

Green—all things dealing with money, business, prosperity or luck; money will come, business prospects are good, a new job or career is in the works or finances are looking up, or luck coming (luck can also be symbolized by orange to avoid confusion).

Red —love, passion, intense emotions; romance is blooming, an existing romance will (or needs to) flourish, a new romance is in the air, it's time to get passionate about something, or follow a passion.

Orange—luck, energy or revitalizing; luck is coming, time to take a chance, time to renew or revitalize something, or time to put forth the energy into something (like a project).

Yellow—wisdom or enlightenment; education should be or is being sought, the querent will receive or give wisdom to someone, think hard about the problem at hand and use wisdom or intelligence to resolve it, or it represent religious enlightenment.

Brown—the color for worldly and earthly things as well as grounding; the querent is too focused on materialistic things, an object (gadget, home, land, toys, furniture, etc) will come to the querent, or the querent needs to focus more on home and stay more grounded (keep their head out of the clouds).

Blue—peace and serenity; a peaceful resolution, querent will find peace, meditation is suggested to resolve the problem, peace and serenity is around the querent, or maybe the querent needs to take some time to themselves.

Purple—royalty and spiritualism; spiritualism is sought, a person needs to focus more on their spirituality or beliefs, spiritual enlightenment, or regality (being regal) is required to deal with the current situation.

Black—negativity, but unlike popular opinion, it is not a bad thing (when tests results come back 'negative' it is a good thing, so think of black in color magick as a good thing). In this case, it could mean that someone around the querent, or the querent themselves, is negative and this negativity needs to be released or protected against or it can simply mean 'no'.

Low Vibe and High Vibe Stones

Gather a few rocks that appeal visually, tactilely, and that fits neatly in the palm. Sit in a place that is comfortable and undisturbed. Hold a rock in the projective hand and meditate on it by feeling its texture, its temperature, the shape and the hard or softness of it; feel it and visualize it. Feel the warmth and vibrations coming from it, it may be like a pulsing or vibrating on the flesh or even just a sense within the mind. Determine if the vibrations are high or low. Do this with several stones and store them separately, when needed a stone of specific vibrations its easy to just grab one, charge it with intent and go on with the magickal workings.

High vibration stones will have fast paced, vigorous or erratic rhythms and the energies are quickly dispersed. They work best for quick-acting spells where an immediate result is needed or where the effects don't have to last a long time (need money fast to make a payment but not a steady income, for example).

Low vibration stones exhibit slow and sedate rhythms and the energies are slower to be dispersed which makes them perfect for spells or rituals that take longer to complete or where long-lasting effects are needed (needing a job with steady income rather than receiving a one-time amount quickly).

Communication

To send a message (telepathically) to someone use a high-vibration stone and a piece of chalk. Write a brief message or a symbol on the stone and bury it deep in the earth while visualizing the person's face and the need for contact. The message will be sent through the earth and the person receiving the message may either 'hear' it telepathically or just get that urge to call or write.

Keep in mind that this is not a perfect form of communication and should not be used in emergency situations but more in a situation of having lost contact with someone and wanting to get reacquainted. It is also good practice for increasing psychic abilities. Make arrangements with a friend to send each other messages for a specific time period, such as a week. Each person should keep a log of when they sent or felt they received a message including date, time, and for the receivers, how the message was received.

Examples of receiving a message might be the sudden urge to call, seeing their image mentally, a dream, or even just coming across their name somewhere (like in movie credits or a book). Compare the results and then wait a few days and try again. Eventually the times between sending and receiving may mesh together so that at the moment a message was sent, the receiver was getting it.

Magick for the Earth Witch
Section VII

Plants and Trees

All herbs, trees or flowers can be considered of the earth element since they are living plants, but each element also has its own plant correspondences based on the similarities between the properties of the plant and of the element. For example, a passionate herb or flower such as a rose might be of the fire element.

Ellen Dugan has a book titled "Garden Witchery" that is a great source for all garden magick and even includes non-magickal gardening tips such as layouts, seasons and care. Any of the herbal books on the market are good, but one I highly recommend is "Cunningham's Encyclopedia of Magickal Herbs" by Scott Cunningham. It has folklore, common and scientific names, and the medicinal or metaphysical purposes accompanied by sketch drawings for easy identification.

Herbs and flower scents act on two different levels: aromatherapy and metaphysical. Aromatherapy is the use of oils extracted from plants to alleviate an array of psychological, physical or emotional states and disorders. Usually it is used through massage (oils or lotions) or inhalation (incense, diffusers, and sachets). It is a common practice among people even of monotheistic beliefs and is recommended by the medical fields as well as therapists.

In metaphysical terms, because trees, herbs and flowers are living plants, they have a life force of their own and that when this essence comes forth through the plant (even when dried out or turned to oils or incenses) these plants will empower us with the same qualities.

Plants and trees have a wide variety of uses both mundane and magickally. Trees are used for shelters and firewood, plants and edible flowers are used for food, and they can be used for decoration. Magickally speaking, they each have their own metaphysical or homeopathic uses and most plants or trees have more than one use. Sage is a favorite among pagans for its cleansing properties, and it also can be used in foods. Trees might be made into wands or staffs in pagan practices, but are also used to make furniture, tool handles and lumber for our homes.

There is no harm in using natural vegetation for use in magick or mundane practices but make it a point to either use what has fallen naturally, grow it for a specific use, or replace what was used. Think of magickal plants the same way as a garden: we grow veggies, pick them, and replant more the next year. Also, know which plants in the area are poisonous or which plants in stores are poisonous to animals; some of the plants we purchase can be harmful to our pets but not necessarily harmful to us. Also, keep in mind that in some state parks it is illegal to pick the plants, so just gather what has already fallen from the stalks.

Herb Magick

If possible, obtain these plants from their natural environment; they are even more powerful especially if homegrown since personal energy goes into care and harvesting. But store-bought herbs can be just as good if fresh are not available. Plants and herbs are used in essential oils, dried plants, in sachet bags or charm bags, or mixed into incense. Potted herbs make great additions to a home that serve as protection when placed in kitchen windows, near the front door or any room of the house and they a readily available supply of herbs by simply pinching off what is needed.

Essential oils are difficult to make, it is best to leave this up to the experts and buy oils from metaphysical shops or online. There is also a difference between essential oils and fragrance oils. Fragrance oils are used in room deodorizers or to scent potpourri, they are not 100% plant essence. Essential oils are pure plant oil and sometimes can be found in health food stores or sections. Tea Tree Oil is 100% plant essence and I purchase a large bottle for $7.00 at Wal-Mart. It is a topical aid as well as a conditioner when added to lotions or shampoos, so it is sold in health and pharmacy departments. Oils can be used in burners, a few drops added to the melted pool of wax on a candle, or to anoint and bless people and objects. Some oils can cause rashes or allergic reactions so it is best to dilute them first if anointing a person with oil. They are also not for human consumption.

Incense is easier to make and the book "Kitchen Witchery: A compendium of Oils, Unguents, Incense, Tinctures, and Comestibles" by Marilyn F. Daniel has wonderful instructions for loose, cone and stick incense. Loose incense must be burned on a charcoal disc (not the type used for outdoor grills) and cones or sticks are lit, the flame blown out and left to smolder. Incense is always recommended as an aromatherapy tool and often used in alternative health facilities, such as for massage therapy, to help relax clients. Incenses can be used for ambience, to represent the air element, used in meditation, divination (in the smoke), as ambiance, or aromatherapy. Dried herbs also come in the form of smudge sticks, which are tightly, bound, dried herbs (including leaves and stems) that are burned like incense. The most popular among pagans and in Native American practices is to use white sage. But, at times regular sage and even lavender have been used or the smudge stick is a combination of herbs.

For charm bags, place a few herbs that correspond to the intent into the bag. Typically, these herbs are added as a supplement to the stones, to further enhance their power, however, in Voodoo, it is believed that the charm bag has to be 'fed' and herbs would be dropped into the bag periodically as a way of feeding the magick. Another way to look at this is that it is really just re-charging the bag; we eat when we need to recharge, so the bag needs to eat to re-charge. Sachets are usually the herbs only and made more for their scent than anything else.

Dream pillows can also be considered sachets as they are small pillows (about six inches) that are filled with herbs known for their relaxing qualities such as lavender, chamomile or celery seed.

Sachets can be hung in a room, placed in drawers or hung in a car in order to add a pleasing scent. They can also be carried by the person and sniffed when needing a boost in whatever the herb provides, for example, there is a sachet bag spell involving cinnamon that when sniffed will increase romantic feelings. My favorite thing to do with a sachet is to fill it up with good-smelling herbs and toss it in the dryer. It scents the clothes and acts as a mild static reducer (it doesn't seem to work well on very static-inducing materials such as fleece).

The Language of Flowers

In the Victorian Age (mid 1800's to early 1900's, named after Queen Victoria of the UK), the language of flowers was a very popular concept and messages could be sent with the offering of one single flower. They also inhabited much of the décor of the Victorian age and prominent homes would have gardens for spending leisure time or in order to keep fresh-cut flowers in the home. The status or wealth of a person could often be seen in the extravagances of their garden.

Today, the most common flower to give as a gift is the red rose, which symbolizes love and given out most often on the American holidays of St. Valentine's and Mother's Day. Today, people don't think about the color of flowers but instead go with the basic red or with a floor that is the recipient's favorite. However, in the Victorian age, doing this could get a person in trouble. A yellow rose meant the giver was jealous and white roses were a sign of purity or chasteness. Pink meant that love was there, but not in a marrying capacity (more like friendship or familial love). No girl would want to receive the jealous rose of yellow or the brotherly love of pink from a sought-after beau.

Like all phases and trends, the Victorian language of flowers has gone to the wayside of beliefs and is nothing more than cute folklore. However, as with gemstones and herbs, there is a folkloric legend or metaphysical meaning behind every flower. Often they are correlated with herbs since many herbs produce flowers (such as lavender). Take the time to know local vegetation and also the specific properties of a variety of flowers that can be purchased in metaphysical shops.

Naturally, there are hundreds of flowers and it is impossible to remember every last one of them and their folklores. But I recommend going for a walk, even just in the yard, and noting the different flowers. Take a picture and write down a description in detail. Later on, research the flower and find its medicinal, practical, and magickal uses. Often the stems, leaves, wood, and flowers can all be used and we record each of their qualities. We often do this in my family, and I type the information up and add it to our own personal herb Book of Shadows.

There is also a way to use flower magick that doesn't require memorizing different flowers but instead is to attach color meaning to the flowers. Similar to the magick involving candles, gemstones or feathers, the flowers can be used for their color correspondence.

Flower Color

Green—this is the color of the element of earth, of fairies, healing, money, luck, prosperity and fertility.

White—the color of the maiden, it is an all-purpose color used for purity, protection and moon magick. It is the color of the goddess or all lunar deities.

Pink—this color is for friends, children, affection and innocence. It is a lighter shade of love so it encompasses love that is innocent and less-inhibited such as family and friends.

Red—this is the color of the mother, the element of fire and it represents all things passionate such as love, lust and sex.

Yellow—the color of the element of air, it is used for wisdom, mental powers, divination and communication and for to represent the sun, as well as solar or male deities.

Orange—revitalizing and full of energy, orange can be used for vitality, success and stimulation.

Purple—this is the color of power, psychic abilities, and spirituality.

Blue—the color of the element of water, use blue flowers for healing, sleeping, peacefulness and calming.

Browns or shades of it—home, stability, grounding, animals or pet magick and hearths.

Blacks or all dark shades—this is the color of the crone, use it for banishing, breaking hexes, and removing negativity.

Tree Magick

Those of pagan faiths, involved in the Eco-friendly movement, or of the 'hippie' generation have often slanderously been called "tree-worshippers' or 'tree-huggers' as a way to criticize beliefs. This is a misnomer; trees are not actually worshipped as a God, but like all nature worship, are honored and revered for their natural energies. Trees have always been held sacred, especially to Druid or Celtic traditions, and each one has a magick and lore of its own.

Wood nymphs, known as Dryads, are said to live in trees, or even be the spirit of the tree, and it is believed that the superstition of knocking on wood to advert bad luck comes from knocking to gain the Dryads favor or permission for something. It may also come from a belief that a person is making an appeal to Christ's cross and to not tempt fate. Trees have a long life and have outlived many a man and seen many things.

In the mythology of the Zaire people of Africa, there are tree spirits known as Biloko. They live in the hollows of trees and dress only in leaves and instead of hair they grow grass on their bodies. Biloko are not as nice as Dryads but are frightening with their piercing eyes, sharp claws and a snout that can open wide enough to swallow a man whole, dead or alive. It is said that they will put spells on people who pass by their trees unless that person is protected by a stronger counter-magick.

Each individual tree has its own properties and folklore, and like flowers or herbs, it can be overwhelming to memorize them all. However, color magick won't work in this instance unless using the color of the flowers or fruit that the tree grows. Again, I suggest learning a few common trees or learn just the trees in the nearby area. If planning on using these plants in magick and in their natural form, it does no good to learn about a tree that only grows in a foreign country that is not likely to be visited anytime soon.

Spells and Rituals

The spells and rituals involving plant magick are very beneficial because of the natural energies of the plants, and they can be used in a variety of ways. As mentioned earlier, plants can be used in oil form, as incense or in charm and sachet bags. But, the parts of a plant, flower or herb can also be used 'as-is' without alternating it a powdered, dried or oiled form, as the spell below shows.

Leaf Spell

This spell is to be used to attract an item that is desired (not for finding a lost item, but for gaining an item previously not owned). Draw a stick-figure style symbol of the item on a leaf using a charred stick (place the tip of a stick in a fire or candle until sufficiently charred). Tie the leaf around a tree with a vine or twine made of natural fibers. Walk around the tree three times while reciting:

> *I call upon the element of the Earth,*
>
> *That's older than time can tell,*
>
> *Bring to me the object I desire*
>
> *And work my magick spell.*

Continue reciting this verse until three complete circles around the tree have been made. Then, walk away leaving the vine and leaf there. As the leaf and vine dry out and eventually fall off the tree, the magick will be released and soon the object will be found for purchase or given as a gift.

St. Frances' Flower Sachet

In a craft book I used to own there was a neat sachet, called a tussie-mussie that was in honor of St. Frances (not to be confused with St. Francis of Assisi). Frances was known for learning a hard lesson between what she wanted to do and what God wanted her to do. A common prayer said to her is: "Saint Frances of Rome, help us to see the difference between what we want to do and what God wants us to do. Help us to discern what comes from our will and what comes from God's desire. Amen." This can be adapted to fit with a specific pagan belief and recited during times of struggle between right and wrong, or doing the right thing even if it's not what we want to do.

I have revised the craft slightly to become a spell that can be done anytime a person needs to feel spiritual enlightenment or at times when it may be necessary to stop working so hard towards a goal or desire and let the divine step in and give aid. Sometimes situations call for letting go of the worries and just living with a faith that things will work out for the best. It is one of the hardest things in this world to do.

For this spell whole and dried flowers can be used since they are going into a sachet. If wanting to make loose incense out of the flowers they can be crushed in a mortar and pestle and burned on charcoal discs rather than put in a charm bag. Recite the following verse as each flower is added:

Give me strength and inner peace (add Lily-of-the-Valley)

When hatred infests let love soon grow (add a Rose)

Where injury occurs there shall also be pardon (add Hyssop)

If doubt is cast let faith reside (add Violet)

Where there is despair, let hope blossom (add Daisy)

When the darkness looms let light shine forth (add Rue)

And when sadness takes over let joy be remembered (add Marjoram)

When the sachet is filled hang it in a prominent place in the house or carry it as a reminder to let the divine take over and make things right.

Herbal Bath Ball

This is a great spell or craft to make when there are a few bits of herbs left over from various magickal workings. There is no set combination of herbs to combine, but try to pick ones that smell good together or with similar intents. It's no good to put two opposing herbs together if they just cancel each other out, unless using them for their scent only and not magickal intent.

Mix together left over herbs (non-poisonous please!) and place two or three teaspoons in the center of a 6-inch square of cotton or muslin material. Pull the four corners up and tie with a ribbon. During a bath, toss the ball in and let the aromatic and magickal pleasures of the herbs wash over the senses through the water and steam.

Cinnamon Love Sachet

This spell is not for making a person fall in love, but to enhance romantic feelings already in existence or to spice up s love life. Powdered cinnamon or cinnamon sticks can be used for this, and a red square of fabric with red lace is also needed. Lay the fabric out flat and place the cinnamon in the center of it. Bring the corners up and tie it with the red lace. Set the sachet on a pentacle (the soapstone or wood-engraved pentagrams mentioned earlier are good for this, but a hand-drawn pentacle will work too). With hands placed around, but not touching the sachet, visualize the intent and recite the following verse:

To spice up my love life,

To place fun in my heart,

To bring to me excitement

Is what this spell with impart

Carry the sachet or place it near the bed and when needing to feel a little romance or love, sniff the bag and breathe its spicy and heady scent. Cinnamon is known to increase vitality, circulation and re-energize; the aromatherapy aspect of it works the same as ingesting it and the spicy aroma will increase these three qualities, which aid in feelings of romance and excitement.

Ash Good Luck

Ash part of what is known as the "fairy tree trinity" (hawthorn and oak being the other two) and it can be used in a good luck spell. Leaves with the same number of divisions or segments can be used with the following verse, which comes from basic superstition, for good luck. At the recitation of each verse, pluck a leaf off and the either wear it or carry it around:

"Even Ash, I do thee pluck,

Hoping thus to meet good luck,

If no good luck I get from thee

I shall wish thee on a tree."

It is advisable to use a leaf that has fallen, but if plucking from a live tree ask permission of the tree spirits first.

The Fair Maid

Hawthorn, or May Blossom, is another of the fairy tree trinity (a belief that where the three trees grow, fairies can be seen). Because of its association with fairies, permission to cut it must be received from these wee folk first. It is a tree of protection and the dew collected on or near it at Beltane (May 1st) can be used in a multitude of concoctions for protection, beauty or longevity. This idea is seen in the following Mother Goose nursery rhyme:

> *The fair maid who, the first of May,*
> *Goes to the fields at break of day,*
> *And washes in dew from the hawthorn-tree,*
> *Will ever after handsome be.*

It was believed that the dew collected under this sacred tree was sure to keep a woman's face beautiful and youthful and was a tradition that was actually practiced as recent as the Victorian Age. Try collecting some dew to use for anointing persons in a ritual or magickal tools.

Divination, Meditation, Scrying

Divining with trees and plants can be one of the most rewarding because of the natural life forces already evident in them; their magickal energy empowers the divination process. The leaves, nuts, petals, and twigs can all be used to divine and scry with. As children, we did this with daisies and the refrain "he loves me, he loves me not" as petals were pulled off. The words said when the last petal was plucked was the answer. This can still be done today by concentrating on a question and plucking the petals until none remain. However, do so with a flower that has a lot of petals rather than one of only a few. It is too easy to "stack the deck" and start with a particular answer first to guarantee that the last answer is the one the diviner wants to hear.

Acorn Divination

Another simple method of divining that can be done anywhere is with an acorn and a bowl of water (or a deep puddle). Name one acorn 'yes' and the other 'no' or give each one two possible outcomes such as "custodian job" or "librarian job." It might be easiest to mark them with a permanent marker or use one with a cap and one without so that it is easy to remember which acorn stands for which answer. Place them both into the center of a basin of water, make sure there is enough water so they can float, and concentrate on the question. The one that floats away towards the far edge of the basin is not the answer and the one floating towards the closer edge is. If they both float an equal distance in either direction (to or fro) it means that the answer cannot be revealed at this time and should be tried later.

Leaf Divination

In the autumn, a simple leaf divination can be done that is entirely in the hands of the tree spirits. Underneath a deciduous tree (the type that loses their leaves) use a stick to draw a square or circle bisected with a line in the dirt. On one side write YES and on the other side NO then concentrate on the question needing answered. Walk away for a few hours or even until the next day and then return. The side that has the most fallen leaves in it is the answer. If neither side has any leaves or is equal then the question cannot be answered at this time.

Counting Rings

Counting the rings of tree stumps is one method of determining its age; this can also be used in divination purposes by counting the rings and interpreting an answer determined by an odd number or even number of rings. Sit by a tree and meditate on a question, calling upon the tree spirits that dwell within. When the focus of the intent is clear and well-defined, break a stick off from a branch and count the rings within.

If the rings are not easily discernible, try counting the segments or shoots that are on the broken piece. An even number is a negative answer and an odd number is a positive answer. This can also be done by asking a question that is answered in a number such as "how many days until I find true love" or "how many children will I have." A stump that is already cut can also be used, and is easier to count the rings on. Sit on the stump and meditate on the question. Feel the energies of the stump and of the life force it still harbors. Keep in mind that the larger the stump the more rings there are. Obviously, this method might not be appropriate for questions involving number answers because the numbers can end in hundreds (and who wants a hundred children?!) but it works well for divining an answer based on even or odd numbers.

Basic Meditation

The best way to meditate with trees or plants is simply to go for a walk and spend some time among them. Observe them, smell them, touch them and listen to them and just let the thoughts flow uninhibited. Spend some time in a wooded area and observe the animals in the trees, try to discern the different bird calls and what the bird might look like. Watch the squirrels or chipmunks playing and try to keep an eye on their rapid movements or jumping from tree to tree. Listen to the wind in the trees, the rustle of the leaves and try to hear messages the sounds might bring. Or, lay back and look up into the canopies. Similar to candle meditation, patterns can emerge in the tree tops or the mind will just 'go blank' and allow subconscious thoughts to flow into the conscious.

The Grass Journal

Quite a few years ago I read a message board post about a "Grass Journal" in which the writer described sitting amongst a grassy area and letting the thoughts flow freely as their hands played in the grasses. At one point they would pluck a piece of grass and whatever the thoughts were at that moment were what was written about in a diary. An entire diary could be done this way or as just a few added entries in a journal, diary or book of shadows. It is a very peaceful, easy and non-restrictive form of meditation and great inspiration when unsure of what to write about.

Magick for the Earth Witch
Section VIII

Mythology and Folklore

Since the earth element is inclusive of our planet earth the folklore and mythology regarding it is endless. Worship of the planet has been around since before written history and how the planet and its living inhabitants were made is truly the stuff of legends. It seems that every religion has an origin myth of the planet and our existence in it. There are numerous gods of the earth as a planet, gods of different components in the universe such as the sun, moon, skies, waters and stars. There are also numerous gods that encumber more obscure aspects of the earth element such as agriculture, crops, animals, hunting and harvesting. Artemis, Greek goddess of the hunt, is usually considered an earth goddess since she is of hunting and often also associated with agriculture. Hecate is also considered an earth goddess since she is of the hearth and home, which are earth attributes.

Since earth is an element that encompasses everything that is not of fire, water and air, all of the superstitions and folklore attributed to rocks, trees or animals can also be included in the mythology. For the purpose of this book I have tried to focus on just those that deal with the earth as a planet or with its soils since those are more specific concepts to work with.

Earth Creation Stories

Among the folklore and mythology of earth as a planet is perhaps one of the most heated of debates: its creation. There is no right or wrong answer; it is all dependent on a person's beliefs. Science and religion are in constant battles to prove the planet's age, creation or the purpose of human life. Each practitioner will have to judge for themselves which set of theology or science is "right for them." I have only included the two most popular (creationism versus evolutionism) and then one more obscure earth-creation that I found interesting when I came across it.

Christian Bible

The Christian Bible starts off with earth's creation in the book of Genesis. It is said that "in the beginning, God created the heavens and the earth. Now the earth was formless and empty, darkness was over the surface of the deep and the Spirit of God was hovering over the waters" (Genesis 1: 1-2) He then goes on to proclaim, in turn, each of the things earth needs: animals, plants, etc., and he creates the earth in six days, resting on the seventh. This seventh day has become a time for rest and worship and in mainstream Christianity and is observed on Sunday, but various other sects or religions may hold a different day of the week as their Sabbath. In Wicca and Paganism there is not any one day of the week that is considered to be holy, but each practitioner may have a specific date set aside that is important to them.

Scientific "Big Bang" Theory

Without getting too technical, this is a scientific theory of the creation of the universe based on the premise that it was created from primordial ooze and is continually expanding. Georges Lemaitre developed this theory with the aid of Albert Einstein's studies of general relativity and simplifying assumptions. Known at the time as the "hypothesis of the primeval atom" the term "big-bang theory" came about in 1949 during a radio broadcast by Fred Hoyle, who coined the phrase. It is based on observing the universe and our own planet and hypothesis on how things were made and what they are made out of. It is science's best logic for creating something out of nothing; whereas religious creation stories start with either a planet and adding life to it (like adding "sea monkeys" to water), or with a god-like energy that creates everything.

Adro and Adroa

In the mythology of the Lugbara people of the West Nile region of Uganda Africa we get the earth creation myth of Adro and Adroa. Adroa was an all-good creator of everything in the world, including of his self. He divided himself into two in order to create the earth. By splitting, his all-good self remained in the figure of Adroa but his other self, Adro became all-evil (assuming that there was no good left for the 2nd self, and the absence of good is evil). Adro became an evil earth-spirit that lived and swam in the waters of the world. His children, the Adronazi (water-snakes), were evil and swam the waters with him drowning and eating people. Adroa went on create all of the good things in the world.

This myth gives us a clear concept of "good versus evil" much like that of Christian lore with the concept of God (good and light) and Satan (evil and dark). Unlike the Christian lore, Ador and Adroa were not two separate entities as Satan and God were but came from the same being, this also shows us that humans all have a good and bad side to them, sort of like the 'evil-twin' theory that is often joked about. It also shows that without evil we do not have the good.

Elementals

Gnomes

Gnomes have their fair share of fame in popular media and literature and have even come to decorate our lawns. Today, especially in home décor and as the mascot for Travelocity, gnomes are seen as wearing blue or green outfits and with tall, red and point caps. Historically, gnomes were cave and earth dwellers usually are depicted in clothes made of natural fibers or leaves and their skin is an earth-tone color. There is a belief in some Wiccan and pagan traditions that a person can project a thought form in the shape of a gnome as an aid for doing long-distant work, particularly that of healing.

Holidays

Since earth, as a planet, is our home it has its own holidays to revere it and show respect to it. Both of the holidays were created decades ago as a way to get the word out about our planet, its resources and how we can preserve it. However, it seems that the honoring of the holidays has gone through cycles. In my youth in the 80's we had never heard of "Earth Day" but we did plant trees on "Arbor Day." In the late 90's and certainly in the year 2000 on up, Earth Day has become a dominant holiday due to the eco-friendly movement and Earth Day implies honoring all of the planet rather than just one aspect of it, like Arbor Day and trees.

Earth Day and Arbor Day

Earth Day is celebrated by the United Nations (UN) On March 21st, the Spring Equinox, and on April 22nd by the remaining world. It is estimated that over a billion people worldwide now honor earth day and it has become a state holiday in many places. It is one of the few holidays that honored simultaneously around the globe by people of all religions, nationalities, ethnicities, culture and race.

In 1969 peace activist, John McConnell founded the tradition in the UN using the Spring Equinox as the day and on this day, a Japanese Peace Bell is rung on this day (a gift from Japan). A second Earth Day was founded in 1970 on April 22nd for all of the public as a way to teach environmental concerns. By the year 2000 the number of celebrants was approximately one billion and Earth Day was observed in over 180 countries. Communities often host talks or events that discuss environmental concerns or show others how to recycle and why protecting the earth is important.

This is a good day to connect with the earth by getting more involved in recycling, gardening, or beautifying the neighborhood or city. In honor of the UN's traditions, ring a bell prior to any spell work or ritual. Me and my family planted snapdragons in honor of Earth Day and my local pagan group gathered to do a ritual to bless the earth and we planted flowers. My family also attended an earth day event in town. There are plenty of ways to honor the earth and with Arbor Day not far away the two days can be incorporated together.

Arbor Day is a holiday in which people are encouraged to plant and care for trees. Originating in Nebraska City, Nebraska it is celebrated in various countries on different dates but in the United States it is always the last Friday in April. It is considered a civic holiday and was founded by Julius Sterling Morton.

Johnny Appleseed, an American who has reached folkloric status, planted Apple trees as an effort to raise conservation awareness and for the symbolic importance of apples. Born John Chapman on September 26, 1774, Johnny Appleseed was a nurseryman who made it his mission to plant trees in Ohio, Illinois and Indiana; although legends today say that he went across the entire country. His story is a good lesson to teach children or others about the importance of planting trees.

To pagans, both days can be equally important and while not a Sabbat on the Wiccan Wheel of the Year, they can be incorporated into pagan practices with a ritual or spell designed for blessing or healing the earth. Remember, the earth is over a million years old; so respect your elders.

Gods and Goddesses

As mentioned earlier, there are many Gods or Goddesses that can be associated with the element of earth; any one of the patrons of agriculture, home, hearth, prosperity, cycles, animals, hunting or any other such area. Similar to the element itself, any deity that does not fit in with the elements of water, air and fire can be said to be of earth. I have chosen just a few to show some of the stories of Earth Gods or Goddesses and I have tried to pick ones that are actually "of the earth" or related to earth-creation stories.

Proserpina

Proserpina is the Roman Goddess of the Earth, and her Greek equivalent Persephone, is legendary with why we have springtime. Proserpina, daughter of Ceres (Goddess of agriculture) and Jupiter (God of thunder and sky) is married to her uncle Pluto. Much like the well-known story of Hades abducting Persephone, Pluto abducted Proserpina and forced her to live with him in the underworld. Her mother went searching for but found only a belt floating in a pool of tears wept by nymphs. At her every step during the search, the ground turned to desert land and Ceres stopped all agricultural growth. Pluto finally allowed Proserpina to return to the land of the living, but for only six months a time and the other six were spent with him in the underworld.

He achieved this by tricking Proserpina into eating Pomegranate seeds because they caused a living person to be able to exist in the underworld but never fully being allowed back into the world of mortals (thus, the joint custody between him and Ceres). Ceres is so happy upon her beloved daughter's return that she allows everything to blossom again (spring and summer) and when Proserpina must return to the underworld Ceres' sadness causes everything to wither and die (fall and winter)

Titans

In Greek Mythology, the Titans are the creator Gods who gave birth to what most people consider the Greek Gods such as Hera, Zeus, Ares, Aphrodite, Poseidon and Apollo (these Gods are known as the Olympians). The Titans are pre-Olympian gods and are the twelve children of Uranus and Gaia, who were the supreme rulers of the Universe until being overthrown by Zeus. It is thought that each God is responsible for some aspect of the creation of earth, for example Oceanus is the personification of a wide and lone river that encircles the earth (the oceans and seas) and Uranus is the sky god.

Some diversity exists among the stories of the Titans depending on what source is being used. Some sites indicate that Chronus or Cronus is the leader alongside of Gaia and as he is thought to be the basis for Father Time, another folkloric character often connected to Mother Nature. Gaia then may have mated with her son Uranus to further create the remaining Titans.

The Titans ruled the earth until Zeus and his sibling overthrew their power and banished them to Tartarus, one of the deepest regions of Hades.

Mother Nature

Even though Mother Nature is a depiction of Gaia, the very term and ideology behind it deserves its own section since she has transformed into her own unique folkloric character. The worshipping of Mother Nature may have started in Neolithic times (8000 to 5000 BCE) as earth-mother worship which gave way to the Indo-European invasion and led to the Hellenistic invasion. Mother Nature has become an iconic figure in popular media such as television or movies and even in commercials. The popular saying "it's not nice to fool Mother Nature" came about from the commercials for Chiffon Margarine (1971-1979), in which the narrator is trying to convince her that what she is eating is margarine and not butter. Played by Dena Dietrich, Mother Nature was a matronly woman dressed in a white gown with a crown of daisies in her hair. She is depicted as a nymph-like forest dweller but one who can release lightning and thunder in her anger at being fooled.

Mother Nature is typically portrayed in such a fashion, usually in earth-tone colors with leaves or flowers adorning her hair or clothing and with lots of animals surrounding her. In the 1974 stop-n-go animation movie "A Year without Santa Claus" she is depicted as the mother of the Snow Miser and Heat Miser who control the climates of the world. Often believed to be in control of all weather conditions, growth and cycles she controls everything having to do with the natural order of things. This means the good as well as the bad and for this reason she is a force to be respected and somewhat awed.

If using Mother Nature in spells or rituals remember to respect the earth and to be very specific, such as in weather spells. Calling on a little rain to harvest crops can go wrong if a specific amount or time limit is not stated; weather is not a force that can be easily controlled and great caution needs to be taken. Mother Nature, in popular media, is often depicted as being the wife of Father Time.

Bhumi

In Hinduism, Bhumi is the depiction of Mother Earth and the divine wife to Lord Varaha. She is often depicted as being seated on a square platform that rests on the back of four elephants. Each of these elephants represents the four corners of the Universe; a similar concept seen in the four points of the universe in Aztec lore and to Egyptian God of Shu or Greek God Atlas who hold up the skies with the aid of four pillars in each of the cardinal points.

She has four arms (multiple arms are a common theme in Hindu mythology) and in each one she holds a pomegranate, water vessel, a bowl of healing herbs and a bowl of fruits and vegetables. The fours arms perhaps represent the four directional points or the four pillars holding up the world or sky. The items in her hands are representative of each element with the pomegranate for fire because of its red interior and its already established connection with the underworld; the vessel holds water; the herbs when burned would be of the air element; and the vegetables are of the earth.

Geb

Egyptian God of the Earth, Geb is the son of Shu (God of the Sky) who holds up the skies. It is said that Shu stands on the body of his son in order to hold up his daughter, Nut the Goddess of the Sky. As a god of the earth, he was one of the more important of the Egyptian Gods. The son of Shu and Tefnut (Goddess of moisture) he is grandson to the creator Gods of Isis and Osiris. His body forms the earth and for this reason he is often depicted in drawings as laying on his side on the earth with plants or leaves growing up and around him. It is said that earthquakes are the result of his laughter.

Magick for the Sea Witch
Section I

The Water Element

Water is a powerful element with both mainstream and ancient religions making use of it in the forms of blessings, naming ceremonies, and inductions into religions as a way to cleanse the soul or purify the body. Many cultures boast of their magical springs, wells, lakes or a Fountain of Youth; Spanish explorer Ponce de Leon (1474-1521) was looking for such a fountain in Florida. Popular legend says that the "sunshine state" of Florida was discovered in Ponce de Leon's quest for these mystical waters, although this legend did not surface until after his death. In the "Historia General y Natural de las Indias" (General and Natural History of the Indies, circa 1535) Gonzalo Fernadez de Oveido y Valdes wrote that Ponce de Leon was looking for waters of vitality-restoration properties in the area of Bimini in an effort to cure his own aging.

Water truly is life giving, we need it to drink, to cook and to bathe in; with 70% of our bodies and 75% of the earth being made up of water it is the key to our survival. In addition to blessings and anointing, it is said to be a deterrent for evil spirits. The belief is that they cannot cross running water, such as in the scene in Washington Irving's tale "The Legend of Sleepy Hollow." When Ichabod Crane is being chased by the Headless Horseman he runs across a bridge and the headless demon stops, not being able to cross over the water. Running water is also said to stop the ghosts of suicide victims and criminals or the walking dead of if the bodies are buried nearby.

As a water sign, or just with an affinity to water, a person might be like the seas on a still day and be calm and deep or they might be a stormy sea with a fierceness that can't be matched. Maybe they are a smaller brook or creek that goes about its business without bothering a soul, staying hidden and yet a joy to those who know it's there or maybe they are a large lake that is visible to all and a place where people go to have fun and mingle. Perhaps a person is like a river that everyone knows about and is very prominent and yet also very shallow, or they are a stream hidden in the depths of caves and hold many secrets. Maybe they are like water in that they can easily adapt to any vessel (situation) that they are placed in, taking the form of first one vessel and then another as situations allow.

Regardless of where it comes from, water gives life to animals, plants and humans; it is warm and relaxing; cool and refreshing; it nurtures and nourishes; it cleanses and cleans; it anoints and blesses and it is an essential element that we, as humans and pagans cannot do without.

Magick for the Sea Witch
Section II

Correspondences

Traditional

Water is generally associated with the west, the color blue, femininity, purification, the chalice and the elemental beings of Undines, which are what we think of today as mermaids. It is symbolic of the womb (birth) and life-giving. It stands for creativity, free-flowing, uninhibited actions, and the ability to adapt. Traditionally, it is linked with the season of autumn but, in our family we associate it with summer because of water play or sports and trips to the beach that occur then. Water magick centers on the subconscious mind, love and emotions because they are fluid and consistently changing like water; they ebb and flow like the waves or tides (emotions is used in the general sense of the word since individual emotions can be specifically placed with the elements, such as anger or passion with fire).

Alchemy and Ancient Medical Practices

In Alchemy the water element is represented by a downward pointed triangle and its chemical element is mercury. Ancient Greek medicine associated it with the season winter and is on the western point of the compass (which coincides with traditional practices). Water is also significant of absorption and germination for plants.

Zodiac and Astrological

Water is a symbol of the Cancer, Pisces and Scorpio birth signs and people under these signs tend to have positive personality traits of being emotional, deep, nurturing, sympathetic, empathic, imaginative and intuitive. On a more negative aspect they tend to be sentimental, oversensitive, escapists (daydreaming, fantasies, always wanting to escape the mundane world) and irrational.

Greek and Roman Mythology

Poseidon (Greek) and Neptune (Roman) are generally considered to be the rulers of the sea. There are many legends surrounding the oceans and seas and it would be safe to say that every polytheistic, pre-Christian belief system has a god of waters, rain or seas in some fashion. Poseidon is the son of Oceanus, a Greek Titan, and is the father of Titan…both of which are also gods of the oceans and seas. There are also numerous nymphs and sprites of the water.

Hinduism

The word 'Ap' is Vedic Sanskrit for water and in Hinduism this element is associated with Chandra (moon) or Shukra (Venus). It is associated with a northeast direction and in the Tattva it is seen as a crescent moon of silver or purple coloring.

Ceremonial Magick

In Ceremonial Magick water is usually represented with a cup or chalice but sometimes a bowl or cauldron can be used, as long as the vessel being used is actually holding water or some type of a liquid. Its archangel is Gabriel and angel is Taliahad. The ruler is Tharsis and the king is Nischa. It is passive and represented by the symbol for Scorpio and is placed on the upper right point on the Supreme Invoking Ritual of the Pentagram.

Wicca

In Wiccan practices water is in the western quadrant of an altar or sacred space. It is associated with autumn and can be symbolized by the white crescent moon, a chalice or cup, a bowl of water, shells, sapphires or a cauldron. It represents wisdom, the soul, emotions and femininity. The elemental creatures for water are known as undines, which are similar to the modern concept of mermaids. However, undines are thought to be made up of water droplets, waves or sea foam and not creatures who simply make the water their home.

Other Symbolism

In dreams, natural running water represents happiness and creativity. If it is seen in a man-made feature such as a toilet, drain or faucet and is running then it can be a sign to be careful with money like the old adage "throwing money down the drain." If trying to cross water or are drowning it could mean that there are burdens to cross or overcome, think of the idea of being "drowned" by something (too many events going on, work is too stressful, etc). Stagnant water can mean life has gotten stale or of being in a rut. Something may be holding the dreamer back or keeping them from realizing something. Life may need some revitalizing such as a move, new job, a new hobby or project, and even maybe just a new hair style.

Magick for the Sea Witch
Section III

Tools of Water

Chalice

The chalice, or the stemmed cauldron, is a tool of water that holds this element, or some form of liquid. Chalices are the most common altar item but cauldrons, bowls or glasses have also been used to hold the water element. In Kitchen Witchery a common drinking or wine glass can replace a fancy chalice. However, for those of a traditional flair, chalices or goblets give us an 'old-world' feel and can be from very plain to highly decorative. It is the feminine counterpart to the male athame and the symbol of all womanhood symbolizing the womb. The water it holds is considered the elemental water of life and is held sacred. It is also a representation of the cauldron of the Goddess Cerridwen.

The Holy Grail of Christian lore is the most famous mythical chalice and one that is searched for in both real life and Hollywood (as seen in the movie "Indiana Jones and the Last Crusade"). It is thought by some to be the cup that Jesus drank from at the last supper and by others to indicate a woman (often that of Mary Magdalene of whom it is believed Jesus secretly married, consorted with, or was a sibling to). In Dan Brown's "The DaVinci Code" it is said that the Holy Grail is indeed Mary Magdalene and he goes as far as to say that the person immediately to the left of Jesus in Da Vinci's painting of "The Last Supper" is Mary Magdalene. To prove his point he states that the space between Jesus and this other person (believed by most to be a male disciple) is in the shape of a "V" which is symbolic of a chalice's shape.

Cauldrons

The cauldron, along with a broom, is often associated with witches. Part of this comes from earlier times when cauldrons were what people had to cook in, do laundry in, or even bathe in. They were a common household item and a person could have one without being proclaimed a witch simply for owning it. Today, the cauldron is sacred to the Goddess because it represents the womb. It is a container of transformation and abundance and can be used for scrying (D.J. Conway has some excellent scrying spell in her book "Celtic Magick"), burning incense, candles, holding water, or mixing herbs in. It can also be used for cooking or as a mortar and pestle. However, if planning on using it for any edible substance then have a separate cauldron for edibles and a separate one for non-edibles.

In Wiccan-based paths, the cauldron is often placed with the earth element because it is a working tool but with Druidic paths it is a tool of water. I also place it with water because the properties associated with it (abundance, over-flowing, and divination) are also properties of the water element. Also, in older times cauldrons were typically used activities requiring water or liquids (cooking and cleaning). When using a cauldron, be aware of what its intent is at the time. Is it holding a candle? Then place it in the fire quadrant. Does it have incense burning in it? Then it is of the air element. Know whether the cauldron is just the vessel holding the element or if it is the element. Standing alone it can be earth (a working tool) or water (it is cup-shaped). I have a collection of cauldrons made of various materials and quite often there are five cauldrons on my altar each holding an element (for spirit it holds an offering such as grain or seeds).

Traditionally, a cauldron is made of cast iron, supported by three legs and its mouth is smaller than the widest part of the cauldron. However, many cauldrons sold in metaphysical stores have a wider opening for convenience sake and I have seen (and own) cauldrons that are plastic, brass, ceramic and copper. Any cauldron works as a tool on an altar, but keep in mind that not all materials are good for cooking in and plastic cauldrons cannot be used for heat sources (incense or candles).

In lore and mythology the cauldron is known as "Cerridwen's Cauldron" (Celtic Welsh) and the ancient Celts used it for food or ritual and to them it symbolized divine inspiration and sustenance. According to a medieval legend known as "The Tail of Taliesen" Cerridwen's son, Morfran, was hideously ugly so she sought to make him wise and poetic in order to give him worthy attributes. She had a magickal cauldron that granted the gifts of wisdom and poetic inspiration to the potions or foods made in it. She created a special mixture that had to boil for a year and a day that by the blind Morda and a young boy, Gwion. The year and a day concept may give rise to the tradition to study for a year and a day before considering themselves initiated into a coven or path.

The first three drops of the potion would give anyone wisdom and knowledge but the remaining portions were poisonous. While Gwion stirred the concoction three drops of the scalding liquid bubbled and landed on his thumb, instinctively he stuck his thumb in his mouth to ease the pain which gave him the knowledge that should have gone to Morfran. Cerridwen was so angry at this that she chased Morfran, each of them turning into various animals in order to get away. Finally, Morfran made the mistake of turning into a grain of corn and Cerridwen turned into a chicken and swallowed Gwion up. She became pregnant and knew that the child was Gwion. She decided to kill him upon birth but it is said that he was so beautiful she could not do it. Instead, she sent him off in the ocean tied in a leather bag and he was later rescued by a prince. Legend says that Gwion-reborn grew into the gifted bard Taliesen.

This story is reminiscent of the Disney movie of "The Sword in the Stone" (1963) in which Merlin and Mad Madam Mim turn into various creatures in a battle and also in the story of Finn MacCool and the "Salmon of Knowledge" in which Finn bursts a blister on the salmon and inadvertently gains wisdom and knowledge that was meant for his master. It is also similar to that Moses in Biblical lore who was supposed to have been killed but instead sent off down a river in a basket.

In addition to Cerridwen, the cauldron has been associated with the Goddess Brigid, of Irish mythology. In an effort to convert pagans to Christianity, Goddess Brigid gave way to, Saint Brighid in the Catholic religion. She is the patron of poetry, wells, women, childbirth and inspiration and the cauldron is her tool. She is honored on Imbolc, February 2nd by pagans of Wiccan or Celtic based belief systems.

There is also a belief that Celtic warriors would take the dead during battle and place them in cauldrons to revive them. The revived soldier could then fight again, despite having no soul or voice, until either killed again or the battle ended. In Irish lore it is believed that leprechauns kept their treasures in cauldrons, usually called pots or "Pot o' Gold," and they have become a symbol commonly seen at both Halloween and St. Patrick's Day in the United States.

Magick for the Sea Witch
Section IV

Working with Water

Water is the rivers, streams, lakes, oceans and all natural bodies of water that criss-cross this earth. Any natural body of water is the perfect source for this element and a great place to visit to connect with it. However, water is also linked to certain weather conditions, specifically snow, fog and rain since they are all made up of water droplets, and anyone working magick with these weather conditions can said to be using the element of water; whereas weather conditions such as wind would be under air. Rainbows could also be considered a correspondence of water because they are seen after rainstorms and are a result of reflections in the droplets. Another correspondence that may be surprising to some is that of mirrors; they are reflective surfaces like water and appear to have a depth to them like bodies of water do.

Before practicing Sea Witchery get to know the local laws or regulations regarding the bodies of water, the vegetation and animals. For example, here in South Carolina it is against the law to pick the sea grasses that grow on public beaches. On Folly Island, South Carolina in the months of May through October there is "lights out" law that says all lights facing the beach must be turned off at a certain time. This is so the sea turtles that hatch in these months won't be confused between the moonlight, which they use to find their way back to the ocean, and houselights. Also, it is illegal in many places (especially oceans and seas) to take wildlife away from the waters or sands away from the beaches. A small jar of water is generally not a problem but never take more than is needed and always be respectful of the earth and litter laws. Some spells ask that an object be tossed into the water, but this could be considered littering and may pollute waters. An alternative would be to bury it or place it in a bowl of water until the magick has worked.

In Sea Witchery reference is often made to the 'seas or oceans' but keep in mind that if not living near an ocean or a sea any naturally occurring body of water, a well, pond, fountain or even the water from the faucet can still be used in water magick. Collecting rainwater is also an excellent idea for obtaining 'natural' water (versus the filtered tap water). Leave jars or buckets outside during a rainstorm to collect it and then store in a fridge (labeling it so it is not accidentally drank) and use it in a chalice on an altar for the water correspondence and for blessing, anointing or cleansing objects.

Indoor Spaces

For a small indoor space try setting up a little Zen garden to look like a beach instead of the usual rocks and sands. In a shallow box or pan, place a layer of sand and instead of rocks purchase dried, plastic or glass sea critters. Sand can usually be purchased where craft or aquarium supplies are sold. On one end of the tray a shallow pan of water, dyed blue for effect, can also be placed; this makes the ocean and the sand is the beach. Zen gardens are then raked with fingers or a small rake for meditative and relaxing purposes. Try raking until reaching an object in the sand, then turn or rake around it. It becomes sort of like a puzzle to get all of the sand raked around the objects without lifting the rake and 'jumping over' them. Start at one end and try to get to the 'ocean' at the other end. Rearrange the objects, smooth the rake marks and try again.

Aquariums are another great way to connect with the water element, but they do require a certain amount of care for its water and the critters living in it. They can be worth it for someone with the time and money to invest in them because they have a soothing and meditative quality, and help connect with the water element by involving the creatures of the water and not just the liquid itself.

Table-top fountains require less care, take less space, are decorative and with their soothing sounds can be great for meditation. Usually, normal tap water is placed in a fountain but water collected naturally can also be used. Fountains need to be refilled periodically because the water does evaporate over time and motors can burn out. They come in a variety of styles and sizes and are perfect for someone with little space. They also make great altar centerpieces or small ones can represent water on an altar.

Baths and showers are other ways to connect with water and can be used to metaphysically cleanse the body of negativity or be used as mild forms of meditation and relaxation. Often the bath can be the ritual, sometimes it is prep work before a ritual. Jewelry that is worn in a shower or bath will also be cleansed, and gemstones can be placed in a mesh bag and tossed into a bath as well. The properties of the gems will be transferred to the person taking the bath.

Outdoor Spaces

Natural bodies of waters such as ponds or creeks can be used for rituals or meditation. If lucky enough to be near a natural body of water, spend some time near it and watch the nature occurring around it. Hold gatherings near the water to tap into the natural energies it holds. Water can also be collected from it to use in magickal purposes. Scrying methods involving water often suggest getting water from a natural source instead of using tap water. Again, rainwater is also natural water and can be collected if there is no body of water nearby. Natural water should never be used for human consumption due to contaminants that may be in it, but it is acceptable to us it for anointing, blessings, cleansing or scrying.

Swimming pools and fountains can also connect a person to the water. Similar to taking a bath, the pool can either be a ritual or prep work for a ritual. Floating in a pool is also a form of meditation and can be very relaxing. Decorative lawn and garden fountains are another great feature that represent water, similar to a table top fountain these larger structures can be placed in the west part of the property to represent water. Coming in a variety of designs, even some depicting the ancient gods and goddesses, these make an excellent addition to a ritual or sacred space.

Water sports are also great ways to connect with this element: swimming, sailing, jet skiing…all activities taking place in the water connects a person to the element. Even a simple walk along a beach or stream bed creates a connection. There isn't necessarily a need to get in the water, but just to be near it and observe its sights and sounds is enough.

Rituals and Spell work

Often a sea witch is drawn to the Ocean Mother and responds to the pull of lunar energy or tides; therefore also working with moon lore since the moon controls the tides. Mastery of this form of magick gives a person the ability to use the flow of energy to obtain goals and be fruitful in their endeavors. Water magick is useful for spells of love, pleasure, marriage, childbirth or fertility, healing, sleep and dreaming, friendship, meditation, purification, emotions and feelings, dreams, freedom and psychic acts. It can anoint objects or people and be sprinkled over statues of the God and Goddess, an altar, or sprinkled around a circle. Ice, the weather, mirrors, the seas and any work with essential oils all are of the water element. It rules over divination, dream work, and hypnotism. Native American sweat lodges, sacred springs, and natural bodies of water all empower this element. Spells or rituals can also be done by drawing symbols in the sand (as the tide comes in and takes away the symbols, the magick is being released); using drift wood, shells, sea glass or other beach-found objects.

Altars

It is represented in a ritual or at an altar by the practitioner holding their hands down at their pelvic area with thumbs and first-fingers touching (like a diamond) to represent the womb and the shape of a chalice. Water can be used to pour over objects to cleanse them, in brew making, healing spells, ritual bathing, tossing objects into water, blessings and cleansing.

To set up a water altar simply place an extra chalice or bowl of water in the west quadrant of an altar. However, a more advanced altar can be created in which each elemental object is relevant to both sea and its element: Earth can be represented by sand, aquatic vegetation, rocks taken from bodies of water, sea salt, sea life and seashells. Air is seen in the breezes so a picture of waves, a sailboat model, or a sea-bird's feather can be used. Fire can be represented with a bowl of sand (and the warmth of the sun that it retains), any red sea object such as a shell, a floating candle, a lighthouse (the light is fire) or by a blue candle. Water is, of course, represented by a bowl or chalice of water but also by seashells or other sea life.

Find a nice picture of the sun setting over the ocean, with a beach visible in the picture, and hang it behind an altar. In this one oceanic view all of the elements are seen: earth (beach), the water, fire (sun) and the air all around (or, better yet, find a picture with birds in it for air). If visiting the shores of a body of water at sunset or sunrise, remember that this can be a very powerful time to do spells or rituals because of all the elements being present and it is an in-between time (the sunset or sunrise is in-between day and night). It is also an "in-between" time which is good for Fairy Magick.

Magick for the Sea Witch
Section V

Sea Salt and Water

The water element has many components besides just the water itself. It is the creatures that live in it, the salt in oceans and seas, the seaweed, and even the tides or currents of the water are an aspect of it. A person working with water can use it in so many ways besides just for altar correspondence or using the liquidity of it. Factor in all the components of water such as its personality (is it a slow-moving stream or a deep pool); everything that goes into making that water (is it salty or fresh, what animal and plant life is in it); the location of the water (is it a mountain stream or fed by a lake or larger river).

Connecting with the element as mentioned in the previous section will help a person to know and understand all of the aspects of it and be able to then relate those to spell work and other correspondences. Even when not near the water, it is possible to evoke the feelings and emotions of it by picturing a specific type of water (deep ocean, quickly moving stream, etc.) and pulling the energies from that image.

Tides

The tides can be used in magick just as the moon's phases can be used. The high tide is like the waxing moon because it is coming in, is getting fuller in a sense, and can be used to bring things towards a person, drawing power or gaining something. The low tide is like the waning moon that is going out; it is getting less full and can be used for pushing energies away, banishing or getting rid of negativity. To use the tides or seas simple rituals or spells can be done on the beach during the appropriate tide or surface condition. Often these spells require tossing an object into the waters, but goes against litter laws and can be harmful to the animals in it so choose an object that is organic, for example, beach debris such as rocks, shells, or driftwood.

The Currents

Currents of streams and rivers can be used in the same way as high and low vibration stones seen earlier. A quickly moving current is the same as a high vibration stone and should be used for spells when immediate results are needed, and a slower moving current is like a low vibration stone and used when a spell needs to have longer lasting effects, such as romance or a career.

The personality of the bodies of water can also be used in spell work. Calm seas can be used for meditation, spells of protection, wish manifestation, peace or to bring calming influences. Angry seas can be used to vent frustrations and angers or be used to get rid of bad influences or negativity in life. Again, it may not always be possible to be near the seas or any boy of water, but visualizing the personalities of the waters can help bring those energies to any ritual or magickal workings.

Sea Salt and Salt Water

Sea salt and salt water are very powerful components in magick and easier to obtain then one might think. In this health-conscience age sea salt can be purchased near regular table salt in grocery stores and is fairly inexpensive and salt water can be made by adding salt to a glass of water (if possible, obtain some water from the ocean as natural salt water is more powerful). Both sea salt and salt water represent two elements in one are very powerful because of this.

Sea salt (as just salt, not salt in the water) can be used to 'draw' protective circles around a sacred space; added to water to bless it, to mimic ocean and sea water, or to represent earth on an altar. Sea water act as a purifier, aids in protection, connects one to the seas, can be used for blessings, consecrations, or to represent both earth and water. When table salt is added to water and gargled it is a natural remedy for sore throats and laryngitis and can be used as an antibiotic for tooth aches, cuts or burns in the mouth.

Natural seawater is more potent in magick then tap water with salt added because of the natural energies in it. It also harbors the essences of the animals and plants living it int. But, tap water that has salt added to it or has been blessed by the practitioner is a great substitute when waters from the seas cannot be obtained. There are some great tips for blessing water later in this section.

Scented Water

Water scented with herbs, fresh flowers, or oils can be used as replacement for incense, which is a great solution for people allergic to incense smoke or living in areas where smoke is not allowed (college dorms, for example). To make scented water, fill a shallow bowl with water and any choice of herbs, flowers or oils. Prior to a ceremony or spell dip just the fingertips into the bowl and flick the water around the room, altar or the sacred space as a way of cleansing the area (be careful with oils as they can cause stains on cloth).

Scented or salt water can also be used to cleanse ritual items by filling a container with blessed water, holding the item to be cleansed over a shallow pan and pouring the blessed water over the object. Continue to do this until the object has been cleansed (this will just be a sense the practitioner gets, there is no visual way of knowing this). If the blessed water runs out do not reuse the water in the pan, it has collected the negativity from the object and will only put it back if re-used. Instead, fill the container with more blessed water (the cleansing may be interrupted if more water needs to be blessed) and then continue the process. When the object has been completely magickally cleansed, retain the blessed water for a future use and pour the used water outside the ground (or in a body of water), giving it back to Mother Earth.

Rose Water

Rose water is a distillate made with water and rose petals; the petals and hips of roses are edible and their uses are quickly coming around in homeopathic and natural remedies. Rose water or rose syrup has a very distinct flavor and has been used in some cuisines, especially that of Iranian sweets and in Lebanon it is added to lemonade for a unique thirst-quenching drink. In health uses it is a mild astringent and an excellent toner for dry or fair skin. For metaphysical purposes it can be used as an elixir, as an anointment or blessing water and to cleanse tools in. A practitioner can also wash their hands in rose water prior to magickal workings; this washes off the mundane world and prepares one for the magickal world.

Here is a simple recipe for making rosewater than anyone can do at home:

Gather rose petals, picking them in the morning when the dew is still on the petals, and place them in a large colander. Rinse them with cold water and then place the petals in the center of large cheesecloth (available in grocery stores or craft stores) and bring up the sides, securing it by tying it or winding a rubber-band around the top. The petals can either be steeped in a pan of water on the stove, or placed into a bowl and boiling water poured over the cheesecloth.

Once the petals have steeped in the boiling water for approximately fifteen minutes cover them in a bowl with plastic wrap and let it sit over night. In the morning, squeeze the cheesecloth to extract the excess water. The rose water is done, simply pour it into a jar and store in the fridge for up to two weeks or freezer for six months. Try experimenting with the colors of roses for different intents, for example; pink can be for friendship, red for love, and white for blessings. Waters can also be made with other edible herbs or flowers such as mint, lavender, or orange blossoms. Use the waters to anoint objects and people, cleansing objects, or for making elixirs.

Holy or Blessed Water

In Catholicism, holy water is a very sacred item in rituals, cleansings, and exorcisms. Holy Water is usually used in Christenings or Baptismal as well, which are rites that cleanse a person of past sins and are basically an initiation and commitment into the faith. Because of its long connection with both Christian and pre-Christian faiths, holy or blessed water has its own set of superstitions and folklore unique to ordinary water. In the days of witch persecution, when it was believed that a black cat was either a witch incarnate or the devil's familiar, a cat would be placed in a bucket of holy water. If it jumped out it was 'proof' of it belonging to a witch's or the devil. If it stayed in the water it meant that it was just an ordinary cat. This is an unfair form of justice, like so much of the witch trials were, since most cats seem to hate water and will jump out of it.

In popular media, such as movies and novels, holy water has become a weapon against the undead, especially vampires of whom it will burn like acid. Who can forget in the 1987 movie "The Lost Boys" when Corey Haim and Corey Feldman used Super Soaker water guns to defend their home against the vampires? Or, the poor sucker (again, excuse the pun) who was pushed into a tub of holy water?

While it does not have such dramatic and gory effects in real life, holy or blessed water can be used by pagans today. Another belief says that holy water can drive out evil, heal a variety of ailments or drive out rats from a home. The idea is to place holy water in three corners of the home and they (the rats) will exit out of the fourth and unblessed corner. This can be revised for modern practices to drive negativity out of a home by placing bowls of holy or blessed water in three corners and asking that the negativity leave with this simple verse:

Negativity and ill-intent shall leave my home

and cannot plague me in the days to come.

Once the negativity is perceived to be gone, dump the bowls of water onto ground, giving it back to the earth.

To Bless Water

In Catholicism, blessing water is done by a clergyman and the water becomes known as holy water. In Paganism, while this can be done by an ordained minister of a Pagan faith, it can also be done by anyone practicing an earth-based path and is usually referred to as blessed water. Water on an altar, whether blessed or not, should be changed periodically as it will go stale and evaporate. Each time that the container if refilled the water needs to be blessed; remember it is the water receiving the blessing and not the container holding it. When the water is used up, the blessing is gone.

The easiest way to bless water is to fill a cup, chalice or bowl with water and add a clear quartz crystal or moonstone to the container. Another method would be to charge the water in either the sunlight or the moonlight (this can be done with a crystal in the water as well). Drawing sigils or symbols onto the chalice or bowl can also help to bless the water contained within it (drawing with just a finger can replace using something that will actually mark up the container). The final way to bless water is to hold the container filled with water and recite a charm or prayer:

Blessed be are the waters of the sea

Consecration, Protection and Serenity;

Blessed be are the waters of the sky

Psychic awareness of the mind's eye;

Waters of the sea, waters of the sky

Bless my magick else it goes awry;

Waters of the sky, Waters of the sea

I enchant you now so mote it be.

Another verse that can be used is:

I call upon the elemental undines

to bless this water of mine;

a mere drop from the seas both great and small,

bless this water once and for all;

bless it pure and bless it through,

bless it for all the magick that I do.

The words or method is up to each person and should fit with their own practices and beliefs as long as it is blessed it in some fashion, refill the vessel periodically and use the blessed water only in magickal workings.

Chinook Blessing

There is also a blessing from the American Chinook tribe that is beautifully written; it is just a small a piece of a longer blessing that can be found on the internet but is appropriate for blessing water or as a way to call upon the element of water in magickal workings

"I call upon the waters that rim the earth horizon to horizon;

that flows into our gardens and fields, and ask that they teach me the way."

The Chinook tribe is of the Northwest Pacific area of the Columbian River. Like most Native American beliefs, their religion and faith is derived from their livelihood. For the full blessing of more on the Chinook tribe check the Bibliography for web addresses.

Wishing Wells and Fountains

Wells are novelty items now and not something we see in town squares where the while village gathers for their daily supply of water and gossip. Wells were once the focal point of many communities and were a communal source of water and it was believed that they had their own guardian spirits. Many cultures and spiritual beliefs have their fair share of magickal, or even ordinary tales, about wells. Today they act only as decoration (with the exception of well-water used in rural areas) and are seen mainly in tourist attractions. I remember the Perkins restaurants years ago had small wishing wells, without water, and children were allowed to reach in a pick a prize. When we travelled we always visited a Perkins restaurant.

Many of us are 'guilty' of tossing a coin into a fountain or wishing well in the hopes that some wish will come true. This is probably from the belief that coins were once considered payment to the Gods of the seas and sailors would toss a coin into the seas as an offering to gods like Poseidon or Triton and this belief has carried over to wishing wells and fountains. I know that in my family we always toss a coin into a well or fountain and make a wish. It wasn't until recently that I realized this can be turned into a spell. The original superstition also states that the wish must never be spoken aloud lest the spirits of the well refuse to grant it. This goes along with the belief that magick should never be spoken about until the outcome is achieved. The belief is that doubt will enter and cause the magick not to work

Wishing wells were often used for scrying by those wishing to get a sneak peek at their immediate future. Stones would be dropped into the well and the condition of the water would determine a future. If the water became cloudy it meant trouble was brewing but if it bubbled then everything was fine. While the Goddess (or Saint) Brigid is usually associated with wells there is another fascinating legend of a saint and might be the basis for the well-scrying.

This story takes place in the 5th century and involves St. Dwynwen (circa 460 CE). She was one of twenty-four daughters born to the Welsh kin, and later saint, Brychan Brycheiniog of Brechon. As virtuous as she was beautiful, Dwynwen, or Dwyn, fell in love with the Welsh prince known as Maelon Dafodril. He had every intention of marrying her but legends muddle the reasons why this never occurred. Some say that she fended off pre-marital advances by Maelon and was so distraught over his attempts that she devoted herself to her God instead. Others say that her father had previously promised her to another prince but rather than marry someone she did not love, she ran off. Yet one more story states that even though she was in love and wanted to marry Maelon she had already promised a life devoted to her God. Whatever the situation was, the marriage did not occur and she devoted her life to the Christian God.

After fleeing from Maelon she dreamt she was given a sweet drink that eased her heartache but that the same drink was given to Maelon and froze him. While still hiding in the forest she prayed until she was finally granted three wishes: 1) for Maelon to be unfrozen, 2) she would never feel the desire for marriage again, 3) God would honor all requests by lovers made on her behalf. Her wishes granted, she continued to devote her life to God.

She started a convent on the present-day Llanddwyn Island off the Isle of Anglesey. Her holy well, a fresh-water spring called Ffynnon Dwynwen, became a wishing well and place of pilgrimage. From this grew a tradition that an eel lived in the well and could foretell the future. Visitors would ask a question and watch which way the waters turned. Women were also known to scatter breadcrumbs on the surface of the water, lay their handkerchief over the breadcrumbs and then wait. If the eel disturbed the handkerchief it meant the woman's lover would be unfaithful to her. If the eel left it alone then her lover remained true.

Spells and Rituals

Wishing Well

This can be done at a public or private fountain or well, a table-top fountain, or a simple bowl of water. While holding a coin in the projective hand visualize a wish or intent and think of the fountain as a place of power where the energies emerge and submerge as a small piece of a greater whole (the seas). As the coin is dropped recite the following verse:

Guardian's power of the deep my inner secrets you will keep;

Bless this water with your power as I charge my magick upon this hour.

It is best to use a penny for two reasons: 1) it's not worth much and 2) copper is a good conductor not only for electricity but also magick. This spell can be done whenever the need to feel the powers of the waters or for simple wish-making arises. If using a bowl, do not remove the coin until the wish has been fulfilled. For yard decorations of fountains or wells, several coins can remain in the feature and removed at a later date. However, do not spend the coins, it is bad luck, but instead take them to a donation box or scatter on the ground in a public place.

Moon Waters

These spell really belongs with moon magick, but since the moon controls the tides and the waning moon is similar to that of the low tide and waxing moon to high tide, I thought it would be a good addition to this section. Any drinking glass will do, but a sacred chalice is preferable.

Fill a glass with drinkable water on a clear night when the moon is visible. In the projective hand hold the glass out so that the moon so that it is reflected in the water. Gaze at the moon's reflection, visualizing what the intent or need is, and then drink the water. The time when this spell is done varies according to the intent: for making a wish, desire or event to occur, perform the spell prior to the full moon (2-3 days is good) and visualize the need coming to fruition as the moon waxes into full. To get rid of something, like negativity for example, perform this spell on the eve of the full moon (it starts waning the next day) and imagine all negativity dispersing as the moon wanes (grows smaller).

This could also be done at the time of high or low tides, except that there won't necessarily be a moon (or anything) reflecting in the water. However, use the tides the same as the moon phases but instead of drinking all of the water, leave a small amount that can be tossed into the tide and as the waters come in or recede they will disperse the magick and intent.

9th Wave Spell

Superstition says that throwing stones into the sea will cause great waves and storms, and sailors might engage in this if needing the rough seas to thwart and enemy or cover illicit actions. The 9th wave is a powerful omen in sailor and sea-faring lore, and often it would be used to bring about favorable winds in order to sail at a smoother or faster pace.

If requiring the powers of the seas wait until the 8th wave has passed and then toss a stone into the water and envision the waves bringing forth the magick while reciting the following verse:

As I cast this stone into the sea, the waves (or rain) will come to me;

They will stop when the task is done and they will harm not a one;

This is my will so mote it be.

Remember, weather spells can be very powerful and hard to control; only envision as much as is needed and not torrential downpours or rogue waves.

Bottle Protection

In Voodoo, there is a belief that a person can fill bottles of water (glass works best) with fresh rain or spring water and a pinch of salt (if using ocean or sea water then don't add the extra salt) and hang them from a prominent tree to protect the home from evil. Try blessing the water in one of the methods already discussed for some added protection. Bottles can be emptied and refilled as needed, but should not be drank or used in magickal workings since it will have actually absorbed the negativity or evil that has attempted to come to the home.

Divination, Meditation, Scrying

Water Scrying

Fill an object with filtered water or water from a natural source. Objects should be at least four inches in diameter but can be anything from a large shell, to a bowl, or a cauldron. There are scrying bowls that can be purchased in metaphysical stores and are quite beautiful. The scrying bowls sold in stores often come with instructions indication that it should never be touched by the sun, so wrap it up in a sacred cloth and store it where light won't hit it. Shells, cauldrons or regular bowls can also be stored in the same manner. It might be advisable to not use the object for anything but scrying to avoid damaging it or altering the effects of the divination.

Set up the scrying bowl in a place with relative quiet and where the lights can be turned low. Lean over it and position the face so that only the facial features are seen and not any background of the room. Also, there should not be any lights reflected in the water (candles, sunlight, or house lights). Water scrying can have two methods: concentrate on a question that needs to be answered, or simply gaze and let images emerge. The face will be the first reflection seen, but after that it will transform and other images take its place. Breathe comfortably, attempt to let the mind go blank (except for the question at hand, if using that method). Don't try to interpret what is seen or felt, the time for that will come later. Continue scrying for as long as is comfortable and then stop; record any impressions, images, or feelings that were experienced during the session.

Ceromancy

This is a form of divination that many pagans are familiar with, or have at least heard of. It requires one candle and a bowl of cold water. It can fall under the categories of either fire or water since it requires items from both elements. However, the candle is not used for divination as in fire gazing but rather from dropping liquid wax into water, which makes it of the water element.

The diviner must let the candle burn for a few minutes, then ask a question and tilt the candle over the bowl so the wax drips into the water. The cold water makes the wax harden instantly and it will float on top. Messages are divined from the symbols seen in the wax. It is best if someone can guide the practitioner's hand over the bowl so that they cannot purposefully drip wax in the form of an image. But, if divining alone then simply hold the candle over the bowl first, then close eyes and tilt the candle, wait a few seconds and then tilt the candle upright.

Then, either divine by the symbols seen or the number of individual droplets of wax. An odd number is a positive answer and an even number is a negative answer. Symbol divination is based on general symbol meaning or use a dream dictionary to decipher meanings. Look for symbols of animals, shapes, common symbols such as hearts, crosses and dollar signs.

Magick for the Sea Witch
Section VI

Sea Shells, Seaweed and Sea Life

Beachcombers often hit the shores of the oceans just as the sun is coming up to look for a treasures tossed up by the sea. If fortunate enough to live near the ocean, make this a daily or weekly practice. For those not near oceans, shells and starfish can be purchased in craft or aquarium sections of department stores. Like with all magick, it is best if the items are obtained naturally but store-bought items work too. Either way, keep in mind that items mentioned below are basically the remains of the once living animal and while it is acceptable to retrieve the shell or sand dollar skeletal remains, it is not okay to take a living creature out of the oceans.

Sea Shells

Seashells are probably the most common item found and tourists can't resist picking up a shell or two on their visits to a beach. They can be used in crafts, for jewelry, as charms or amulets, placed in charm or medicine bags, large ones can be filled with water and used for scrying, they can hold water on an altar, or be used as smudge pots of loose incense. When we went to Wisconsin a few years back to visit family I carried a sea shell in my charm bag as a connection to the South Carolina shores (it was found at Myrtle Beach) and to help us return safely to our home. With such an endless array of uses, I recommend to everyone to keep a few shells in their magickal supplies; a person never knows when they will come in handy.

Like gemstones, shells and other sea novelties can have different meanings in spell manifestation or to add power to magickal workings. I have included a few spells for the different beach riff-raff listed below but for most of these items they will be used in only one of three ways: worn or carried as an amulet, placed on an altar or carried in a charm bag. However, other spells or magickal workings could be derived from the information here so feel free to be creative.

Abalone

Abalones are an edible invertebrate shellfish and the inside of the shell is often used in making or adorning jewelry. Abalone shells are great for all general purposes, similar to sage in herbology or quartz crystals in gemstone therapy, and can be used when no other shell is available. It can also power herbs, stones or other magical items if placed with them either to charge them or to remain with those items.

Clams

Clams are a 'bi-valve' invertebrate ocean animal with a muscular foot that burrows into the sand to escape predators. Clams are great to use for purification or love and a rune or magickal symbol can be painted onto the surface. They are also great for secrets because of the clichés "as quiet as a clam" or "clammed up" and can be used to stop the wagging tongue of someone who might tell secrets or gossip, or use it to protect magickal workings and documents. Place a clam with anything that is to remain private, setting it on a book or stack of papers or storing with magickal supplies.

Because of their two halves they are perfect for spells to strengthen the bond of friends, family or a romantic couple. Both people must be a part of the spell and willing participants, and it can only be done by two people at one time. This is similar to making a wish on a wishbone but with a different intent. Each person holds onto a piece of the shell, focuses on the same intent (strengthening a bond, staying connected, etc.) and then at the same time pull on the shell, separating the two halves. Each person can carry their half on them in a charm bag, in a locket or amulet, or place it where other magickal items are stored. As long as both people keep their halves the bond will always be there. This same concept is often seen in couples who keep their half of a movie ticket (my husband and I did this while dating) or in those 'best friend' necklaces popular in the 80's where each person wears half of a pendant and when placed together they make a whole.

Conches

A Conch shell is mainly a shell of the tropics, it is brightly colored and has a large spiral. They are popular in tourist shops for their size, color and design and are the shell of childhood lore where it is held up to the ear in an attempt to hear the ocean. Children inevitably marvel at the magick of the huge ocean being contained in one handheld shell, until they grow up and science (and common sense) tells them that it is only the sound of blood rushing through veins and amplified by the shell. To bring back a little piece of that magickal moment, try this simple divination method involving a large conch shell.

Find a quiet space, light a candle and hold onto a large conch shell. While holding the shell, meditate on a specific question or keep the mind blank for a general message to come unhindered by the gods. If desired, call upon a chosen sea deity, then place the shell up to the ear (getting as tight a seal as possible) and 'listen' to the shell. A message might pop up mentally or the sounds heard may actually seem as if they are forming into words or phrases, both of which are ways of the subconscious relaying information.

Cone Shells

These shells come from a type of sea snail with a cone-shaped shell. The shell is vividly marked and the snail often has a poisonous and sometimes fatal sting. These snails are mainly native to the South Pacific and Indian Ocean. Because of the poisonous defense of this ocean critter the shell can be used for protection or to counteract any spell, hex or curse. Wear it as an amulet or in a charm bag to ward off ill-intent.

Cowries

Cowries are another tropical invertebrate sea animal with a glassy and brightly colored shell and a long, central and toothed opening. The shells are very smooth and cowries can be identified by the almost-serrated edge at the opening of the shell. In the cultures of Africa, South Asia and the South Pacific cowries were actually used as payment. Because of this, cowries should be used for spells of prosperity, money, luck or to enhance spirituality. They can be carried or worn as an amulet or placed on an altar when doing a prosperity spell.

Mother-of-Pearl

Mother-of-Pearl is the hardy, pearly layer inside of some mollusk shells (clams and oysters) that is prized for its shiny appearance and is widely considered lucky if one owns a piece of it. This attributes to the popularity of it sold as novelty items or used as decorative inlays. If able to obtain a piece of mother-of-pearl, keep it where magickal items are stored, on an altar or carry it as a good luck piece similar to a lucky coin or rabbit's foot.

Olive Shells

Shaped like pointed olives, these smooth and symmetrical shells are often used in jewelry and ornaments. They are a nocturnal creature with limitless patterns and colors. Use them for all nocturnal or moon magick or any spells or rituals for healing all mental or physical problems. Due to their vast array of patterns and colors they can also be used for inspiration and creativity. Place one near where crafts or painting are done, on a desk where writing is worked on or anywhere near a place where a person shows creativity.

Oysters

Oysters are known as a shellfish with an edible muscle. The shells are rough, irregularly shaped and have a 'bi-valve' like clams. The muscle is widely believed to be an aphrodisiac making the shell useful in fertility spells. The shell can be carried around or ground into a powder to be used as an aphrodisiac or in a love spell. In parts of the United States there is a superstition that carrying an oyster shell is good luck. Because they have two halves they can be used in the same manner as clams. Oyster shells that are broken up are even used around plants and in driveways. This use makes it part of the earth element and good for all plant magick. Place one piece of a shell in a garden or flower part to promote the growth of plants.

Scallops

A bi-valve mollusk with a fan-shaped shell that has radial ribs and wavy edges, this shell is the epitome of all seashells. It is used in logos, clipart, and other popular media, as well as in décor and jewelry to represent shells or sea life. Perhaps because of the way they move in the water or because of the way their shell 'fans out' they represent movement and travel. On a sea or water-themed altar the scallop could also represent air because of its fan shape.

Similar to tossing a coin into a wishing well, a wish or desire can be obtained by using a scallop of medium size with a decent surface area. Draw a symbol of the intent on the shell and meditate on that intent while holding it. Then, focus on putting personal energy, feelings and desires into it, then toss it into the ocean as far as possible. As it floats, sinks and moves about the ocean the magick will be released and the desire manifested.

Slipper Shells

These are among my favorite of all the shells. They are a flatter, smoother shell then the others mention and on their underside is either convex or concave shelf that is about half the length of the shell. This little shelf makes the shells look like household slippers and my girls and I like to imagine that sea nymphs use them as shoes. The Slipper shell attaches itself to a hard object, often other mollusks, and lives in that one place filtering food through the water.

Because of their tendencies to remain in one place and their co-existent with attaching to other creatures, slipper shells could be used for stability or co-dependency. Wear them as an amulet when in need of stability or when dependence on another person or the gods is necessary. It can be difficult to allow others to help out, but sometimes it is necessary and the slipper shell can give a person the confidence in letting the universe, gods or trusted person to handle things. They are also great for keeping magickal documents or tools safe from prying eyes. Place them near where magickal items are stored or on an altar.

Whelks

The last of the more common sea shelf is the Whelk; often confused with a conch shell, this is a mollusk with a conical spiraling shell. Some types of Whelk are edible but it is not a common shellfish seen in seafood restaurants. Whelks, along with scallops and conches, are the more common and easily recognized of the shells and very common in tourist shops or as craft and aquarium accessories. Try using a whelk when in need of a dramatic but positive change in life (moving, a job, a raise, marriage or children). Because of their pretty design they also make great jewelry adornments.

Sea Critters

Coral

Dating back to ancient Rome, gifts of coral necklaces were given at Christenings to help protect the person from evil. Coral is a marine organism that lives in colonies known as coral reefs. It is another novelty sold in shops and can even be purchased as a craft or aquarium accessory. Carry some coral as jewelry or place it on an altar to ward off evil and negativity. Large pieces of coral can also be placed on a porch, in the yard or near the front door. Because of its deceptive quality in looking more like a plant than an animal it can also be used to guard a secret or the identity of something sacred and magickal.

Red coral helps to deter evil and protects houses and ships from damage in severe storms. If worn as an amulet or jewelry it is said that the coral turns pale in color when the owner is sick and regains color as they recover and heal.

Sand Dollars

I have yet to see a sand dollar on the beaches, but do see them often in novelty shops or even in craft sections of department stores. My personal desire is to find a sand dollar because of their lore and their use in magickal practices. They are also very decorative and can enhance room décor by being hung on walls or placed in a vase or bowl. Another thing I love about the sand dollar is that like the apple, it has its own pentagram.

Sand dollars are a flat, round sea animal native to coastal waters of North America and are related to the star fish and sea urchin. It is enclosed around a white shell with an imprint resembling a five-pointed flower. The flower has wider and more rounded 'petals' but when the animal dies it leaves behind this sandy textured disc with a five-pointed design that has more slender and pointed rays making it look more like a star. If broken, there are tiny pieces inside that range in color from a pure white to a creamy white and are called "peace doves." These are really just little parts of its internal structure that break off when the creature dies, but legend has it that they are doves and finding them is believed to promote piece.

Crypto-zoological folklore tells us that sand dollars are used by mermaids as money but Christian mythology has taken over with a legend of its own. An anonymous poem (see bibliography for website to read the entire poem) tells how the five slits in the sand dollar, which is actually only seen in a Keyhole Sand Dollar, represents the four wounds of Christ plus one slit for a Roman's spear. The star in the center of the dollar is the Star of Bethlehem and the five doves inside spread good will and peace.

There are different species of Sand Dollars but they all share the common link of having a star-shape that is evident on both the living organisms and the skeletal remains. In paganism they can represent wisdom, peace, goodwill or can be placed on a water-themed altar as the pentacle or pentagram.

Starfish

Often animals are named something that leaves us scratching our head "why?" but in this case the animal was aptly named. An invertebrate echinoderm, the starfish has five (or sometimes more) arms radiating from a central disk. There mouth is on the underside of their body and they feed on mollusks on the seabed or the shores. When the animal dies its 'skeleton' is left behind in a roughly textured star-shape.

Starfish are another must-have item for anyone practicing sea-witchery as it is its own pentacle (minus the circle). It can be placed on an altar to represent the pentacle or just to adorn it. They can be purchased in tourist shops, craft stores and a variety of other places. It could also be used by anyone combining sea and nocturnal magick because it is a sea critter but in the shape of the stars that adorn the night sky. In ancient Christian times the star was used to represent Christ and mankind because of the four points. The top point was the head of a body, the side points the arms and the two downward points are the legs. This also makes it a great pentacle for those of Christo-pagan faiths.

Other Sea Riff-Raff

Pearls
The birthstone for June, pearls are steeped in tradition and superstition. They are small, lustrous spheres of calcium carbonate that form around a tiny grain of sand in an oceanic organism, most commonly in an oyster. Prized as a precious gemstone, it may not be possible to obtain a real pearl, but a fake one will work just as well because it follows on the law of sympathetic magick (the item or spell simulates the real thing). Pearls can be used for love or when placed under a pillow to help a couple conceive, they guarantee a long life if given to an infant, or can cure madness and depression if worn as an amulet. Ironically, there is a superstition that pearls are unlucky if worn by brides because the pearls represent tears. So, it would seem that women shouldn't wear them on their wedding day but be given pearls as gifts on every other day in the year as a way to combat depression. Sounds like a nice idea to me!

Driftwood
This is broken pieces of wood that floats up to the shores of rivers and oceans. Maybe ythee are from trees or branches that were broken apart among the rolling waves, or perhaps they are pieces of long-ago ships that have drifted for years on the ebb and flow of the tides. Either way, driftwood is almost a type of wood all unto itself, originally it would have been a common tree such as oak, elder, maple, elm but because it has been on the seas for quite some time it is its own creation now; the salt and the waters have changed it into something truly unique.

Often found in nautical décor, driftwood is a gorgeous addition to any sea-themed altar. It can be used to represent earth because it is wood, but is also from the seas so it is of the water element. It also bobs along on the water, going with the flow of the tides and currents, and if useful for spells involving flexibility, relaxation or a 'going with the flow' type of attitude.

Seaweed

Seaweed is that slimy, gross and unidentifiable green sludge that we inadvertently, and unwillingly, either step on in the water or catch on our fishing poles. It is often ignored due to its slimy nature. But, it is vegetation and just as useful as any other plant from the dryer realms (no, not that the realm of the dryer where lost socks go, but dry terrains). There is a superstitious belief that seaweed can be used as a weather omen by hanging some dried seaweed outside and checking on it periodically. If it shrivels it means that the upcoming weather will be dry and sunny, whereas if it feels damp or swells then the weather coming will soon be wet.

There is another superstition that originally comes from British coastal dwellers but is also listed as a magickal tip that I read about on a pagan website. It is believed that dried seaweed kept in a house will drive away evil spirits. Hang some in the kitchen or near the prominent door of a house to keep away negativity and evil spirits.

In Wiltshire there comes a superstition that a person who carries a bit of seaweed on their person is never without friends. Based on this, dried seaweed would be a great item to place in a charm or medicine bag.

As I said earlier, this section of the book is intended for all people and not just those living near an ocean, so if it is not possible to get seaweed then I suggest buying or picking Spanish Moss. Again, this is an item available in craft stores or can be obtained naturally by those in the southern states. Biologically it is not really the same thing as seaweed but it will work as a negativity trap because both plant types are a tangled mass and those tangles act similar to the weave of a dream catcher, catching and trapping the evil.

Or, try this simple spell bottle for seaweed: gather fresh or dried seaweed, a jar (a canning jar works great), some whiskey or rum (or a non-alcoholic version would be to use apple cider vinegar but since this is not meant to be consumed it doesn't really matter). Place the seaweed in the jar, fill it with the liquid and store in the kitchen to attract good fortune and health to the home and its residents.

Shark's Teeth

Unless purchased in a tourist shop, shark's teeth are not easy to find or at least not always recognizable as a shark's tooth if found on the beaches. I will never be forgiven by my teenager for tossing back a triangular shaped hard piece of beach riff-raff that we later decided may have been a shark's tooth. They are easier to find in tourist shops and often adorn jewelry or used for other decorative purposes.

Shark's teeth will draw money towards a person who carries one around and if worn as a necklace it will protect the wearer, bring prosperity and good fortune, and keep away evil spirits. Surfers also believe that wearing a shark tooth necklace will keep them safe from shark attacks or protect them from other surfing mishaps.

Spells and Rituals

Basic Sea Spell

Walk along the beach looking for different debris that floats up. Any stone, seashell, driftwood or other debris will work for this spell. Once an appealing piece of riff-raff has been found, pick it up and hold it in the projective hand. Push personal energies into the object, imbuing with it the power of the intent. Face the ocean and wait eight waves to come into the shores. On the ninth wave recite the verse:

Ninth wave of the sea,

Bestow your magick on me.

Toss the object into the sea releasing all of the power and visualizations along with it. As it drifts or settles with the tides the magick will be released and carried forth. This spell goes along with the belief that the ninth wave has magickal powers.

Stone Castle

This is a great spell to use when in the process of looking to buy or rent a new house. Walk along the beach for a few moments until a spot that is undisturbed and peaceful can be reached. Clear an area of the beach of all beach debris, and then either from the debris cleared or from debris in other areas of the beach, collect shells, pebbles, driftwood, seaweed or dried sea critters (starfish, sand dollars). Gather as many things as possible and take them back to the cleared spot.

In the sand, outline a house with the items found. The house doesn't have to look realistic or artistic, just so it looks like the general shape of a house. Think back to the simple square house with a triangle roof we all drew as children. Decorations or additions can be done as seen fit, maybe driftwood becomes a sidewalk, seaweed is some shrubbery in front of the house, or sticks become a picket fence. As the masterpiece is created, visualize all the aspects of moving: finding the house, packing, loading and unloading everything, unpacking, and finally being settled in the new place. When the house in the sand is complete, walk away and don't look back. As the tides come in and then recede, they will take the image with it and the magick will be released.

Divination, Meditation, Scrying

There are many forms of divining with water such as hydromancy (water scrying), Ceromancy (dripping melted wax into water) and Lecanomancy (throwing stones into a basin of water). Quite often, cauldrons or scrying bowls are used but anything capable of holding water will do. The Palo Mayombe tribe use large shells or coconut halves rather than scrying bowls or cauldrons for divination and have even been known to cap the horn of a sanctified animal with a mirror and use it to scry. I think a coconut half would be a terrific way to scry, especially for those living in tropical places or from tropical descent.

Scrying With Sea Shells

Just as a person might scry by using a scrying bowl or cauldron, a large shell can work just as well. A clam shell would work best since it is most resembles a dish, if it refuses to sit flat try hot-gluing a flat disc to its bottom such as a lid, small plate or piece of wood. Fill with water and light a candle choice of incense. Sit where the shell can be directly looked into without other reflections being seen and scry in the same manner as a scrying bowl.

Shell Prophecies

Much like the divination in the Earth Magick section, shells can be used for divining in the same manner as the stones. Instead of the words 'stone, rocks, or pebbles' (as seen in the Earth Witch section) try replacing with the word 'shell' and any of the methods listed. Another method might be to sit on the beach and meditate while digging hands through the sand. Without looking pull up a shell and look at it, referring back to meanings of shells earlier, interpret the answer to the question. For example, a cone shell might indicate that someone means ill-intent or harm. This method doesn't require a specific question but gives a general feeling of what the near future holds.

Magick for the Sea Witch
Section VII

Physical and Metaphysical Health

It would be impossible to have a section on water and not talk about the health benefits of it. Not only do our bodies require water, or some liquid, to stay hydrated but water helps skin retain its elasticity and youthfulness and since it has no calories it is great for those watching their weight. Water is frequently associated with good health and there are is a bit of folklore and home remedies out there regarding when and how to drink water for health.

There is the Welsh belief that a spoonful of sea water taken every morning will increase longevity and regular tap water with salt can be gargled as an antiseptic for mouth burns or to ease the rawness of sore throats and the pain of toothaches. There are also beliefs about the items found in natural bodies of water such ash pebbles gathered from a stream having the ability to cure everything from sciatica to thrush, if rubbed on the affected area. Minor irritations such as warts and other skin ailments are said to be curable if the affected part is bathed in water that is reflecting the moonlight. Then there is the common idea of drinking a full glass of water without a breath as a cure for hiccups.

Whether any of these methods work or not, water is crucial to our survival and should never be taken for granted. Since we need to drink water, and as a society we need to increase the amount of water drank and decrease the amount of sodas, we might as well add a little bit of magick to the water we drink.

Adding Magick to Water

Natural Flavoring

Water is something we all know we need to drink more of and by adding a little bit of natural flavoring a person can add to the taste as well as add magick to the water they are drinking. Head to the local farmer's market or grocery store and purchase fresh mint leaves, lavender buds, oranges, lemons, grapefruits, or limes. Mint adds a boost of happiness, as well as freshens breath and aids in digestion; lemon is good for protection, and the sourness of lemon or lime juice aids in alertness of the body and mind; lavender buds aid in spirituality, psychic connection and also have calming and relaxing effect; orange and grapefruit aids in a person's general health as well as creativity and revitalizing.

At a local gathering we had a "Healing Day" which teaches about alternatives to medicine, such as massage therapy, aromatherapy and Reiki. Since I am skilled at none of those I brought along some mint leaves, oranges, lemons and limes. Everyone was encouraged to create their own flavored water. We squeezed the citrus into the water and then tossed in the squeezed fruit (the same as if adding lemon to water or tea at a restaurant). For the mint leaves we just threw them in as is.

The children in the group had the most fun with this and enjoyed making an array of combinations. The favorite seemed to be all of the items at once: mint, lemon, lime, and orange. It was a wonderful way to encourage children to drink more water and they had a great time bonding as they sliced, mixed, stirred and sipped. We used cold water but this could also be done with hot water to make a tea on cold days.

Elixirs

Elixirs are defined as a "quick or magical cure" and are the wares that travelling salesmen tried to sell to villagers proclaiming wild and fantastical possibilities such as age-reversal, immortality or a cure-all for everything. Today, elixirs are still used by pagan practitioners but have taken on less exorbitant claims, although they are still considered magickal. Typically, elixirs are made either on a new or a full moon and must steep for a full month (from new moon to new moon, etc.) but what is known as a "single-dose elixir" can be created in an hour. Elixirs today are usually made with water and gemstones.

There are two ways to do this: 1) meditate over the stones in a collection or in a metaphysical store and let instincts choose the stone) or, 2) choose stones that are based on a specific need. The first method is perfect if a person is trying to determine where they need assistance in their life. My family did this and my daughter instinctively chose stones concerning communication. Later that week she was both on television and was chosen for an award for her science fair project; the communication elixir was useful for both occurrences. The second method should be used in the person knows they have an area of weakness and want to diminish it.

Regular tap water or even flavored bottled water can be used (keep in mind that the flavors added to water might alter the stone's properties, so choose flavors fitting the intent). Place an opal or a moonstone in the water to charge it and then pour it over the stone in a bowl or glass of water. The stone must be completely covered by water. If doing a single-dose the container can be covered with clear plastic wrap and for the full dose use a jar with a lid. Set the elixir outside and leave it for the specified time. When it is done, remove the stone and drink the water. For single-doses (which are not as powerful) all of the water can be drank but for a full-dose it is recommended to take only sips of it. Store the water in a refrigerator and take a sip daily or whenever the need for the magickal properties is felt.

Always use stones that are made up of quartz crystals and somewhat transparent as these are fairly safe; clear quartz, citrine and amethyst are a few examples of quartz crystals. Avoid stones that are black, green or opaque such as hematite or malachite. These stones often have chemicals or minerals in them that are unsafe (such as lead or copper) and can leach into the water causing it to be toxic. Polished stones are also safer to use then raw stones; there is something about the polishing process that decreases the ability to leach toxins.

Bathing and Bath Salts

In writing this book I wondered where to draw the line with water—do

I include mundane things such as bathing and cleaning because they deal with water or do I stick with natural bodies of water and spells or rituals involving it? But, then I read this cute superstition of American folklore "wash and wipe together, live in peace together" and I knew I had to include a small chapter about mundane uses for water. If we all get back to coed showers and baths we can all live in peaceful; not sure it is a trend that will catch on but it is a neat thought.

The act of bathing has had its ups and downs in the past. In some eras it was bad luck to bathe because it would wash away one's fortune and good luck. But, other eras have given us the idea that bathing not only cleansed a person of dirt from his body but also sins from his soul. When people did bathe it was in rivers and lakes and early Greek and Roman civilizations used bathing houses, in which people bathed communally. Eventually this led way to bathtubs in the home and bathing has become (mostly) a solitary event. In today's times we know that it is a requirement for good health and it is done daily rather than on a weekly or monthly basis.

Bathing can also be used in magickal workings either as part of a ritual, as the ritual itself or as a cleansing prior to the ritual. For me, it combines two things in one: a literal cleaning and a magickal cleansing and I love multi-tasking. It is also a great way to relax the mind and body so that it is ready for magickal workings. Bath salts or sachets (mesh bags filled with herbs) are a great way to empower a bath, although not necessary. The bath alone can be enough if the intent is one of cleansing the aura or mind. However, there are many wonderful bath salt recipes out there and they can even be made at home. I often make one with tea tree oil to help my children when they are stuffed up from a cold. Below are two recipes for a base salt in which individual oils, herbs or colors are added per choice, or pick up one of the following books for recipes: "Kitchen Witchery: A Compendium of Oils, Unguents, Incense, Tinctures, and Comestibles" by Marilyn F. Daniel or "The Complete Book of Incense, Oils and Brews" by Scott Cunningham.

Salt Base Recipe #1

1 cup fine sea salt

½ cup of Epsom salts

½ teaspoon of liquid glycerin (for moisturizing)

Salt Base Recipe #2

3 parts Epsom salts

1 part sea or table salt

2 parts baking soda

For either recipe, combine all the ingredients and let it dry on a flat surface for a few hours. Oils, dried bits of herbs and flowers, or food dye can be added to increase the power or just for appearance. To use bath salts add approximately 1 tablespoon to ¼ cup of the salts to the bath water. Keep in mind that large bits of herb may get stuck in the drain so use a mortar and pestle to grind the herbs up in small bits, almost like powder. Add oils and food coloring a drop at a time until it reaches the desired color or scent.

Spells and Rituals

Simple Cleansing

If time is limited or a full bath is not warranted (for small rituals or simple spells) then a pagan practitioner can simply wash their hands in a silver bowl filled with water. Think of it as 'washing one's hands' of something, negativity or mundane influences. Just as we wash our hands prior to eating or a doctor washes prior to surgery, we also can wash our hands prior to magickal workings as a way to ensure that whatever we touched or did with them in the mundane world will not have any affect in the magick we work.

Take a large, silver bowl (a color symbolic of both water and the moon), fill it with water and bring it outside to sit where the moon is reflecting in it. Recite the following:

> *I wash my hands in this dish;*
>
> *O' Goddess do grant my wish;*
>
> *and release me of all negativity.*
>
> *This is my will so mote it be.*

While washing, visualize the negativity being washed off and away. Then, Dump the water harmlessly on the ground or into a running body of water.

Purification Wash

Combine three parts crushed rose petals, one part bay, and one part lavender with either of the base salt recipes listed earlier. Powdered quartz crystal can also be added by rubbing a crystal on a metal nail file. Only a small amount will need to be used, just a few filings from the crystal, do not try to file the entire stone. Sprinkle this bath salt into bath water in order to purify the mind, soul and body. If showering, the salt can be omitted and the same amount of oatmeal placed in the bag instead. Place ingredients into a sachet bag and tie it over the shower head so that as the water flows it hits the sachet and brings with it its powers. Visualize the water cleansing every part of the body and reaching every part of the mind and soul. For bathers, splash water on the face or hunker down in the tub so that the face, or most of it, can be covered with water. In a shower, let the water wash over the face or splash water in the face.

When finished, visualize that the negativity and impurities are running down the drain with the water. Step out of the shower or tub knowing that the body, mind and soul are fully cleansed. This is the perfect ritual to do before a larger Sabbat ritual or a High-Magick ritual. It can also be done anytime a person feels negativity, stress or if they have been psychically attacked.

Self-Nurturing Bath

A person's physical, emotional and magickal energy needs to be maintained and cared for at all times, and one way to do this is through self-nurturing. Pampering never hurt anyone and is, in fact, very beneficial for all areas of personal energy. Combine a few drops of rose oil and a quarter-cup of sea salt to a warm bath and then place either a rose quartz, carnelian, or red jasper stone into a mesh bag and place it in the tub. Relax with the steamy water and let fantasies and visualizations roam free, as long as they remain positive. Push away any negative thoughts and picture being the perfect person; content and happy with successes made, proud of accomplishments, as a beautiful and wonderful person, or any other positive affirmations that come to mind.

As the water starts to cool, remove the stones and let all negativities drain away as the water drains. Feel rejuvenated and like a brand-new person with new goals to meet, places to see and people to meet. Carry the stones in a pocket, purse or around the neck as a reminder of the need to self-nurture and positive affirmations.

Divination, Meditation, Scrying

Divining or scrying does not come easily in a shower or bath, unless a person adopts a way to divine in a steam filled room or mirror in a manner similar to fire or smoke gazing, but showers are perfect for meditation and relaxation.

During a shower or bath visualize that all of the negativity is being cleaned away from the aura, showers work best because the sight of watching water fall down off the body aids in visualization process, but there is nothing wrong with a bath to cleanse metaphysically. As stated earlier in the last few spells, visualize all of the negativity and 'magickal dirt' draining harmlessly away as the water drains. This clears the mind for meditation and the body for relaxation.

Another method for meditation is to take a "Bath Elixir." Elixirs generally are tonics that are imbued with a certain stone and then drank, but in a Bath Elixir the stones are placed into a mesh or cloth bag and then placed right into the tub. Add no more than five stones to a bag and toss them into a bath that has no oils or soaps added (instead, try adding Epsom salts or baking soda) so that the stones do not get damaged. The properties of the stones will empower the bath water and give those qualities to the bather.

Stones (or even shells) should fit the intent, such as rose quartz for love or an amethyst to increase psychic awareness, and stay in the tub through the entire bath. If leery of placing the stones in water, then they can be placed near the tub and the steam of the will still cleanse them and the bather will receive benefits of the stone by being near it and by visualizing that the steam is carrying stone's properties   Remove the stone prior to the plug being pulled and as the water drains away imagine all negativity or mundane occurrences draining away with it.

Magick for the Sea Witch
Section VIII

Mythology and Folklore

There is no end to the folklore and mythology associated with the seas. Maybe it is because of their vastness and their depths, maybe because we are fascinated with them or maybe because they are yet so unexplored. For whatever reason, the folklore abounds from every culture, religion and belief system. Even the Christian Bible has its fair share of stories of the sea from "Noah's Flood," to Jesus ability to walk on water, to "Jonah and the Whale". The sea was both a livelihood and yet something to fear and it is no wonder that people have become superstitious of it.

Water Creation

Many of the earth creation stories start with water as the dominant matter, and much of life either springs from the waters or the Gods that created life on earth were water-creatures (such as Titamia in Bablylonian lore). This is not surprising since scientists surmise that the planet may have been all water at one time and that currently three-fourths of the planet is still water.

The debate exits about why our planet is mostly water and where it came from. Was earth a giant ice ball that melted? Was it all oceans and seas that eventually receded, leaving the land that we now walk on? Perhaps our waters were tears wept by some giant like in Lewis Carroll's novel "Alice in Wonderland" when Alice wept tears that flooded the Dodo bird and his companions (explaining why the sea is so salty).

All we really know that we need it to survive and that it is a cyclic event: it evaporates and falls as rain which goes into the oceans, which evaporate and fall as rain…because of this it would seem that water is eternal because there is no beginning and no end to it cycle. Most stories involving water creation involves creatures coming from the water, rather than creation of the water itself. So, even in our mythologies we still do not get tales of where the water came from. But, the legends of sea-creatures or beings that came out of the waters and created life is a lot like the scientific theory of evolution that states aquatic animals crawled up from the sea, grew feet and learned to adapt to breathing air. They continued to evolve until species resembling mammals, apes and finally humans emerged.

Elementals

Undines

These are female spirits that live in the water, similar to mermaids, and the elemental creature for water. It is said that they can become human if they bear the child of a human male. While most pagans agree that they look like mermaids, some texts claim that undines are not creatures living in the waters but rather are made up of the waters and can be seen in the foam and waves of the waters. Undines are thought to be more of a water sprite and reside in freshwater such as pools and waterfalls rather than their salt water cousins, mermaids and sirens. Usually they are depicted as playful and fun loving water spirits. If using water as a source of meditation or divining or even just to sit and watch a peaceful stream or waterfall, try to be open-minded and see if an undine can be spotted in the waves or droplets.

Sea Beings

Along with the above monsters of the seas, there are other beings that are more human in appearance but still make the seas their home. Belief in these creatures has gone more to the side of folklore and superstition than science, but they are fascinating stories.

Mermaids

Known as beautiful creatures of the deep, stories of these half-human and half-fish creatures have existed for centuries. The first known mermaid "tale" comes from Assyria circa 1000 BCE and sailors have been coming back from the sea with legends of mermaids ever since. Science has never proven their existence and eventually it was believed that manatees behind mermaid sightings. Manatees will come to the surface and have been known to have a flirty and playful demeanor. Their bottom halves do resemble what we typically think of as a mermaid, but I still find it hard to believe that we can go from the real creature of a manatee to the beauty and sexual appeal of the folkloric mermaid. Sailing life must be hard indeed.

Sightings of mermaids have occurred as recent as the 1870's and 1890's and there is even a vague report of a sighting occurring in 1967. Belief in mermaids is so great that P.T. Barnum fooled circus attendees with the Fiji Mermaid. Millions flocked the circuses to see the 'real' mummified remains of a mermaid. However, what circus-goers saw was only a clever trick of taxidermy in which a fish and a monkey were fused together and then made to look as if mummified.

Sirens

Sirens have a more ominous role in Greek Mythology then mermaids or sea hags since they were known for leading sailors to their deaths. These beautiful, yet dangerous, sea nymphs were described in pre-Christian times as being half-woman and half-bird but in later Greek tales they were depicted more aquatic, like a mermaids or as humans. Either way, they were said to sing beautifully and hypnotically and they would do so at every passing ship. The sailors would be so bewitched that they would steer straight into rocks or coral reefs, and to their doom.

In the famous legend of Odysseus, he and his men were said to avert the allure of the sinister and seductive sirens by blocking his crew's ears with beeswax (so they could not hear the siren song) and he was tied to the mast so that he could not reach the helm and steer towards the Siren's, the men controlled the ship with oars. Today the term is used in regards to a woman whose sexual appeal is said to be dangerous.

In 4th century Christianity the belief of Sirens was highly discouraged and the word came to mean temptation rather than a real being. However, in the 17th century some Jesuit writers asserted their belief that sirens were real creatures that actually existed. They fought this belief to the point of arguing that Noah had them on his ark in the time of the Great Flood. There speculations were never taken seriously and eventually the Sirens fell to the way of folklore.

Sea Hags

Television and popular media, such as comic books and movies, have turned the sea hag into a gnarled, ugly, green and evil entity that is thought of as a 'direct cousin' to the folkloric and commercialized Halloween witch. Perhaps the most popular of these beings are the Sea Hag from the "Popeye" cartoons comics and the eight-limbed, overweight octo-human named Ursula from Disney's "The Little Mermaid." Both are evil and bent on getting what they want out of people.

In Greek myths the Sea Hags are not evil or ugly but are as beautiful as the fabled Sirens however, instead of luring sailors to their death with their songs and beauty, Sea Hags helped the sailor's control the winds. They would give sailors knotted ropes or cloth and untying the knots could control the winds. If a sailor untied one knot it would release a strong breeze, two knots would release a strong wind and three knots a gale force.

Sea-faring Lore

Sailors are a superstitious lot and avoiding death, specters and other mishaps is something that sailors try to control in a variety of superstitious ways. Because of the tragedies at sea and its vast depths the ghost stories out there are as numerous as haunted house stories. There are also numerous superstitions that involve the weather at sea or the fate of the crew and ship. Numerous superstitious acts were done to ensure safe voyages and fare weather so that no one would end up in the sea-bearing afterworld. Many of these superstitions are still believed or honored today.

Davy Jones' Locker

A sailor who died from violence or being lost at sea was said to go to Davy Jones' Locker. Davy Jones may have been a real person, but is most likely is a pseudonym. The first time this phrase is mentioned (which typically means the depths of the ocean or the bottom of the sea) is in the 18th century. It may be a combination of the West Indian word 'duppy' (devil) and the common English surname of Jones. The name Jones itself may be a derivation of Jonah from the Bible. Davy Jones is also thought to be a malignant spirit who has power over the seas and may be responsible for some of the deaths or losses in his domain and in present-day is thought of as the very personification of the sea. The name has even taken on the personification of characters in popular media such as in the movie series "Pirates of the Caribbean."

Fiddler's Green

Similar to Davy Jones' Locker, this is the after-world of sailors and other sea-farers but unlike the ominous locker, the Fiddler's Green is a paradise of eternal mirth where fiddlers always play and the dancers never tire (Irish). This is similar to Norse mythology and Valhalla; a great hall where Viking heroes who died in battle go for their eternity to spend the day in battle and the night in drinking.

It is also said that sailors with over fifty years of service will go to Fiddler's Green when they die. However, some legends do state that a serviceman can find this paradise by walking inland with an oar over his shoulder until he comes to a place where people stop and ask him what he is carrying. Similar to this idea is one we find in Homer's "Odyssey" in which Tiresias tells Odysseus that the only way he can appease Poseidon and find happiness is to take an oar or a winnowing fan (used to separate grain from its chaff, such as in wheat) and walk until he is asked what he is carrying. At that spot he is to make a sacrifice to Poseidon.

Earrings

The stereotype of pirates or sailors wearing earrings comes to us from superstitious lore in that one who works on the sea cannot drown if wearing an earring. Obviously, there is nothing to support this superstition but it can make a wonderfully charming spell for anyone leery of a boat ride or voyage.

Earrings can be worn to ensure good luck and a safe return home. Of course, this does not mean to ignore all boating safety precautions such as wearing life vests, safe driving or any other such rules and common sense. Purchase a pair of earrings or use ones from a jewelry collection already owned, anoint them with salt water, blessed water or an essential oil such as patchouli and as they are anointed recite the following:

> *Earrings of luck, keep me safe as I roam*
>
> *on the high seas and back to my home.*

Wear the earrings for the entire voyage (they can be taken out at night but should be put back in the next morning). Incidentally, a similar stereotype of sailors and tattoos may come from the belief that tattoos would ward off disaster and evil spirits.

Silver Coins

A silver coin placed under the masthead of a ship will ensure a successful voyage, typically done as the ship was being built, this could be done by placing a silver coin near the mast head or if owning the boat, nail the coin to it. As this is done, recite the following:

> *I call upon (name of a God or Goddess) for safe passage on your seas;*
>
> *Bless all those aboard this ship and bring us all home safely;*
>
> *This is my will so mote it be.*

This belief comes from the idea that coins were used to either pay the passage of deceased sailors across the river Styx, or as a payment to propitiate the Gods. This belief is so widely held that it is said the US Navy casts special coins in a formal ceremony when the mast is set on newly commissioned ships. When older ships are stripped for salvage or in need of repair it was not uncommon to find something under the masthead.

Christening Boats

The belief that boats should be christened before their maiden voyage is widely held and popular. It is so ingrained in people's beliefs that in 1912 when the ill-fated Titanic sank it was rumored to be the fault of not having properly christened if before if left port. Christening a boat is a way to appease the Gods of the seas when launching a new boat and therefore will protect it on the seas. In ancient times this was done by smearing human blood over the prow and as it dipped into the waves on its voyage the blood mingled with the water and acted as a sacrifice to the Gods. The

Vikings of Scandinavian and Germanic lore took this one step further and actually crushed their prisoners under the keels of the longboats.

Eventually, and thankfully, this custom gave way to using red wine and then to champagne (used today) because it is believed that the more expensive the beverage the more honor and respect bestowed upon the boat (and the Gods). The bottles are usually broken on the ship's prow and the boat is either stated by name or dedicated to a person, group or purpose and then launched. For anyone on a boat as a guest, there is no way to tell if the boat was properly christened or not, so for extra assurance that the gods have bee appeased another superstition says that pouring wine onto the deck is also seen as a libation to the Gods and will ensure a safe or successful voyage. For all practical purposes, try sipping a glass of wine from an altar's chalice and make a toast to the sea God of choice and ask for a safe and successful passage.

Leaving Port

Another superstition involves leaving port and the belief that it is bad luck to look back as the ship departs. This is similar to a belief that when performing certain acts of magick in which the practitioner has to bury an object (such as witch bottles) and is advised to not look back at where the bottle was buried. This causes doubt that the magick will work and with ships I imagine it causes doubt that the port will be seen again, so the voyager looks back for one last sight. When departing on a voyage stand facing away from the port or harbor and recite the following:

If the harbor I do not see, the (name of ship) will bring us home safely.

Try tossing a coin over the right shoulder as this is recited this as a further act of favor to the Gods of the sea.

Gods and Goddesses

There were many ways to gain favor through the Gods when venturing out on the seas, christening a boat or tossing coins to the seas were just a few. It is believed that the flags on masts date back to pre-Christian times when boats were decorated with wreaths of flowers in order to appease the Gods. It was also believed that if a man fell overboard the Gods of the seas meant to have him and it would anger them if anyone on board ship attempted to rescue him. The Gods would either take the rescuer instead of or in addition to. Often gifts of fruit and meat were given near any important navigational point, such as the equator, to propitiate the Gods and allow safe passage. This is a tradition that is still honored by many cruise ships today.

Tiamat

In Babylonian creation myths, Tiamat is the personification of the sea. She is considered to be a monstrous embodiment of the primordial chaos (the seas) and is depicted as a sea serpent or sea dragon. Tiamat is responsible for giving birth to the first generation of deities but when she made war upon them she was killed by the storm God, Marduck. Her body was divided up and became the Heavens and the Earth.

Ancient texts do not refer to her appearance but in the Enuma Elish (creation myth) she is said to have given birth to the dragons, serpents and a general array of monsters such as mermaids and scorpion men. She is also described as having a tail. In the 1970's, with the advent of the role-playing game "Dungeons and Dragons", we get the description of Tiamat as a multi-headed dragon.

Oceanids and Oceanus

In both Greek and Roman lore the Oceanids are known as ocean nymphs but are also the three-thousand daughters of the Titans Oceanus and his sister Tethys; the oceanids are patrons of all bodies of water. Some legends say that they have three-thousand brothers known as Potamoi and some legends claim that the Oceanids are three-thousand children of both male and female genders. Oceanus is known as the God of the oceans and also the name of his domain, with the belief being that the ocean is a giant river encircling the world.

Nereid, Naiads and Nereus

Nereus, a Greek god of the sea known as "the wise old man of the sea," is said to have had fifty daughters with his wife, Doris. Nereids are sea nymphs said to be helpful to sailors, especially during storms. Naiads are a type of nymph of only freshwaters such as lakes, rivers, springs and fountains. Also of Greek lore, the Naiads are nymphs skilled in music and dancing and are said to have healing powers.

Anna Perenna

Anna Perenna is mainly thought of as a river nymph and the moon-goddess of the current year is, she is also the Roman Goddess of the New Year. Her festival, or feast day, was celebrated on March 15 (Roman God Mars' feast day is also on this date), otherwise known as "The Ides of March." Ides, or idus, is thought to simply mean the day of the full moon which was considered an auspicious day to the ancient Romans. Her name may be derived from 'amnis perennis' (eternal stream) or from 'annis' (year) and 'perenna' (lasting many years) and may be where we get our words annuals and perennials when referring to plants, which makes her a great deity for garden magick.

Because of her association as a river nymph she can be honored in sea witchery with any spell involving running water or by setting up an altar in her honor (or, for the earth witch try working in the garden on this day). Anna is concerned with cycles of renewal and connecting the past to the present. In past times, on the eve of the 15th people, would gather to camp out, dance, feast, sing, and drink. They toasted to long life and health. It was believed that one would live as many years as the cups of wine they could drink.

Neptune, Poseidon, and Triton

It was said to be bad luck to cut hair or nails at sea because those items were considered offerings to Goddess Proserpina, Roman Goddess of the Earth (her Greek equivalent is Persephone) and the Roman God of the Seas, Neptune would become jealous if these offerings were made to her while in his kingdom. Considering that he controlled the seas and the fates of the sailors on them, it would not do to anger him. Fisherman would also insert a coin into one of their floats as a payment to Neptune in return for ensuring that they had a good catch of fish. His brothers were Pluto, Jupiter and Saturn; all of which are names of our planets (yes, I still consider Pluto a planet).

Poseidon is the Greek equivalent to the Roman God Neptune and was the god of the sea, water, earthquakes and horses. He is relied on by sailors for a safe voyage and lives on the ocean floor in a palace made of corals and gems. He is often seen carrying a trident and sometimes confused with Triton, who is actually his son. Poseidon is said to be responsible for all the trials and tribulations that Odysseus endured on his journey to get back to his home a Ithaca. Poseidon is not usually considered as a nice or caring God but rather as vengeful and angry. He is the cause of tidal waves, rogue waves, tsunamis, violent storms and any other aggressive oceanic condition.

Triton, or sometimes referred to as King Triton, is thought of as the King of the mermaids (made popular by Disney's animated movie "The Little Mermaid,") but Triton was actually a Greek God of the sea. It is believed that he had the tail of a fish and the upper body of a man (mermaid). He is the son of Poseidon and Aphrodite and was seen as a messenger of the sea and carries a trident but is also known to blow into a conch shell to calm or raise the seas. He is seen more as a fatherly figure and less of an angry and vengeful god than his father is.

Sedna

Sedna is the Inuit Goddess of the Deep, sometimes known as the Goddess of Life and Death. She is sometimes referred to as the Seal Goddess and though mortal at one time, she became a goddess under tragic circumstances involving betrayal.

Her father, a widow, was trying to do right by his daughter and find a suitor to marry her. Sedna did not like any of the suitors and refused them all. One day, a sea bird came to Sedna and promised to take her away from it all and to his home where she could live in luxury. Sedna agreed and against her father's wishes she eloped with the sea bird. However, his home was a dirty nest and Sedna was made a slave. Realizing she had been tricked and not happy with her new life, she begged her father to come and rescue her. He did, but he had to take a boat to get to where she was being held captive and on the way home a flock of sea birds surrounded them and the boat. Their wings made such waves that her father feared it would capsize. In an act of self-preservation, he threw Sedna overboard to appease the birds and save his own life. Shocked, cold and betrayed she tried to climb back into the boat but her father cut off her fingers. When she tried again to climb in he cut off her hands.

As she sank to the bottom, the blood from her dismembered limbs turned into the seals, whales, fish and other sea creatures that we have today. She descended all the way to the land of the dead Adlivum; where she remains to this day as the Queen. Sedna is bitter but when she is feeling good she keeps a continuous supply of sea animals in the ocean so the hunters can catch food. When she is feeling that she has been disrespected she sends sickness, storms, and starvation to the land. When this occurs, Shamans must descend into Adlivium; passing through dangers such as abysses, cauldrons of boiling seals, and a ferocious dog that guards the entrance. If they survive this, they are required to massage her aching limbs and comb her hair. Once she is fully appeased she fills the seas with animals once again so the hunters can hunt.

Aegir

This is the Norse King of the Sea and he was both worshiped and feared by sailors because he would rise to the surface and randomly take ships, men and cargo. Sacrifices were made to appease him in the hopes that he would leave the ship alone. Aegir was also known for his lavish entertainment and parties given for the other gods. At such an event one of his faithful servants was killed by the god Loki, a god of mischief and tricks. He seems to be the very personification of the power the seas and tides hold.

Magick for the Air Witch
Section I

The Air Element

Air is our breath; it is our very existence and life. If we are sitting in our houses without water near us, no fireplace and our feet are not touching the bare earth we are still in the air element. It is all around us and is vital to our existence. We can live three days without water, two weeks without food (earth) and an indeterminable time without fire but we cannot live without air but for a few precious minutes. Yet we cannot see it, smell it or taste it on its own. We can hear it and feel it when the winds blow, but we see things moving in the air and not the air itself and we smell things wafting on the air but do not smell just the air.

Perhaps we are like a small breeze wafting in silently causing very little bluster and infinitesimal changes but are as important in its minute changes as the strong gales that come in and blow everything around with fury and fervor. Maybe we are like the subtle winds that blow from off shores and push along the bird in its current, or bounce along the balloon or kite floating up to the skies, or even cooling a person on a hot day. Maybe we are stronger winds that cause greater changes by filling the ship's sails or powering windmills. Hopefully, we are not like the forceful winds that blow in quickly, destroy everything in their path, and blow on out without a care to the destruction left behind.

However like the air, people with a kinship to this element are inspirational, creative, free-flowing and inhibited. They like to follow along on a current to see where it leads and then drift off again on another current when they can. They are fairly flexible in that they bob and float like a leaf in the air and a ship at sea. Air and water have a lot of similarities, but unlike water which has substance and depth, air does not have any substance and is difficult to see or discern and yet we know it's all around. It is also eternally expanding and reaches far wider than we can perceive, and yet still it has no depth or substance to it.

To commune with air sit outside when there is a good breeze blowing, feel it on all part of the body: the face, blowing strands of hair, on arms and legs, feel it all around and touching every surface. Try to pick up sounds or smells that come to on the breezes; if possible sit on a hilltop to feel the breezes. Opening doors and windows in a house can also be a way of letting air in and connecting with it as an element. Spending recreational time outside flying a kite or model airplanes is also a relaxing way to commune with air. Hang-gliding, flying and hot air balloons are ideal methods but not always available to the general public; however, if the chance arises, remember that it is of the air element and relish the experience.

Magick for the Air Witch
Section II

Correspondences

Traditional
This element is masculine and usually represented in the east quadrant of an altar. Predominantly the color yellow is used in symbolism, but air may also be represented by light blue or any pastels and even light gray. Its elemental beings are sylphs (similar to fairies) and stones might be moonstone, turquoise, and rhodachrosite. Herbs such as wormwood, parsley, mint, lemon verbena, lavender, dandelion and anise can be used in magickal workings when dealing with air as well as broom (plant, not a besom) for use in wind spells and saffron for raising the winds.

Alchemy and Ancient Medical Properties
In alchemy air is symbolized with an upwards pointing triangle that is bisected by a horizontal line; a symbol commonly used in pagan practices today. In ancient Greek medicines it is attributed to the season of spring and on the northern point of the compass.

Zodiac/Astrological
Anyone of an air element is born under Gemini, Libra or Aquarius sign and exhibit positive personality traits of kindness, intellect, communication, socializing and helpfulness. On the negative side they may be

cold, superficial, impractical and insensitive. I had to double check the signs for this element since I know that Aquarius is sometimes known as "the water bearer" but it is indeed of the air sign because it is not the water itself or a water creature such as Cancer the crab, Pisces the fish or Scorpio the scorpion (lobster) are. It is the person carrying the water, just as Gemini is two people and Libra is a set of scales (the only inanimate object) often depicted as being held by a person. If we think of air as ethereal or as spirit, then these signs all depicted by people, are of the air.

Greek and Roman Mythology

Greek and Roman mythology symbolize air with swords or daggers, which is where modern practices get their usage of knives to symbolize this element. This is perhaps because of the imagery of swords being swished through the air in battle or it might come from an old adage of cutting air with a knife, such as the saying "the fog was so thick you couldn't cut it with a knife." For those basing their practice on Greco-Roman studies, bladed weapons would be of the air, or at least the athame alone would be of the air.

Hinduism

Hindus also symbolize air with swords and it is known as Vayu (air), Vata (blown), or Pavana (wind). Prana (breathing) is the primary deity who is the biological father of Bhima and the spiritual father of Lord Hanuman. In the Tattva air is represented by a blue circle.

Ceremonial Magick

Within Ceremonial Magick the dagger or athame (a ceremonial knife often used to represent air or the God; an athame is never used for carving or cutting) is said to be painted yellow with the magickal names or sigils written in violet. This contradicts what most practitioners adhere to today with the athame's requirements being a silver, double-edged blade and a black handle (Wicca). The archangel is Raphael, the angel is Chassan, ruler is Aral and the king is Paralda. Air is considered active and represented by the symbol of Aquarius, by man and on the upper left point of the pentagram in the Supreme Invoking Ritual of the Pentagram.

Wicca

In Wicca the colors of air are pastels, mainly yellow, and its direction is east with the elemental tool being the athame. Air is also the element of the sunrise (which occurs in the east), childhood, springtime and new beginnings. The elemental being is a sylph, which is similar to fairies but often thought of as being made up of air currents rather than than a creature that can lives in air.

Other Symbolism

In East Asian cultures it is usually seen as the equivalent of wood and as discussed earlier, it is not one of the five Chinese elements but rather their concept of Chi or Qi is similar to air. Ironically, air is seen in Buddhism as an actual element like those of Wiccan practices, Buddhism is a belief system that does have some of its history in ancient China so its interesting to note the differences.

In Aztec cultures, air is symbolized by a snake, and this is perhaps because their God of Air (Quetzalcoatl) was depicted as a feathered serpent. In the Aztec beliefs the world was flat and surrounded on all sides by ocean with the waters rising up to become the sky. Because of this belief it seems that Quetzalcoatl (sometimes spelled as Quetzal coati) had he ability to go from the air to the seas seamlessly. Considering that he needed to go into the waters he was also serpentine-like so that he could delve into the seas without mishap. Incidentally, the Aztec universe had four directions much like the four directions seen in the elements. These directions all originated from a central point in which their capitol, Tenochtitlan, was erected.

In Christian Mythology it is represented by mankind, again, possibly by the representation of air also being similar to ethereal beings, such as angels, or the spirits and souls of man.

Magick for the Air Witch
Section III

Tools of Air

Bell

Bells have a long line in history and religion and are a common item found in home, either as musical instruments or decorations. They have often been used in the world's religions and social rituals or events. Often the bells used in churches are put through a ceremony of their own that is similar to consecrating a tool in paganism. The ritual can include such things as naming the bells, decorating them with flowers and herbs, or engraving special symbols and words of meaning on them. It has even been noted that the bells have been given reverence as a living thing, which is a belief system known as Animism, and that to insult the bells meant that they would not ring.

Their tones are said to scare away evil spirits; a reason why noisemakers are popular on New Year's Eve. The tradition of noisemakers on New Year's Eve (December 31) were a way of staving off any negativity from the past year and bringing in only goodness for the upcoming year). Bells have also been known to be placed around the necks of animals to help ward off the evil eye and protect the livestock. Bells can help clear an area of negativity and are often used to cleanse an area prior to magickal workings or as a way to intone the beginning of a ritual or to call upon the God and Goddess.

Bells also are said to be critical in the Catholic ritual of excommunication known as "bell, book and candle" in which the bell tolls for the sinner (who is being basically kicked out of the faith). In the movie "Bell, Book and Candle" Shepherd Henderson (Jimmy Stewart) is placed under a spell by Gillian 'Gil' Holroyd (Kim Novak). An author of witchcraft starts talking about his subject, not knowing he is in the room with three witches, and he says "ring the bell, close the book, and light the candle" as a formula for getting rid of witches.

There is really no end to the superstitions involving bells, and they also have an array of uses in pagan practices. Place a bell on an altar in the corresponding quarter and use when calling the quarter by ringing the bell to summon the element of air; or it can be used to cleanse an area prior to magickal workings and because of its shape it can be used as a candle snuffer if one isn't available. Bells can also be used to invoke the God or Goddess, to invoke good energies or to indicate the beginning and the end of a ceremony, rite or ritual.

Wand

The Wand is typically thought of as a male tool and can be used to call the spirits or deities to join in the ritual, to direct energy, to trace symbols for protection, to trace a protective circle that encompasses the working area and to stir the contents of a cauldron. When using a wand, think of it as an extension of the self. It is not going to make things appear like stage magic, but rather it directs and focuses the energy being put forth and helps it to go where it is needed. To put it in mundane terms, it is a lecture's pointer stick or a symphony conductor's baton. Teachers or lectures often have a stick that they use to point to objects or words on a board or overhead projector and symphony conductors use their baton to direct the musicians. It is just a cleaner way of directing attention or ideas (or energy) to an area without getting other fingers or fists in the way.

In Wiccan traditions it is placed with fire because it is an extension of our energies and passion, which are qualities of fire. In Druidic paths it is placed with air and I also place it with air due my association with it modern wands, such as the conductor's baton and a stage magicians wand. Also, the Hollywood and stage magician versions of wands are waved in the air or pointed at objects and literally create things from 'thin air' or change things into something else. In Pagan practices wands are used much in the same way with the exception that they don't make things appear and cannot change a person into a toad (or vice versa). But are used to point and focus energy or to wave in the air to expel negativity energy and cleanse an area. I also think of athames as being forged in heat so for me, they are of the fire element. There is no right or wrong answer here but depends on the practitioner's own beliefs.

They can be made of many different materials such as gemstone, clay, metal or natural wood. Crystal, obsidian or amethyst are the usual gemstones for wand use, but any hard stone can be used and many beautiful designs can be purchased in metaphysical shops. Woods for wands tend to be of cherry, hazel, willow, elder, oak, apple or peach. Metals are usually steel or copper or an alloy metal. Again, these can be purchased in stores but many pagan practitioners take pride in finding a stick and shaping it into a wand. Wands are often decorated with sigils or symbols carved or painted on them; with beads, feathers, buttons or gemstones; with a crystal at the tip (to direct energy); and with either copper wire to conduct energy, silver wire for the Goddess, gold wire for the God or a combination of all these things.

On an altar it should rest in whatever quadrant is associated with the wand, for me it is in air and that is where I will place it when it is not in use. While using it, hold the wand in whichever projective hand and directional quarters can be tapped to acknowledge their presence, the wand can be waved in the air to cleanse a space, or it can be used to draw an invisible circle of protection around the sacred space, to close a circle and to touch objects important in the ritual or spell.

Magick for the Air Witch
Section IV

Working with Air

Air rules over the acts of divination, prophecy and weather watching. Any weather involving winds from small breezes to tornadoes and hurricanes are of the air element. Use it in all spells or rituals that require visualization or positive affirmations. Types of spells to use for honoring the air element might be tossing objects into the air or fanning smoke over an object such as in cleansing.

The key to working with air is to remember that we need it. Do not ever attempt any spell, trick, ritual, or anything else in which cutting off respiratory circulation is asked for. Also, in working with weather magick (regardless of it's with the water or air element) remember that weather magick can be very powerful and can have devastating effects and harm others. Remember the rule "and if it harm ye none" and that it can harm others in ways we might not realize. While it is not the intent to harm others by asking for a sunny day for a picnic, the weather could go awry and cause a drought which will harm the farmers.

Air can also be a difficult element to work with in that it gets mixed up with the ether or void, which are also other names for the spirit element. When working with it, try to keep in mind that it is as an element and not an ethereal being. Concentrate on tangible items related to the air such as the creatures living in it and weather or atmospheric conditions (winds and clouds).

Indoor Spaces

Since air is all around us, the element is always around and all we need to do is manipulate it so that we are aware of it. Hang wind chimes in a breezeway or on a porch or place fans in the home to bring the element of air inside. Feathers can also be used as decorations in vases or wreaths or pictures of insects and birds can be placed around the home. Plants are also good to represent air because they take in and give out air; acting as great filters for the air. Also, open doors and windows to let the air cleanse the house. A common form of house-cleansing involves smudging an entire home and then opening all of the windows and doors to let the smoke out, taking with it the negativity.

Outdoor Spaces

Similar to indoor spaces, air is all around and we only need to manipulate it to see it and appreciate it. Hang wind chimes outside where the breezes can catch them or decorate a yard with windmills and gardens with small toy pinwheels. There are a number of decorative objects sold in dollar stores and garden or home décor sections of department stores such as spinners, chimes or weather vanes. All of these will be manipulated by the air either visually or auditory and will remind a person of the air element. Going for walks on hills, windy mountaintops, or breezy beaches is another great way to connect with air.

Rituals and Spell work

Use this element in spells dealing with travel, memory, intellect, divination, psychic ability, to find lost items, uncover lies, develop psychic abilities, for obtaining knowledge and overcoming addictions. It also governs over the realm of thought, clear and uncluttered visualization, movement and manifestation. Think of the four winds (north, south, east and west) and spring time when working spells or rituals. Air is a cleansing and purifying element and is uninhibited, free-flowing and without form. People who feel a kinship with air might do so for the freedom of movement and uninhibited feelings that air brings or they might be like the forceful winds that come on strong and make a big impact.

Aside from bells and wind chimes, incense is another typical item used to represent air but or anyone who cannot have lit objects in their room/apartment or may be allergic to the smoke there are alternatives. Try using essential oils by placing them battery-operated oil diffusers, for scenting sachets, or pour a small amount into a spray bottle with water and spritz it around the room. Dry potpourri will smell nice just sitting in a decorative bowl, and looks good on an altar, or electric potpourri burners can be purchased . Because all of these place odors into the air they can be considered of the air element.

Altars

On an altar it is represented by incense, a feather, bells, whistles or any woodwind instrument, and by statues or effigies of winged creatures. To create an air altar try adding an extra item that represents air, for example in addition to the usual incense burner add a feather or a bell in the east quadrant. Please remember that feathers should be found naturally and never plucked from a bird.

A more complex altar might include each of the four quadrants can have an item that represents both the natural element of that direction and air. For example, in the north (earth) any winged animal or fairy effigy could be placed since the being represents earth and the wings represents air. An incense diffuser (sticks placed in a liquid that give off a scent without smoke) can be placed in the west for water or a bowl of herbs can be used (basically and scented water because the liquid is water and the scent is air). For fire, a yellow candle can be placed in the south since it is the traditional color of air and a candle gives off a little bit of smoke or try placing a statue of a winged and fire-breathing dragon in the south.

While standing at the altar, or casting a circle or in a group ritual, air is symbolized by the arms extended straight up and slightly out like a 'V,' think of bird's wings when picturing this hand sign. Hold the arms up when invoking this element and then lower in order to ring a bell or light the incense.

Magick for the Air Witch
Section V

When the Winds Blow

People across the ages have been fascinated with the winds, maybe because they are not seen unless observed by the objects they move. Only through mechanical devices that produce wind, such as windmills or fans, can we attempt to control and harness it. Wind also plays a big part in mythology, such as with Odysseus of Greek Mythology, and for centuries man has desired to fly without the use of contraptions, such as planes or hot air balloons. We envy the birds their flight, and it is an unachievable act for humans. Because we feel the effects of wind but can't control it, we are fascinated with it.

Wind chimes, spinners, weather vanes and flags are common decorations in yards and are the perfect way to 'see the air.' It is tricky working with air because, like spirit, it is not always a tangible form. However, we can see it with a few cheap decorative devices and we can feel it anytime we step outside. The air is always there and there are always currents. Sometimes we don't feel the breezes, sometimes they are just enough to cool us of on a hot day, and sometimes they are destructive forces that can blow things down or tear things up.

We also have an internal air that no one considers to be 'of the wind' and is often taken for granted, until we don't have it. Take a deep breath and then blow it out: we have wind in our lungs. Our breath can be used to replace the wind in some magick and it is the only wind we can adequately create and control. We use it to cool our food, blow out a candle, or for deep breathing exercises, and now it can be used in magick.

Wind Correspondences

In calling quarters for ritual, each of the directions is named along with the element that they represent. In air magick, each of the directional winds is believed to bring their own magickal properties to a spell or ritual. When performing a spell or ritual all upon a specific wind or stand and face that direction when performing the act. If the winds happen to be blowing that day, the winds can be used similar to the way moon phases. If there is no wind, spells or rituals can still be done by visualizing the correspondences that the winds bring and imagining the winds coming from that direction.

The northern winds are known as the 'mysterious winds' and are the coldest winds. They can be used to banish bad habits, destroy disease or rid a person of negativity. The correspondences for northern winds are the season of winter, the color black, element earth and the time correspondence is midnight.

Southern winds are the hottest winds and are used similar to their elemental correspondence of fire: for energy or changes. Its season is summer with colors of white or yellow and a time of noon (usually though of as the hottest part of the day). Be careful with southern winds because they can bring about more than asked for or expected.

Winds from the west are cool, moist and can be used for love or fertility rituals and spells. Use western winds to contact spirits or seeing the future (there is a divination spell for western winds later in this section. Its correspondences are water, the colors of green or blue, a season of autumn and the time of twilight.

Eastern winds are perfect for renewal or for a fresh start such as a new job or home. Its correspondences are springtime, air, the colors of crimson or pink and also the time of dawn. Use these winds anytime that changes, renewal or rebirth are needed. Think of 'spring cleaning' when we clean out clutter from a home or how the springtime brings about new life.

Wind in Folklore

Talk of the winds is also seen in nursery rhymes, superstitions and folklore, such as in the Mother Goose rhyme:

"Mister East gave a Feast,
Mister North laid the cloth,
Mister West did his best,
Mister South burnt his mouth eating cold potato."

There may be a possible correlation of this rhyme with weather divination by stating what the winds do (more on this in the divination section). Nursery rhymes were often ways of communicating with each other in times when many people were illiterate and could not read or write. Meteorologists did not exist in these times so weather patterns were watched and then the information was passed along either in rhyme form or was translated to rhyme in the collection of these tales. This rhyme perhaps indicates what the winds will bring when it comes from a certain direction.

There are also old adages regarding the wind and weather such as "when the wind comes from the east; 'tis not good for man nor beast" or the popular "when the wind comes from the west, the fishing is at its best." Often these adages have scientific value because; meteorologically speaking, certain winds bring about certain atmospheric conditions.

Try using some of the folkloric superstitions or the correspondences mentioned earlier to create spells involving the wind or even try making an outdoor wind altar in which all of the items on it will blow or move in the wind and include objects corresponding to the directions. At the very least, a weather or wind vane is an ideal tool to keep outside in order to keep up with which way the winds blow so that the appropriate spell or ritual can be used.

Spells and Rituals

Much of air magick might be used either in correspondence, divination or weather magick. But, there are a few spells that require either a person's breath or the actual air currents, which can be used similar to the tides and the phases of the moon.

Fast currents are the perfect time to do a spell that needs to be acted upon quickly and for immediate, short-term effects. Slower currents are for spells that may take longer to manifest and when the effects or intent needs to last longer than a fast spell's results.

It is also possible to use one's own breath as a way to rid the self of negativity, such as in the balloon spell below. This concept is similar to burning paper to rid the self of negativity such as a bad habit or illness. The practitioner is still ridding themselves of something unwanted, but it is being done with their breath and not fire. Remember that in the divination methods and spell work in this section is not an attempt to control the wind or air, but only to use what is already present. Working with the wind is a tricky aspect of pagan practices because it is not something that can be easily created or controlled, the easiest way is by using our own breath to blow intent into a spell. Some candle magick requires blowing out the flame rather than using a candle snuffer because it blows intent into the spell (think of making a wish and blowing out birthday candles).

Balloon Anger Release

Who knew that those fun-loving, colorful and festive staples of any birthday party can actually be used in spells? There are two different versions of using balloons to release anger. The first one is based on a spell in Llewellyn's Magickal Almanac 2007 and only requires a person to imagine a balloon, which is great practice for visualization, and can be done anywhere a few moments of concentration can be met. This is meant to be done by anyone who has had 'one of those days' and doesn't want to take their troubles home with them (from work, a meeting, volunteering, or just everyday stress). I think this is a great spell to teach children and something that they can do at recess, on the bus or anytime they don't have to concentrate on schoolwork.

Imagine a non-blown up red balloon (red for anger) being placed to the lips. Mentally blow up that balloon and with each breath expel all the troubles, angers, frustrations or anything else that is a bother. Keep doing this and with each breath expel another trouble, concern or worry into the balloon and visualize it getting bigger and bigger.

This balloon is very flexible and can get as big can be imagined, even as big as a hot air balloon! Once it is as big as is needed to fit all troubles and concerns inside, visualize tying a string onto it or simply tie it off. Look at the balloon and see all the troubles in there bouncing around in images or words. They are separate from the self and are no more annoying than mosquitoes. When ready, let the string or balloon go or use an imaginary pin to pop the balloon which lets all the troubles float harmlessly away.

The second method is similar to the above but uses a real balloon and is great if having trouble visualizing a balloon. Blow up a red balloon and imagine all negativity and troubles going into the balloon. Visualize everything negative going into that balloon and that it (anger) is no longer harmful. When the balloon is as big as it can get, recite the following verse:

My anger is released with harm to none, so mote it be.

Then pop the balloon with a pin and 'see' all of the frustrations float harmlessly away into the universe. However, please remember to pick up the pieces and then discard them in the trash so that animals will not be harmed by them. An alternative to popping the balloon for those who hate that sound (raising my hand here) don't tie off the balloon but instead just let it go. All of the air will come whizzing out and the balloon will dash about the place, as it does so imagine all of the troubles dispersing harmlessly outwards.

Balloon Wish

When we were little we liked nothing better than to eventually let a helium balloon go and watch it float up to the sky and disappear. In school we attached cards to balloons that had our names, ages and school address and released them. My card was found by a farmer in Iowa, living in Wisconsin at the time we estimated my balloon flew some 500 miles. I don't know where I got the idea that if letting a balloon go a wish can be made on it, but it was something I always told my own daughters. Maybe it was just a way to placate them when they got upset at losing their much-coveted balloon, maybe it my subconscious writing its first spell, or maybe I just fear popping balloons so much that I don't want them in my house. (It is a fear I am endlessly teased about but glad to know that it is legit, it is called globophobia, which is the fear of balloons, or ligyrophobia, which is the fear of popping noises in general).

Regardless, I started telling my daughters they could let a balloon go and make a wish. The wish would be carried up to the stars and would granted (imagine my horror at the screams that abounded when a balloon got caught in a tree, fortunately their daddy managed to release it and it continued to carry the wish up). This can be done with any helium-filled balloon and is another great one to teach children. Just before releasing the balloon think of the wish (intent) or draw a symbol onto the balloon that shows intent. Recite the following verse:

Balloon of fantasies; balloon of flight;
Grant me this wish that I wish tonight.

Let the balloon go and watch it until it is out of sight; when it has popped from atmospheric conditions the magick will be released and the wish granted.

Kite Magick

Kites are a great way to honor the air element and season of spring, which is the best time to fly kites because of the windy weather and is a season often associated with the air element. Purchase some kites and have fun with friends and family flying them; be mindful of trees and power lines, always keeping safety in mind. If lucky enough there might even be a kite-flying club or event locally. Just by accident we discovered that the Boys and Girls Club in our town hosts a kite-flying contest. For $1.00 admission we were entered into the contest, won a door prize and got a free hot dog and drink. There was no age limit and our oldest contestant was in his 80's and the youngest barely able to hold the kite strings by himself.

Like the balloon spells, this is another great spell for children and teaches them that while it is appropriate to be angry, there is also an appropriate way to deal with it. This spell is not limited to children but can be done by adults as well; there are many adults who take up kite-flying as a hobby. In the book 'Magickal Household' by Scott Cunningham there is a similar spell mentioned regarding the use of a kite for releasing anger.

Cunningham recommends making a kite so personal energies can be poured into it, but if not crafty enough to do this then go out and buy one. Add energies to it by holding it for a few moments and putting intent into it, similar to charging an object such as a candle. Or as the kite is released into the air on the string the energies and intent can be placed into it. As the kite dips and sways in the breezes the negative energy is being released harmlessly into the air. As it flies about recite the following verse:

Kite that bounces and floats up above

Fill my mind and heart with only peace and love

Continue flying the kite until either the winds are no longer good for it, or the feeling of being purged of negativity comes.

Leaf Spell

Find a large leaf, preferably one already fallen from the tree, and with a charcoal stick (a stick charred in fire) get to as high a place as possible and wait until a good wind is blowing. Visualize a need and draw a symbol on the leaf that represents that need, for example a dollar sign can represent money or heart for love. Throw the leaf into the wind and if the breezes catch it and take it away then the power has gone forth and the wish will come true. If not, then it is not meant to happen for the spell can be tried again later with a new leaf. A permanent marker also works in place of a charcoal stick and might be easier to use.

Divination, Meditation, Scrying

Air divination is done by atmospheric conditions such as wind, weather, fog, rainbows, or clouds. There are various forms of divination by air depending on the area being focused on but in general it is referred to as aeromancy. It is basically a method of interpreting these conditions based on imagery or behaviors of them.

Air divination can be difficult because in all of the forms of it there is no clear 'yes or no' method, like in the earth divination techniques, but rather is an interpretation of patterns and events. This type of divination takes a lot of imagination, creativity and knowing the inner self in order to interpret accurately.

Austromancy

Divining by wind is known as Austromancy, which is interpreting the force and direction of the wind. Weather folklore and superstition says that the wind on New Year's Day indicates what type of year it will be. Southern wind means prosperous times are ahead, a wind from the north means bad weather for the year, an eastern wind forebodes famine and calamity and western winds indicate plentiful and fruitful harvests. Calm winds or very little wind at all means a prosperous and joyous year ahead.

Based on the above weather lore, the nursery rhyme previously mentioned may possibly be interpreted as such: "Mister East gave a feast" could actually mean famine because the wind ate up all the crops for himself, leaving none for the people. The phrase "Mister North laid the cloth" could be a way of saying that extra clothing or blankets were needed due to harsh weather coming and "Mister West did his best" is surely a sign of the plentiful and fruitful harvests. Finally, "Mister South burnt his mouth eating cold potato" could be an obscure reference to the idea that the crops are so bountiful it's possible to get hurt by the overabundance such as theft of crops, rotted foods (can't be eaten fast enough) or some other calamity.

If using this type of divination, use the correspondences mentioned earlier to determine what the winds are trying to say. Stand outside and ask or concentrate on a question. Once the visualization is complete ask that the winds give an answer. With eyes closed, feel which way the breezes are blowing. They may be small breezes or feisty gales, once the direction has been determined use the correspondences to determine what the message is.

Scrying the Western Winds

Try this ritual for scrying anytime there is a conflict in decisions, an uncertainty about the future, or for meditation. On a day that the winds are blowing in from the west, go outside to a place where they can be felt at their utmost intensity (while still being safe, don't try this under hurricane or tornado watch conditions). Stand to face the winds and hold arms straight out as if preparing to embrace it. Feel it blowing in hair, on skin, ruffling clothes, etc. and relax the mind so that it slips into a slightly meditative state. This allows the subconscious to come out and reveal its self. When a relaxed and meditative state has been reached, recite the following verse:

When the western winds blow,

My future I will know.

Let them blow with all their might

And let my future come into sight.

From west to east they travel so

From present to future I will know.

Let the winds blow steadily for awhile and move into a deeper meditative state. Don't think of anything, just focus on hearing and feeling the wind.

This works similar to that of candle meditation or fire gazing (both of which will be mentioned in Magick for the Fire Witch). The subconscious will be able to reveal information buried deep and help resolve a conflict or give some insight as to what may lay ahead. This is not going to give a clear and concise answer such as quitting a job, but rather it acts as guidance or to relax a person enough so that they can make decisions or see their options more clearly.

Ancestral Western Winds

If using the western winds for ancestral communication of guidance, follow the same instructions as above with the exception of keeping eyes closed this time, but still face the western wind. Remember to never call up anything that can't be controlled, and don't even focus on opening portals or calling forth any spirits. Simply concentrate on positive feelings such as peace and harmony. Relax the mind and body so that when messages are sent they can be aptly received.

Once a good visualization (of what needs to be answered) is being met and the body has relaxed into a slight meditative state, recite the following verse (it is best to memorize it so that the eyes can stay shut during this process):

Western winds of spirits past

Guide me where I am lost.

Recite it a few times as a chant or litany and then open the eyes quickly to view the area. Use all six senses (sight, touch, hearing, taste, smells and the 'sixth sense') to explore the surroundings. See the environment, the creatures in it, atmospheric conditions; hear the winds or sounds of life; open the mouth to taste the air and then close it and take a deep breath through the nose to smell the air; feel the winds blowing clothes and hair or caressing skin and, finally; let the subconscious and intuitive mind open up to receive any messages that the spirits may have.

Messages may come in the any of the senses mentioned, but usually sight, sound or the 'sixth sense' will receive the message. However, depending on what the question is, a taste or smell might be experienced as well.

Magick for the Air Witch
Section VI

Winged Friends

Birds and flying insects are wonderful way to represent air because they are the only creatures that truly fly. There are lizards, snakes, squirrels and fish that are called 'flying' but they truly do not fly, it's more like they fall or jump with style. Birds and insects can achieve something of which man has striven for since his very existence and we have yet to achieve it without equipment: they can fly. Even though we cannot fly, we can tap into the energies that the flying creatures harbor by imagining ourselves visualizing a specific creature and using its qualities in our magick. By visualizing the creature, and the attributes it brings magickally or metaphysically, we can empower magick or ritual work.

When working with our winged friends don't attempt to capture wild animals and never try to harm them. A domestic bird as a pet can be used as a familiar, but animals should never be forced or harmed. Their habitats also should not be damaged or destroyed. We can use animals in dream divination, by visualizing their qualities, or by items they have left behind (such as feathers) and without disrupting their environment. Not only can it be illegal in most places, but it goes against pagan policies of "harm ye none."

Birds

Birds were often used as totem animals, spirit animals, familiars and spirit guides. Look around the yard or park for local types of birds that can be called upon or look in bird books for a more exotic flair. When needing the personality of a specific bird, imagine it and bring those qualities to the magick being worked. Eagles might represent strength and nobility, or lovebirds for compassion and partnership.

Feathered or winged birds that do not fly, such as ostriches and emus, are both connected to air and earth because of they have feathers and wings, but yet they do not fly. Penguins are water and air because they are aquatic birds. Legendary creatures like the Phoenix are of fire and air because the Phoenix, at the end of its life cycle, dies in fire or a Dragon because they are believed to fly (air) and breathe fire. In the mundane world, any tropical bird can be of both fire and air since they live in hotter climates. The feathers of birds are also very useful in magick. They can be used for fanning smudge smoke, in divination, as quills, or to represent air on an altar.

Try researching the birds in the area and spend some time bird-watching. A good pair of binoculars works great for spotting them, and even in town common birds such as robins, sparrows, doves or pigeons can often be seen. The flight patterns of birds can also be observed in divination or even weather patterns. Think of when winter is approaching and how the flights of birds are witnessed in the skies. Geese make a V-shape and other birds are just a massive flock. They know when to fly south for the winter, and this site in the sky is not only a minor form of divination but also a scientific fact. When the birds fly south, winter is on its way; when they fly north, warmer weather is approaching.

Insects

Insects can be used in the same manner but most often these smaller winged creatures are used for divination. In divination, they are used by seeing that particular insect repeatedly. I never consider something as 'a sign' until it has occurred three times, and then I will decide to look up the meaning. In writing my first book I was taking my time at editing and getting it sent off to potential publishers. I kept seeing bees near my, when normally I would never see any, and I since bees indicate creativity

I figured it meant I needed to work on my book. And, just a few months ago at work I kept finding ladybugs, including one in my office! Since they denote good luck I am hoping they meant that we will have good luck with the new director we have.

There are literally hundreds of thousands of insects and they all have various mythologies or magickal attributes either as a species or a genus. Anyone having a favorite insect should research the superstitions, mythologies and folklore attributed to it because it can be a powerful tool or animal effigy to use in practices. Insects are also used commonly in talismans and amulets and often people have a favorite insect.

The Scarab Beetle has long been associated with Egyptian lore and was often carved of Lapis Lazuli and gold, which were believed to be materials of the Gods.. Bees are bearers of goodwill and messages from the Gods and always a sign of prosperity, creativity or mean to keep as busy as a bee. Ladybugs, or Ladybirds, have always thought to be of good luck both magickally and are said to be good for gardens and it believed that ladybugs do not fly if the weather is below 55 degrees Fahrenheit so they can be a good weather indicator. Crickets can also be used to find the temperature of the air by counting the number of chirps in 14 seconds and then adding the number forty. Butterflies often are used to represent change in basic divination because of the metamorphic process that they go through (caterpillar, to chrysalis, to butterfly).

Bats

While neither bird nor insect, bats can be included in air because they are a flying mammal. Often seen as a thing of great superstition and in depictions of Halloween scenes, especially haunted houses, they are often thought to be vampires or witches transformed because of their appearance, fangs and nocturnal habits. While there really is a Vampire Bat that does feast on the blood of animals it does not drain them or turn anything into vampires, and they typically seek out farm animals not people.

Bats can be used in air magick and need to be recognized for more than their sinister and dark reputation. Because of their nocturnal habits they are great for anyone practicing nocturnal or moon magick. Bats have various reputations all over, such as the belief in the Isle of Man in which a bat landing on a person's head is considered good luck. Also, carrying a bat's bone will also bring good luck and in China and Poland bats are seen as symbols of long life and happiness. In Australia, to kill a bat will shorten the life of the person doing the killing.

Spells and Rituals

The feathers on birds are as important as the bird itself: on an altar feathers represent air, used as a quill for writing spells or grimoires, fan incense or smudge smoke in order to waft it around sacred space, decorate and empower Witch Ladders and divination can be performed by the colors of feathers found on the ground. Feathers are a good tool for air because birds live most of their lives in the air either living in nests high up in the treetops or by a mode of transportation. They can be purchased at metaphysical shops, in craft stores or found in nature. Even feathers from non-flying birds, such as ostriches, can still be used since there is no discrimination between non-flying or flying birds when it comes to the element of air.

Feathers in Witch Ladders

In Witch Ladders feathers would be tied into the knots to enhance the magick with the use of color correspondence. Similar to using a colored candle to represent intent, the color of the feather would represent the intent of the ladder.

White—purification, spirituality, hope, peace, protection and for blessings of the moon.

Red—physical vitality, courage and good fortune.

Blue—mental abilities, peace, protection and psychic awareness.

Yellow—cheerfulness, mental alertness, prosperity, and blessings of the sun.

Green—money, prosperity, growth, health, luck and fertility.

Green and Red combined—affects finances for the good

Orange—attraction, energy and success.

Pink—attracts love

Purple—psychic awareness and the divine.

Gray—peace and neutrality

Brown—stability, respect, home, grounding.

Brown and White—a protection that goes unnoticed by anyone trying to harm the person.

Brown and Red—brings healing to animals

Brown and Black—balance between physical and spiritual world.

Black—mystical wisdom or mystical insight.

Black and White—union and protection but if mixed with blue it signifies change.

Black and Gray—hope, balance and harmony.

Black and Purple—deep spirituality

LadyBug Wish

Ladybugs are common in folklore and are seen in the rather disturbing Mother goose nursery rhyme:

> *Ladybird, Ladybird fly away home,*
>
> *Your house is on fire and your children are gone*
>
> *All except one, and that's little Anne,*
>
> *For she has crept under the warming pan.*

Thought to be symbols of good luck, a lady bug can be used to make a wish if it lands on a person and then flies away of its own free will. Usually the rhyme was recited, a wish made and then the ladybug would fly away. The following spell can be done anytime a ladybug lands on someone, I have written a kinder verse to recite:

> *"Ladybug, ladybug, fly away, go!*
>
> *Fly off to green pastures or a flowered meadow.*

Observe the ladybug, if it flies away within a few seconds after reciting the rhyme then the wish will be granted. If it flies away before the rhyme is recited or does not leave for quite some time, then the wish will not be granted at this time.

Bird Charm

This spell benefits both the practitioner and the birds and is a great one to perform when needing prosperity, luck or peace and is one that can be done during a person's daily chores. Fill a bird feeder with food, sprinkling a little on the ground for the birds, and fill the bird bath with water. If without a feeder or bird bath just toss some seed on the ground and fill a shallow pan or bowl with water and set it in the ground. As these chores are being completed recite the following verse:

Birds of a feather flock together

through all types of weather.

Birds of a feather sweetly sing

And carry my desires on fluttery wings.

Recite this as each task is completed and know that as the birds come and partake of the offerings they will take desires of peace, luck and prosperity with them and bring it back to the house or practitioner on their next visits.

Divination Meditation, Scrying

Feather auspices are used when finding feathers on the ground. It is said that the color of the feather found can determine a person's immediate future. A person does not necessarily have to set out with a purpose for divination but rather just go on a walk and if one happens to find a feather, pick it up and look up the meaning later. In my home, we keep all found feathers in our magickal supplies so that we can use them later for different purposes.

Feather Color Meaning in Divination

Brown—good health awaits

Red— love is blossoming

Orange—a promise of delight.

Yellow—be wary of false friends

Green—adventure awaits

Blue—good fortune is immanent

Purple—an exciting trip is coming up

Black—possible death, illness or bad news is coming

Gray—peace is near

Brown and White—joy is coming soon

Black and White—trouble has been averted

Black and Green—fame and fortune in the future

Black, Blue and White—a new love is near

Gray and White—a wish will come true

Oomancy

This is a type of divination used with egg yolks; it is similar to tasseomancy (tea leaves) in that patterns are looked for an interpreted in the yolks. It has been widely used in the Celtic British Isles, Lithuania, Eastern Europe, Morocco, Mexico and India.

To try this form of divination hold an egg in one hand while meditating on a question. Then sweep the egg (in the shell) all around the body and aura (this is a Puerto Rican method of both healing and divining) and let the egg take in the person's essence, aura, concerns, feelings and everything else that makes up the self. Acknowledge the egg as an oracle. Toss the egg onto the ground or break it by hand into a clear glass or bowl. Study the shape from as many angles as possible (a clear bowl of glass is recommended as it can be held up the egg looked at from underneath). Look for patterns or symbols that can be interpreted based on instincts, feelings and general symbol divination.

A simpler method of divining is to drop three drops of egg white into a bowl of cold water and divine a future based on the shape the drops make (this basic symbol divination, similar to ceromancy. There are more in-depth and various divination methods with eggs at the site "Matrifocus: Egg Divination." See the bibliography at the back of this book for the website address.

Roman Augury (Orinthomancy—flight patterns or calls of birds)

For an internet venue I wrote an article about the Roman Augurs and their purpose in Roman mythology and history. Here is a brief excerpt of the article I wrote and published on Helium.com:

"In ancient Rome an augur was a religious official who used birds for divination (Ornithomancy) and to interpret omens to guide public policy. The art of the augur was called augurium (augury) or auspicium. Plutarch states that the augur was originally called an auspex and auspice is the act of looking at birds..."An augur worked with the leading officials and his main job was to interpret the divine will by reading signs in nature and by using animal entrails to predict the future. An augur was of great importance in Ancient Rome due to the fact that their sole purpose was to determine whether the Gods/Goddess or divine will approved of the military and political acts that the King was attempting to instill. An augur also used his abilities to seek out and mark sacred areas, known as 'templas'."

The entire article can be read at Helium, my penname there is 'D. Anderson' (see Bibliography for a web address). Suffice it to say that bird divination, augury, is an age-old practice and while practitioners today are not going to use bird entrails other methods can be implored for bird divination such as flight patterns or even the following method.

Bird Seed Divination

One form of bird augury is to toss bird seed on the ground, wait awhile until the birds have had plenty to eat, and then decipher the patterns that emerge with the remaining bird seed. This works best on snow-laden grounds because the seeds will be more discernible than amongst the dirt and all its debris.

To do this form of divination some quiet time and a quiet and secluded space is needed as is some wild bird seed. On the ground a symbol inside of a circle that represents the need, either an elemental symbol (the triangle symbols mentioned earlier) that fits the intent or a more specific symbol such as a heart for love and dollar sign for money. As the need is visualized, toss the birdseed to the ground inside of the circle. As the seeds are scattered recite:

Winged creatures with the gift of flight;

answer my questions, bring them to light.

Leave the area and let the birds eat the seeds, but check back often because there needs to be some seeds remaining. View the patterns of the remaining seeds and let instincts guide the interpretations. If a 'yes or no' question was asked and the remaining seed sort of looks like a 'y' or a plus sign then take it as a positive sign, if it looks like an 'n' or negative sign it may mean no or if the seed looks like a specific shape, such as a heart, interpret it according to basic symbolic meanings.

Magick for the Air Witch
Section VII

Weather Magick

I've mentioned weather spells a little bit in other areas and after much hesitation, finally decided to include information about it in here, mainly because I needed another section for the Air Witch but also because weather magick, even precipitation, falls under air as an element because it is an atmospheric condition. However, weather magick is tricky because it is fooling with Mother Nature, a very powerful force. Caution should always be heeded and rather than attempts to control the weather (of which no spells in here will be mentioned) a person should learn to use the weather that is already present.

Controlling the weather can have adverse affects, such as a person wanting a drought to end might call on rain and either cause it to flood or cause a drought to occur elsewhere. In an attempt to keep the "harm none" creed always at hand, asking the weather to do something it isn't set to do can cause harm elsewhere. Often spells may cause harm that we are unaware of. Such asking that a certain person pays a debt they owe; it might take money from them that should have gone to pay a bill and now they face eviction or lights being turned off. The same goes for weather magick, favorable conditions for us might cause unfavorable conditions later.

For example, it started to sprinkle while we were at a festival. I did the usual "rain, rain, go away, come again another day" nursery rhyme but added more intent into it and chanted it (mentally) like a litany. I imagined the clouds holding onto the water and not releasing it while we were at the festival. On the way home a few hours later I realized it was still not raining. I did a little chant to release the rains. To this day I don't know if I actually performed weather magick or if it was a coincidence, but seeing as how after I 'released' the rains we had a torrential downpour it is not something I am likely to try again. I felt that by holding back the rain it caused it to build up so much that if flooded out of the clouds rather than just maintain a steady sprinkle all day.

When working with weather magick, it is mainly in the form of sympathetic magick, which is an act that mimics what the magickal intent. So, if a person wanted it to rain they would sprinkle water outside. If they wanted it to be windy they might go outside and blow air in any direction. However, as I said earlier, there are a number of spells or divinations that only use what is already there rather than attempts to control the wind. There are a number of weather-controlling spells to be found on the internet, but I am only including two in here; both of which are very specific in their intent. As always, visualization is the key so if attempting to control the weather, be very keen on visualization with nothing left to interpretation.

Often we don't realize the power in storms or the cleansing qualities of the rains. However, think of how fresh the world looks after a good rain and in paranormal terms, thunder and lightning storms are thought to induce activity. Next time it rains, place objects outside to be cleansed or use the power and energies of a storm to perform spells and rituals. Check out the section on lightning in Magick for the Fire Witch for some great spells involving lightning.

Spells and Rituals

Weather magick takes the form of all types of atmospheric conditions such as rainbows, wind, all forms of precipitations, and temperature. Lightning is also a weather condition that is said to be controlled by either Zeus (Greek mythology) or Thor (Norse mythology). In Magick for the Fire Witch there are some great (and safe!) ways to use lightning in magick. Below are a few weather spells that either use the weather or are very intent specific for creating certain weather conditions.

Rainbows

Often a childhood fascination, rainbows are a rare treat for anyone to see. I remember as a child we took off on our bikes hoping to catch the end of the rainbow so we could find a pot o'gold, or at least a leprechaun or fairy. We never did reach the end and, in fact, lost sight of if completely before we got to where we thought the end should be. A thing of superstitious lore, rainbows are associated with good luck, fortune, and the fairy realms. In the Christian Bible the rainbow is known as "God's Promise," which refers to the promise that he would never again flood the entire earth. In Greek mythology, Iris is the Goddess of the Rainbow and often acted as a messenger to the gods. She is usually depicted as having wings or a gown of rainbow colors. Despite being a minor deity, she can be used for all rainbow magick.

Next time a rainbow is visible in the sky think of intent, like a wish, and recite the following verse:

Goddess Iris arched in the sky,

Look down upon me with a kind eye.

In colors of red, orange and bright yellow,

Carry my wish along your arced rainbow.

In colors of green, violet and blue,

As I cast this wish, make it come true.

Thanks Iris and be confident that the message will be delivered to the proper gods or goddesses along the rainbow and in Goddess Iris' capable hands.

Thunder and Anger

Thor of Norse mythology controls both the thunder and anger, and usually it is joked that when a thunderstorm has come up it is because he is angry. The ancient people really did believe that thunder, lightning and other extreme weather conditions were the results of angry gods. Today, we know that they are controlled by atmospheric and geological conditions but that doesn't mean that the gods aren't still out there, or that we can't use these conditions in magick.

To get rid of pent-up anger, frustration or negativity, the next time a storm is brewing use this spell to cast aside all negative feelings. Remain inside where the storm can be heard and its energies felt, but do not attempt to go outside and be directly in its path. Feel the rumble of thunder and hear the snap of lightning and visualizing everything that is going wrong in life, safely expel those feelings by reciting the following verse:

> *Thunder and lighting, lightning and thunder*
> *Take now the feelings that tear me asunder.*
> *Lighting and thunder, thunder and lighting,*
> *I cast them out where they no longer are frightening.*
> *As the winds cease, and the thunder passes,*
> *As the lighting stops and the rain turns to caresses,*
> *My anger is gone; it is spent just like the storm,*
> *To be released without causing anyone harm.*

Recite the poem as many times as needed to expel all of the negative feelings. It might be helpful to recite the words out loud, growing in cadence with each verse or each recitation of the poem. Visualize that the negative feelings are leaving and feel the body and mind grow more relaxed and calm.

To Call the Rain

If needing a little bit of rain to help gardens grow or replenish natural bodies of water, try this simple spell. It is an old superstition that burning ferns will cause it to rain, but be intent-specific and careful about calling on too much rain. Also, never attempt a rain spell just to fill up an outside pool, for ruining plan's a person has, or with the intent of causing harm to anyone.

On a day where the sunny weather has been pretty consistent and consecutive and vegetation is starting to dry up, gather some ferns and place them in a fire-proof container. Light them on fire and as they burn, recite the following:

> *To soothe this parched ground,*

And nourish the flowers all around,

Bring us rain, but only what we need,

and keep all safe with this deed.

Once the ferns have completely burned to ash, scatter them on the ground. The rains will come to wash them away.

Blowing Up A Breeze

From the "Good Spell Book," which is a wonderful book by Gillian Kemp that is all about Gypsy magick and lore, there is a little quip in there about how to get the breezes to blow and help dry the clothes on an outdoor line. I try to always hang my clothes on a line but often there isn't a good breeze to aid in the drying process. Having just read this quip in her book I decided to try it, imagine my surprise when it worked! No sooner had I completed it then the winds picked up to the point where the clothes were visibly moving on the line.

This spell is wonderfully simple and requires no tools; it could be classified as a weather spell since it involves changing the weather slightly. Kemp did not add a chant or saying in her mention of the spell but I have created one that can be said just prior to doing the spell.

Do this only on those days when it feels as if there is no breeze stirring or not enough to adequately dry the clothes. Stand outside for a few moments to determine which way the breezes or air currents are moving. Even if it feels as if there is no wind there will be slight air currents that can be felt on they body or hair, or watch the trees and clouds to determine which way the air flows. Once the direction is determined, stand away from it (back facing the air current or breeze) and facing the clothes line. Take a deep breath and blow in the direction that the winds or air current flows. Try to get all of the clotheslines with the one breathe while imagining the breezes picking up and blowing the clothes dry. As an added step, just before blowing on the clothes recite:

With a huff and a puff and a breath of air

I need the winds to blow gentle and fair.

Remember intent and keep in mind that the winds need only to blow enough to help dry the clothes. Avoid imagining strong, gale force winds.

No one wants to accidentally call up a hurricane! This is a perfect example of sympathetic magick: blowing on the line is an act of showing the divine what we need. The intent is not to get the clothes dry with personal air-power but to simulate what nature needs to do.

Divination, Meditation, Scrying

There is a method of divining what type of weather is around that is one of my favorites, even though it is usually meant as a joke. Often sold in tourist shops as a novelty item, there is a cord attached to a piece of wood with a card that says if the cord is wet, it's raining; if the cord is moving, it's raining; and if the cord is white, it's snowing. Of course, if already looking out to see the cord, chances are the weather condition will also be observed. Before the news and Weather Channel, people had verses and sayings that helped them to predict what type of weather was coming.

Books on omens and superstitions, as well as the internet, are great places for finding this little folkloric weather quips. However, today they are not often used and weather divination my pagan practitioners doesn't involve predicting the weather but involves using the weather to predict more personal outcomes. Similar to bird divination, weather divination is used by observing patterns in the weather or letting the weather decide what the outcome is.

Cloud Scrying

Known as 'chaomancy,' looking for visions in the sky or clouds is something many of us probably spent at least one afternoon doing as a child. This can still be done as a form of scrying or divining by interpretation the images seen. Sit outside in an area where the clouds can easily be seen and, without looking at them; meditate on a question for a few minutes. Once the question has been clearly formulated or defined look up at the skies and interpret results based on the first cloud or image seen; it may take a few minutes to 'see' an image in the cloud but once an image has come to mind, say of a butterfly or a heart, then divine what that means personally and how it applies to the question.

When scrying in the clouds ponder a moment on the Nephelae who are the nymphs of the clouds and daughters to the Titan Oceanus. They drew their rain waters from their father in order to send the rains down where needed. Ask for their assistance in cloud scrying and thank them when done.

Blowing in the Wind

On a slightly windy day, head outside for this simple 'yes or now' divination involving the winds and leaves. Find two leaves on the ground and write Y on one leaf and N on the other one. Hold hands out, palms up, with a leaf in each hand and concentrate on a question. Watch the leaves; whichever leaf blows away first is the answer. If both leaves blow away it can be interpreted as "maybe" or perhaps that the answer cannot be revealed at this time.

Rain Gauge

When rain is impending, label two containers of equal size with a 'yes' on one and 'no' on the other. Or, try writing two possible outcomes such as "get a job" or "stay at home." Set both containers outside where they will be able to catch the rain but not blow away in strong winds. Meditate over the containers for a few minutes, visualizing a question that needs to be answered. Then head inside before the rains come. Once the rain has ceased, check the containers. The one that is more filled with rain water is the answer. Use a ruler to measure if they look close; if they have equal amounts this means the answer cannot be revealed at this time.

Magick for the Air Witch
Section VIII

Mythology and Folklore

Mythology about the air is as abundant as the other elements and has made its way into folklore, superstition, mythology and old adages like "an ill-wind blows." However, it is harder to define mythology about air because it is more about the weather conditions of it or the creatures living in it rather than the air itself.

Air Creation
The creation of air is one of no creation at all. Of all the elements in this book, air is the one that seems to always have been around and was not created by anything or anyone. Fire was given to or stolen by the humans, earth was created by gods, water came from the skies or melted from glaciers, but air was always around and not created. It is one of the elements often taken for granted and yet we can only live a few moments without it.

Elementals
Sylphs
A sylph is best described as a fairy, although that is not an accurate

description. Fairies are little beings that have sentient thought, feelings, emotions, and free-will. A sylph is defined as any female, soulless being that inhabits the air or is made of the air; they are similar to undines because they are of the air (undines are of the water) and not just a creature living in that element. Seeing dust motes swirl in a sunbeam or heat waves shimmer on hot pavement is about as close as a person can get to understanding what a sylph is or looks like.

While represented artistically as fairy-like in appearance, real sylphs probably do not have such humanistic features. Seeing air is not an easy task as it is not tangible like water, fire or earth. We see air only in the things that are in the air or moved by the air, therefore we see sylphs in the same manner and not like we see a bird or fairy that uses the air as a mode of transportation.

Controlling the Air

Both of the following characters were in control of the air in some fashion. Icarus learned to fly like the birds, something man has been trying to re-create ever since, but with ill-fated results. Aeolus, in one version of this man's life, was actually in control of the winds and used them to help Odysseus cross the seas. Being able to control it to our advantage or fly in it with the least-restrictive machine possible have long been goals of man. We can get close in that we have flying machines and we can control the winds with fans and windmills, but we have yet to achieve what Icarus and Aeolus did centuries ago.

Icarus

Icarus has been immortalized as the man who made wings and flew to close the sun, which melted his wings and plunged him to his death. Icarus was the son of Daedalus, an inventor, and Naucrate, a slave. He and his father were imprisoned in a labyrinth by King Minos of Crete because Daedulus had aided Theseus in killing the Minotaur, escaping the labyrinth and running off with King Minos' daughter, Ariadne.

Knowing that King Minos controlled all routes through land and sea Daedalus set their escape route through the air. He fashioned wings of wax and feathers, which he fastened to reeds of various lengths to mimic the curvature of bird wings. Daedalus warned his son not to fly too close to the sun or the waxes would melt, and not too close to the water or it would dampen the feathers and renders them incapable of flight. After their arrival in their homeland, Icarus was so taken with flight that he continued to fly after the day of their escape. He flew higher and higher until he flew too close to the sun and the wax melted in the hot blaze. He fell into the sea and was drowned. His father, upon seeing the feathers floating in the sea, surmised what had happened and named the island (nearest to where Icarus fell) as Icaria and the sea became the Icarian Sea.

This story is a good reminder that while we do not want to live outside of our means, have extreme expectations or reside in fantasy worlds (fly too high to the sun) we also don't want to live without ever daydreaming, of having too low of expectations or never set goals (fly to low to the water). When it is felt that either of these two things are occurring, try meditating and reciting this verse for "flying to high":

Icarus who travelled not by sea or land

Help me to fly lower and stick to the tasks at hand.

Or, if having lost sight of goals and dreams and focusing too much on daily "to do lists" meditate and recite this verse:

Icarus who travelled not by land or sea

Help me to fly higher and unleash my creativity
(or "unleash the inner me")

These verses can be combined with any air ritual or spell and used as empowering words prior to or during the spell. They can also be recited during meditative sessions.

Aeolus

In Greek mythology Aelous is known as "the keeper of the winds" and sometimes referred to as just the king of the winds or a god of the winds (in post-Homeric texts). There are three different Aeolus' mentioned throughout Greek texts and it is confusing as to whether they are different versions of the same person or three different men of the same name. The best known Aeolus (or most accepted theory) is as the one who aided Odysseus in his journeys. He is reputed to have given Odysseus a tightly closed bag filled with winds in order that Odysseus may control the winds of his sails and get back home.

Opening the bag slightly would give a smaller wind and opening it wide would give a great wind. This myth falls into similarity to the oceanic legend of Sirens aiding sailors by gifting them with knotted rope that, when untied, released various amounts of winds to fill their sales. Some say that he did not control the winds, personified by the Anemoi and could only release them at the commands of gods greater then him. Whereas, others say that he controlled the winds and could unleash them at will.

Gods and Goddesses

There really aren't any gods of just the air itself but there are gods of atmospheric conditions such as clouds, winds or weather and there are gods of the skies. Check out the website http://www.theoi.com/greek-mythology/sky-gods.html for a comprehensive list of sky gods relating to the winds, the dawn, the clouds, and other aspects of air or skies. There are gods from everything to the different phases of the sun (dawn and dusk) to space, stars and planets to gods of the winds and their various strengths. For example, Aura (a Titan) and is the Goddess of Breezes and her children, the Aurae, are nymphs of the breezes. There is also Iris who is a Goddess of the Rainbow and the Nephelae, daughters of Oceanus and nymphs of the clouds.

Aether (Aither)

Aether does not just mean "of the void" or "ether" but rather, it is a god who is believed to be son of Erebus (personification of primordial darkness) and Nyx (Goddess of the night sky) of Greek Mythology. Ather has become the personification of the upper skies, space and the heavens. He was a primeval god personified in the shining light of the blue skies at which he (the blue sky) was cloaked by the dark of the night sky, or his mother Nyx. In the morning, Aether's sister Hemera (Goddess of the Day) lifted the dark cloak to reveal him, or the blue sky. He was often perceived as being the substance of light or the layer of bright mist that hovers between the two worlds of heaven and earth.

The Anemi or Anemoi

The Anemoi, of Greek mythologies, are the four gods of the directional winds and also heralds of the four seasons. These gods start giving us an idea of correspondences to the directional winds, seasons, and elements. Despite all of them being considered deities of winds or air and having no correlation to the basic elements, we are starting to see how correspondences come about, that is, how certain aspects get connected with other aspects.

Boreas is the god of the northern winds and the lord of the winter season. Think of Boreas as "Old Man Winter" or even as Jack Frost as he brings the winter on with his cold breath. He lives in a cave in the northern mountains of Thrace, which is a region near the Balkan Mountains and Aegean Sea that encompasses all of Turkey, the northeastern part of Greece and southeastern Bulgaria. When he is ready, he brings the cold winds of winter.

Zephyros, or Zephryus, is the god of the western winds and spring. He is the husband of Chloris, Goddess of the flowers, and the father of the God of Fruits, Carpus. The union between Zephyros and Chloris might lend to the old adage "April showers bring May flowers."

Euros, the god of the east and the season of autumn and Notos, of the southern winds and the season of summer, are believed to be the Typhoeus, who is a monster locked away inside of Tartarus. Aelous could release them at the commands of the gods to wreak havoc (or help) sailors.

Nephelae

These are the nymphs of clouds and rain. They would descend to Oceanus to collect his waters and, carrying them in pitchers, they ascended back to the clouds to fill them with water which then fell as rain to nourish the earth and feed the bodies of their brothers, the Potami or river-gods and their sisters, the Naiades or goddesses of the springs.. They are often depicted as beautiful, young women with long-flowing and billowing robes (resembling clouds). In the Rider-Waite deck of Tarot cards there is a card known as "The Star" in which a woman is seen pouring pitchers of water to both the river and the earth and though she is often nude, she may be a depiction of the Nephelae.

Atlas

Probably one of the more common of the Greek myths, Atlas is known as the man who was doomed to hold up the sky. In some depictions he is seen as holding the entire world on his shoulders and because of this, world maps were named 'atlases.' In some versions he was required to spin the earth on its axis. In Homer's epic poem Odyssey it was written that he was released from his labors and was appointed as the keeper of the pillars in Heaven that Hercules had erected at the edges of the earth.

Shu

In Egyptian mythology, we see the Shu, the God of the air, who is known as "the holder of the sky" because he stands on the body of his son, Geb the God of the Earth and hold up his daughter, Nut, the Goddess of the Sky. He is the God of air, wind, the atmospheres, sunlight and protection and his parents are the creator gods Iris and Osiris. Today, he seems to be more of a personification of the air rather than an actual god but there are depictions of him with an Ostrich feather headdress, as a lion in part or whole, and with either a sun disc on his head or seen holding a scepter and wearing an Ankh (symbol of life and death).

Similar to Greek myth, it was believed that there were four pillars in each of the cardinal points and that these helped Shu to hold up the sky, thus they were known as the "Pillars of Shu." It seems to be a common concept in ancient civilizations that pillars and gods were needed to hold up the sky because it is a solid thing that, if it were to fall, would leave no space between it and the earth for all of the living things. Think back to preschool and elementary school drawings where we drew the sky as being blue up on top, the green grass on the bottom and a white void in the middle of the picture. This was also how the ancients saw the world, the sky was not all around us as we know now, but rather a color-changing 'roof' over the earth and it could fall, crushing everything under it. This belief, as my husband calls it, is "The Chicken Little Syndrome." Chicken Little believed the sky was falling when an acorn dropped from a tree and landed on his head.

Shu was also considered the god of the winds and would be invoked by sailors asking for favorable winds on their journeys. He personified the cold northern winds and was the breath of life into all living things; it is said his bones were made of clouds. He also could lift the spirits of the dead up to the heavens, presumably because he was the pathway or ladder between earth and sky.

Magick for the Fire Witch
Section I

The Fire Element

There probably isn't a cultural or belief system out there that does not have a fire-creation story; fire has a long history of use and its origins are debated in scholarly arenas. It may have been used by Homo erectus as long as 1.5 million years ago, but this would be the use of fire as it occurred naturally and without creation or control. The act of creating fire from flint or friction may not have occurred until Neolithic man circa 5000-8000 BCE. Neolithic man was the first to use polished stone tools and weapons and may have discovered the use of flint in making fire. Perhaps, the creation and control of fire came much later. Certainly, when it did happen it must have seemed like magick and a gift from the gods. In fact, many of the fire-creation mythologies are based on a mortal man either stealing fire from the gods, or a sympathetic god giving fire to mortals.

Fire-people are passionate, have a lot of energy, have high emotions, and can flair up quickly when angered. Having an affinity to fire maybe a person is like the solitary candle that burns all by itself without much flair or heat, but is singularly beautiful and useful in its own right. Maybe they are like a community bonfire built for fun and frivolity, always there to have a good time and be sociable. Or, they are like the campfire that is necessary for survival providing warmth, security and stability to those around it. Maybe a person is like the raging wildfire that flairs quickly with an unmatched ferocity destroying everything in its path But, when it is extinguished it provides some renewal of growth, even though the price to pay was very high.

We are always trying to control fire and most of us like to create fire from scratch just to see if we can. We control fire with lighters in our pockets, matches in the kitchen, and our fireplaces. Fire-breathers and jugglers control it with their talents and skills and amaze the rest of us who are not daring enough to try. It's important for warmth and cooking and without it we'd live, but not as comfortably. Fire can also be used for ambience in a romantic or relaxing way and be a place of communal gathering.

A few years ago we had some neighbors that knew if they saw the fire glowing in our fire pit it was an open invitation to come over, relax, laugh, and eat some roasted marshmallows (someday I am going to incorporate these delectable and sinful treats into a spell).

Regardless of how it is used, fire has a long history in the world and with that comes a long history of superstition, folklore and magick.

Magick for the Fire Witch
Section II

Correspondences

Traditional

Fire is a masculine element with a directional quadrant of south on an altar and it is represented by a candle. The colors of fire are bright reds, oranges or yellows, but if using a candle to represent fire then any color can be used because the lit candle is the correspondence, and not the color of the wax. However, a colored candle can be used to fit the intent of the altar such as pastels for spring or reds and greens for Yule. Fire is the element of will, passion and change, and governs over candle magick and banishing, but in a sense it can rule over all magick since that is a process of changes and fire represents change. It is a primal element of sexuality or passion and is the spark of the divinity which shines within us both of the physical and spiritual worlds.

Alchemy and Ancient Medical Practices

In Alchemy, fire is represented by an upward pointed triangle and its chemical element is sulfur. In Greek Medicines it was associated with the season of summer, masculinity and it is on the eastern point of the compass.

Zodiac and Astrological

Anyone of a fire element for their zodiac sign are either Aries, Leo or Sagittarius and are said to have positive personality traits of good leadership qualities, are extroverted, rebellious, passionate, and enthusiastic. They also harbor negative traits of being moody, hot-tempered, snappy, uncontrollable and angry.

Greek and Roman Mythology

Fire is represented by an apple-bough in Greek mythology because the fire that Prometheus stole from Gods and gave to the mortals was carried on an apple-bough torch. Most of the Gods associated with fire in Greek or Roman mythology is seen in gods of the sun, such as Apollo (seen in both Greek and Roman myths) who pulled the sun across the sky in his chariot. The sun is often personified by Helios, of Greek myth who is debated to either be a Titan or just a son of Titan. The sun is always associated with the male gender and, since it was believed that fire came from the sun, the element of fire is considered male as well.

Hinduism

Fire is linked to the God Surya who is one of the chief solar deities in Hinduism and is said to have hair and arms made of gold. Much like his Greek counterpart, Apollo, he drives a chariot through the heavens that is led by either seven horses or one horse with seven heads. The seven horses (or heads) represent the seven colors in the rainbow and their corresponding seven chakra points (points of energy on the body). Surya has become the Hindu personification of the sun. In the Hindu system of astrology, the Jyotish, fire is also represented by the planet Mars, or God Mangala. He carries a trident, lotus flower and a spear. Fire also corresponds to the southwesterly direction, lightning and in the tattva is symbolized by a red, upwards-pointing triangle.

Ceremonial Magick

In high ceremonial magick the elemental tool for fire is the wand or dagger and the elementals are salamanders. Salamander elementals are not named for the amphibian creatures we think of today, but rather it is the other-way around. Similar to a belief about Undines (water elementals) the salamanders do not live in the fire but are made of the fire. Gaze at a fire and in the licks of the flame the salamanders can be seen. Fire is also dominated by the archangel Michael, angel Aral, ruler Seraph, and king Djin (genie). It is an active element represented by the symbol for Leo and on the lower right point of the pentagram in the Supreme Invoking Ritual of the Pentagram.

Wicca

In Wiccan practices, fire is always represented in the south and the season of summer. Its color is red and its elemental tool is the wand. It is symbolic of the sun, lightning, fire, volcanoes, lava and light and while it's elemental creature is a salamander it can also be represented by the Phoenix, a drake (non-flying) or dragons (flying). On an altar or in ritual it is usually represented by a candle, but in larger group rituals it may be represented by a fireplace or outdoor fire.

Other Symbolism

Aztec cultures represented fire with the flint, which is a stone tool used to make the spark that starts fire. The most spectacular and important ritual in the Aztec culture and belief system was the 'New Fire Ceremony' that was held once every 52 years. All the citizens would quench their hearth-fires, gather together on top of Mt. Huixachtlan and proceed to burn all household utensils. They would also use torches to receive new fire from the bonfire and take it back to their home to re-light their hearth-fires. This, presumably, was to ensure good luck and health to be bestowed upon the citizens. This communal bonfire ritual is similar to Celtic traditions in which all hearth-fires were extinguished and re-lit from a communal fire .

In Celtic practices we also see the custom of building two fires on top of a hill and the people or their livestock would pass between the fires as a way to cleanse themselves or ensure prosperity and good health for the coming year. Celtics, or other neo-pagan sects, today may follow a similar tradition with camp fires. A group may go camping on the eve of Beltaine (May 1st) or on Samhain (Oct 31st) and sometime before midnight a central campfire will be built and all individual camp fires extinguished. They then will gather at the communal fire for a ritual and each person or head of a family will light a torch and carry it back to their personal campfire to relight it.

In East Asia fire is symbolized by the Vermillion Bird which is a mythical spirit creature similar to the Phoenix of Greek and Egyptian lore and has its own correspondence in the Wu Xing system of Chinese elements.

In Christian mythology it is symbolized by a lion, which is Leo on the Zodiac calendar and the same symbol used in Ceremonial Magick. This is, perhaps, because the men who created the Golden Dawn order (who were originally Free Masons) brought their Christian beliefs over into the neo-pagan beliefs. It seems to be a continuous cycle: pagan beliefs were incorporated into Christian beliefs centuries ago, which were then put back into pagan beliefs when Christians left the faith and created new pagan beliefs.

Magick for the Fire Witch
Section III

Tools of Fire

Athame

It is said that every pagan practitioner should have a wand and an athame if they have no other tools. In Wiccan-based paths the athame is a double-edged, silver blade with a black handle and of the air element. It is of the air because an athame is a ceremonial and symbolic knife and never used for cutting or carving; traditionally a bolline is a working knife, meaning that it is used for cutting or carving.

For me, athames are of the fire element because regardless of the purpose, all metal-bladed tools are forged in fire. I also have the title sequence from the "Xena: Warrior Princess" television show stuck in my head in which the narrator says "forged in the heat of battle" and Xena is seen brandishing a weapon at the same time. This scene has metal weapons or tools firmly etched in my mind as being "forged in fire." Ancient Druids and the Scythians also placed bladed tools or weapons in with the fire element. Daggers and swords were also considered thunderbolts (another word for lightning) of the Gods, and I consider lightning to be of fire due to its energy, heat and ability to cause fire.

Often, practitioners of other paths or culturally-influenced religions will use an athame made out of other materials, such as wood. They can be decorated with sigils or symbols and should be consecrated to and used only by the practitioner. Athames are used for storing energy (a fire quality) for later use, casting circles around a sacred space, symbolically cutting doors in a circle so participants can leave the sacred space, consecrating other tools, and when placed in a chalice it represents the male aspect in a male-to-female bond. They can also be used for less common occurrences such as banishing unwanted enemies, for evocation and invocations, and can be used in place of a wand.

Athames of metal can be made by someone with the proper skills, but it is best to purchase one from a metaphysical store or us an ordinary household knife as long as they have been consecrated and imbued with the practitioner's energies. In Wiccan-based paths, steel is the preferred metal but there is a tradition of Wicca founded by Gavin and Yvonne Frost (circa 1968) in which copper or brass was preferred. But, an athame can be as unique as the person using it. My husband's is a steel blade with a bone-handle and mine is actually a letter opener while a few members of my group have wooden, hand-carved athames.

The Candle

Every witch or pagan, or person in my opinion, should have candles. When the power goes out a person may rely on them to see in the dark. They are also wonderful because they are portable, can be used for divination or spells, easily represent the fire element and create ambience anywhere they are lit.

Early occultists believed that the candle represented a human in that the flame was the spirit, the wick was the mind (or intellect) and the wax was the physical form. A candle can also represent all five classic elements with the flame as fire, melted wax as water, solid wax as earth, smoke as air and the spark that created it as spirit.

In magick, I have heard that scented candles should not be used, but I see no harm in it. First of all, unless shopping online or at a metaphysical store it may not be possible to find unscented candles, especially when they are colored. Many department stores do have 'unscented' candles but the color is usually white. I believe that the power of aromatherapy can aid in divination or even in adding power to the spell or ritual, just make sure scents, colors, and intents all correspond.

There are literally hundreds of candle spells out there and are the easiest of spells to create from scratch. I will mention only a couple basic ideas for candle spells, but if interested in more I suggest surfing the internet or books and start a collection of candle spells for a variety of needs. Candles are a great way to practice magick and still be somewhat discreet about practicing the pagan arts. Everyone these days seem to have decorative candles and just seeing some in a home does not mean a person is pagan. Candles are one of the best implements in magick because of their personal energy and they are a common household and store-bought item with multiple purposes. They also come in wide varieties or colors and scents which give a person a lot of variety and any intent a person has can be corresponded to a colored candle.

Magick for the Fire Witch
Section IV

Working with Fire

Fire magick can be a very rewarding practice because of its base, primal instincts and properties. Fire gives us a sense of power because it's the one element we can create from scratch. It also requires two of the other elements in order to flare into existence, oxygen (air) and fuel (earth). If using lighter fluid, then water is also represented in the liquid.

However, as with all magick, caution needs to be heeded because fire can quickly get out of control and it is very dangerous. Safety measures with fire are very basic and made up of common sense such as never leave burning candles or incense unattended or having flammable materials and liquids near an open flame, these warnings even come on the products.

But there are other concerns to be aware of that many people might not consider. If renting or in a dorm room at college check the lease or regulations in case there is a rule against fires on the property or candles being lit. Also, be aware of fire regulations within the city, quite often a phone call has to be made to the fire department to alert them of any open bonfires and in some dryer regions there are "no fire" days due to drought conditions.

Indoor Spaces
Using fire indoors usually constitutes candle magick, but can take

place in the form of cooking (the heat of the stove and oven symbolize fire) or with fireplaces. Most spells or rituals that can be done with an outdoor fire can also be done with a hearth fire such as banishing negative habits (writing the bad habits on a piece of paper and burning the paper) or divining with the fire. Fireplaces are also good for representing the fire element in a group ritual and can lend ambience or lighting to a ritual or gathering. The fire element can also be honored by decorating a home in the bright colors of fire.

There is a particularly cute superstition that I am fond of and may use if I ever move to a house with a fireplace. It is believed that only the residents of the house are permitted to poke the fires for fear of offending the Gods of the hearth. The only exception is any friend that the family has known for at least seven years or any friend that has been drunk with the host at least three times. Not a very practical superstition, but I think it will be fun to mention at the next gathering I have with my friends since all of us are prone to poking the fire when it needs it.

For indoor spaces where candles are not allowed (dorm rooms, for example) or where there are no fireplaces look for Lava Lamps online or in a local department store. Usually they can be found in the lamp and lighting section of department stores or at novelty shops such as Spencer's. They are also wonderful for scrying or meditating with and can represent fire on an altar or a group ritual without the danger of open flames, making them also perfect for a children's space.

Outdoor Spaces

If possible, group rituals should be held outside and a fire can either represent the south quadrant, be used for warmth, or just lend lighting to an outdoor ritual. At one gathering we had, the fire was in the center of the circle and we all stood around it. The four elements and directional points were represented on small tables on the outside of the circle and a candle sat on the table in the south. The fire was not representative of the fire element so much as it just lent an atmosphere to the gathering and as we raised energy everyone could concentrate on the fire in a mini-meditative state.

Fire can also be represented with Tiki torches or Chinese lanterns if a large, open fire is not desired. Garden sections of department stores also sell fire pits that come in a variety of designs and are great for having a fire that is more confined and not on the open ground. Fire pits are also great on porches or other covered outdoor spaces such as garages or barns.

Rituals and Spell work

The element of fire rules over spells of success, passion, love, sex, illness, protection, legal matters, competition, strength and energy. Rituals might include: burning objects; burning images and words on paper; burning herbs; baking or cooking; candle or fire magick; passing objects through smoke; and finally, working with the stars. Places like deserts, volcanoes, fireplaces, open fires and ovens all empower fire magick.

Altars

On an altar either the wand or the athame can represent fire (it is up to each individual practitioner's beliefs) or a candle can sit in the quadrant designated for fire.

To have a fire dominated altar, more than one candle can be placed in the south to show that fire is dominant here. Or, each quadrant can have a candle of a corresponding color (blue for water, green for earth, and yellow for air), a candle for the God and Goddess (spirit) and a red altar cloth. More complex fire altars can have components that all represent fire and the element of that direction. For example, a winged dragon can represent air (it flies and breathes fire), a lava rock (pumice) or ash for earth (made of fire but also considered earth when in rock or ash form), and a floating candle in a bowl of water. If standing at an altar, the hand sign for fire is hands raised over the head and fingertips or palms touching. In this manner, the hands resemble the shape of the flame, the head is the wick and the body is the waxen candle

Magick for the Fire Witch
Section v

Flames and Fire

When a person thinks of the fire element they probably think of a flame or a roaring fire. Fire in the literal sense is the best way to honor the fire element but it can be dangerous, hard to control and in some apartments or dormitories it is against the rules to have open flames of any sort. There are alternatives to open flames for representing the fire element, but when possible use an actual flame for fire magick. It is the purest and most direct way to connect with the fire element.

It can be utilized with a single candle, a bonfire, a campfire, or a fireplace. There are many divination methods and spells that can be done with flames and fires from banishing to candle magick, to candle divination and fire-gazing. Fire is a cleansing element and can be a rejuvenator of life but it can also destroy, so use it carefully and always adhere to safety precautions when near open flames.

Candles

Candles are another item that were a common household object and could be placed in the open without being accused of any misdeeds. At one time, they and natural light were the only sources of light that people had and they relied on them greatly. Today, making candles is a craft but in the past, it was a necessity. Of course there is a fair amount of folklore, superstition, and other lore associated with candles. One of my favorites is a nursery rhyme riddle that was sung by children and has made its way into Mother Goose books:

"Little Nanny Etticoat,

In a white petticoat

And a red nose

The longer she stands, the shorter she grows."

The answer is, of course, a candle. The white petticoat is the wax base, the red nose is the tip of the lit wick and the longer it is lit the shorter it gets as it melts.

There is literally no end to the number of spells in candle magick, so I am only including a few basic samples here and the basic color correspondence. There probably isn't a book out there on magick that doesn't have at least one candle spell in it. This is when a Book of Shadows or Grimoire comes in handy, write down the various candle spells and start a collection of spells, at least one or two for different aspects of life. Also, have fun experimenting and creating new spells.

Typically, candle magick corresponds to the intent or need a person has, think of the stereotypical feelings or moods we associate with colors such as peaceful for blue and red for love or create personal color correspondences as long as they have meaning and are the same each time that color is used. When in doubt about a color, use white. It is the color of protection and is like a 'jack-of-all-trades' when it comes to color correspondence.

Candles should be charged with the intent prior to use, don't rely on the color alone to perform the magick. The color and the candle are the mediums, but the person provides the magick. To charge a candle, take an essential oil of corresponding need, or just any base oil such as olive or grape seed, and start in the middle of the candle by rubbing the oil over the wax up towards the wick. Then, start again in the middle and rub the oil down towards the bottom. While doing this, think of the need or purpose of the candle. Anointing a candle with oil will aid in a more even burn as well as charge it with intent.

When lighting the candle speak words of power from a pre-written verse, a chant or an impromptu prayer. Visualize the need clearly and that it is manifesting with the burning of the candle. Let the candle burn either completely out or for a specified amount of time. Many spells written indicate that a candle should burn completely out and advise using tealights, votives or mini-tapers (about 3-4 inches long) or even a birthday candle instead of the long tapers. However, there are spells that require a candle to burn for only a certain length of time, as seen in the 5-Minute Money Candle in this section.

Either way, when ending the spell thank the divine for their assistance and the fire element for its power. Once the candle has been extinguished or burned out on its own, take the wax outside and either bury it or toss it on the ground to give it back to the earth. Each spell written by someone else may vary in its method, but the above is a very basic way of doing candle magick. Feel free to adapt or change it to fit personal needs, likes, and beliefs.

Basic Color Correspondence

White—protection, healing, spiritual guidance, invoking, peace

Black—banishing, trapping negativity

Brown—grounding, honoring earth element, animal magick

Gray—not used very often, but can be for the 'in-between' space between the mundane and the magickal worlds or as a color to encompass all things.

Silver—to represent the moon or the goddess

Gold—to represent the sun or the god

Red—fire element, passion, love, creativity, anger (pink is used as a milder form of red)

Orange—creativity, zest, energizing

Yellow—air element, peace, hope

Green—earth element, money, prosperity, fortune, luck

Blue—water element, calming, peaceful, relaxing

Purple—psychic work, connection to divine, spirituality

Volcanoes and Lava

Volcanoes and lava flows are a raw-source of fire and highly respected and feared in countries where there are active volcanoes. Mythology is often filled with stories of virgins being tossed into volcanoes in order to appease the gods, while this is probably more in the realms of Hollywood myths because to get to the opening of a volcano is very treacherous, the image has nonetheless stuck with us and gives a sense of the fear that the ancients had of these fearsome beasts. Volcanoes hold fire (lava) but are mountains, so they are of both earth and fire. Lava is also of both earth and fire since it is molten rock.

Volcanoes

If lucky enough to live near a real volcano (hopefully not a very active one) the volcano's power can be called upon for strength and the element of fire that it possess. But, if not a fake volcano can be made and used in a spell or ritual. Made from clay, baking soda and vinegar homemade volcanoes are the stereotypical Science Fair projects in schools (and often not allowed because they are too common) but with a little creativity they can be transferred to pagan practices. Great fun for children and good for a visual effect, they are typically a one-time use and very messy. Do not try this on an altar but rather outside or where clean up is easy. It would also be great for group rituals to honor Pele or the power of the fire element with the ritual leader pouring a libation of vinegar from a chalice into the volcano.

Make a volcano out of clay or other medium (instructions can be found online) and fill the volcano's hole with baking soda; it can be as realistic or as simple as desired. Focus on the intent (remember the attributes of the fire element) and as the vinegar is poured recite the verse:

Volcano of power and element of fire;

Sacred to the Goddess Pele, hear my desire.

State the intent and the 'lava' will carry the magickal energies and intent as it flows up and around the volcano.

Pumice (lava rock)

Lava stone, also known as pumice, is a great stone for abundance, control, healing, protection and it corresponds to fire and Goddess Pele. Pumice is the only stone that floats and is a natural stone that can be used to exfoliate calluses. This stone is great to represent all of the elements because it was created in fire, but is now stone and it floats on water because it has air pockets. Pumice can be used in any of the quadrants when making a fire-altar as a representation of two elements, or can be used to represent all of the elements.

Pumice can also provide a little bit of visual magick and science to children by showing them a handful of stones that sink and then showing them the pumice, which does not. My daughter used this experiment when she taught a class on gemstones to our local group. The adults were as fascinated as the children.

Having lava stones around when working magick can create an excellent psychic shield because the fire element protects and the earth element holds that protective energy in its place. The fire in a lava stone has cooled and makes a good charm to keep on hand for a temperamental person or to help keep possibly volatile situations cooled down.

Brimstone (Sulfur)

Otherwise known as Sulfur, this is the stone of the Christian Hell. Perhaps the phrase 'fire and brimstone' is a familiar one. It is a simile for God's wrath or a preacher's style of voracious sermons. Brimstone is an archaic word for sulfur, a chemical which casts out a heinous and acrid smell and is formed around volcanic vents, hence its association with fire.

In Christian mythology the God destroyed Sodom and Gomorrah amidst a rain of fire and brimstone and it is used as a threat or punishment throughout the Bible. In one reference, God's breath is even said to be "like a stream of brimstone" (Isaiah 30:33). Hell is said to be made up of fire and brimstone and Satan was cast into a lake made up of the same.

On a contrary note, burning brimstone was a practice of Greek Orthodox traditions as a purifier and cleanser. It appears that Brimstone could be used as a cruel punishment or to purify the land from sin and decay.

English superstition says that if one carries brimstone on them it will cure them from suffering cramps. Commonly sold in metaphysical shops, neo-pagans might use brimstone to dispel or prevent a hex, destroy an enemy's power or banish evil. Keep in mind that this is sulfur and does not smell good (rotten egg smell) but it does emit a pretty blue flame.

Spells and Rituals

5-Minute Money Candle

From the book "The Good Spell Book" by Gillian Kemp we find my favorite spell. This is one of the spells that requires a candle to be blown out, so if this goes against a person's beliefs it is better to find a different spell. A snuffer can be used, but the spell requires smoke to exist after the flame is out so make sure that there is a fair amount of smoke drifting up after extinguishing.

Take a green candle, charge or anoint it with the visualization of money or inscribe a dollar sign in the candle. Set it on a fire-proof surface where it will not be disturbed and light the candle, envisioning money coming soon. Let the candle burn for five complete minutes and then blow out the flame. Rub hands together in the smoke and visualize money coming into those hands. Once the smoke has completely dissipated stop rubbing hands. Money will soon come.

I have had this spell work too many times not to be valid, but I have found that it does no good to do this spell on a day when money is a sure thing. Paydays are especially bad days to do a money spell since the money is already on its way; it's like two people voting opposite...one cancels out the other. Most often the spell simply does not work and the energy was raised for nothing. Having "lazy energy," that is, energy that was raised without purpose or incorrectly, lying around the house can clutter a home spiritually and metaphysically the same way dust and debris clutter a home. Or, an adverse affect can happen and the paycheck will not arrive. Suffice it to say, do this spell on a day when no money is expected and only envision as much as is really needed.

Cleansings

Fire can be used to cleanse objects and also people. Objects can be passed through or over the flame (only metal objects should be cleansed this way, never try it with anything that is flammable such as wood or cloth) and can also cleanse people in the form of Beltane fires or by jumping over small fires.

Eventually the rituals at Beltaine and Samhain may have filtered down to jumping over small fires or candles as a way to purify the body and soul. The popular Mother Goose rhyme 'Jack Be Nimble' may even be a left over chant or charm from this simple practice:

"Jack be nimble, Jack be quick;

Jack jump over the candlestick!"

Often practitioners wear robes or cloaks during rituals and it is not advisable to jump over a candle or fire in case the flames catch on the cloth, so adapt this to walking around a candle or fire and changing the rhyme to:

I am nimble, I am quick

as I walk around the candlestick.

Bless me for the coming days

and let nothing hinder my way.

If this is a group ritual in which everyone walks around the candle at one time, insert the words 'we' and 'our' where appropriate as all people speak at once. Or, if each person takes their own turn around the fire or candle, the group can recite the verse but insert the person's name in place of the word 'I' (such as "Terry's nimble; Terry's quick," etc.).

Fire Banishing

Another spell often done at Beltaine, Yule, or Samhain, but can be done anytime, is that of banishing negative aspects a person has. Similar to making New Year's resolutions, a person can write down the habits that they want to be rid of (smoking, biting nails, road rage, etc.) and then burn the paper in a ritual fire (or over a candle for solitaire practitioners). Parchment paper, a quill pen and Dragon's Blood Ink are the preferred writing implements but any paper or pen will work just as well. Concentrate on the items that have been written just before tossing the paper into the fire and as the paper burns visualize those habits or tendencies leaving the body and mind with the drifting smoke.

Chakra Spell

The Chakras are seven points in the body in which there are main points of energy. Going from the bottom up they are: root (feet); sacral (pelvis), solar plexus (chest), heart, throat, third eye (brow between the eyes), and the crown. They each have a color and going from bottom to top again the colors simply follow along the rainbow scheme: red, orange, yellow, green, blue, indigo, violet. A neat trick to remember this is to put the first letters of each color, in order, into the name of "Roy G. Biv." Working with chakras and their energies has become a common practice in New Age, neo-paganism and the Healing Arts.

To do a Chakra Spell involving candles is more for fixing the chakra-based energies within a room or building then it is for healing a person's own chakra energies, although it could be used for that as well. This spell requires all seven of the rainbow colors (use gray or white for indigo unless a deep blue or purple can be found). Line up all seven of the candles in an area free of breezes and drafts and light them. Focus or meditate on the candles for a few minutes, asking that they analyze the energies in the room or the building. After they have burned down almost to completion, analyze how well, or how badly, they burned. Any candle that has a lot of wax drips or burned unevenly is an area that needs work. Any candle with very little drip or that burned evenly means those energies are good.

The colors represent similar qualities to that of the chakra points on the body: red is the base or selfish needs, the natural order of the place; orange is the creativity levels; yellow is the general atmosphere of the house; green indicates emotional or physical states; blue means communication; purple is for intuition and psychic awareness and indigo is spiritual connection. So, if blue burns unevenly or badly it means that the people in the house need to focus on better communication with each other and so on.

Divination, Meditation, Scrying

Fire is a favorite amongst the various techniques whether it is in the form of campfires, fireplaces or a single candle and is generally referred to as Causimancy. Fire divination is not always the most precise way of foretelling the future but it can let a person know if the environment bodes well and is a great way to meditate. Fire divination can occur in a variety of forms from candles to open fires and also in the ashes and smoke by interpreting patterns.

Superstitions about divining with fire are very common and numerous and it is hard to separate all of the superstition and know which is the correct interpretation, but in time a person might develop their own meanings. I have listed several different interpretations of flames (both of candles and open fires) and they can be used, but it is best to use fire as a meditative source or interpret based on images 'seen' in the flames rather than concentrating on the nature of a fire.

In paranormal circles, a blue flame means ghosts or spirits are nearby but Scottish lore says bad weather is on the way if a flame is blue. Most flames have a little bit of blue in the very center of it and it is a natural occurrence. The divination comes in when the flame turns mostly or entirely blue. Considering that paranormal experts tend to agree on the idea that storms can increase paranormal activity, the two divinations may go hand-in-hand.

The best omens in fire-gazing are with fires that burn intensely, flare up or start quickly. Flames or fire that burn to life quickly or with renewed strength usually portend good things such as visitors arriving soon, that all is well, or that a lover is in a happy mind. Fires that have bright and clear flames are also indicative of positive things to come. Long burning flames are also a very good omen, especially if the flame is steady and not wavering.

Usually it is seen as a bad omen if any fire has difficulty in starting, goes out suddenly or just doesn't burn as steady and as bright as it could. A candle or fire that is reluctant to burn shows sensitivity to someone with a bad temper who is causing problems. Any fire that shows difficulty in lighting, especially on Yule, means an unlucky year ahead or is a bad omen when occurring at other times in the year.

Flames that are not very strong are also usually not a good omen with faintly burning flames indicating that there are mitigating factors causing uncertainty. Flickering flames represent a lack of support by the universe for an intended action and constantly moving flame means the situation is in flux.

The other colors of flames can also predict events or outcomes. Predominantly red flames warn of anger, orange flames mean emotions are at an all-time high, and yellow indicates a need to communicate clearly. Along with colors, the appearance of a fire can indicate different events with rings in the flame presaging good news; a smoldering flame implies trouble will follow and a flame that sparks means a message will be received.

Candle Divination

It is important with candle or fire divination that the area in which the work is done is free from breezes. There should be no mistake between a flame that is moving erratically because of the divining message and a flame moving erratically because of the air conditioner. The preferred time for candle divination is at night time and when the lights are low or turned off; this makes it easier to focus just on the flame. There are many different ways to divine with a candle flame from using one candle of a corresponding color (red for romance) to using multiple candles. Here is a basic candle divination technique that anyone can use.

Arrange three candles in a triangle shape; the color is not important as long as the candles are all of the same color and size. Meditate on the question for a few moments and then light the candles. Watch all three of the flames for an answer. If one flame burns brighter than the others then there will be an unexpected stroke of good luck. If any of the flames go out it portends bad luck. If they dance around in circles it could mean enemies are working against the outcome and they spark it could mean being surrounded by enemies or negativity. If all three candles burn steadily then all will go well.

For one-candle divination, observe the candle flame and search for possible signs within the flame and the wick. A dim flame might mean to hold off on plans for the time being (remember the phrase "the future is not bright") while a bright flame is a sign of good fortune. However, if the flame burns bright and then dims quickly it could mean that good fortune is temporary. A candle flame that waves about could mean a change in circumstances or situations is coming soon and a spark at the tip of the wick is foretelling good news.

Another method of candle divination is to watch the wax as it drips down. This can be done with one candle or done with many, as in the Candle Chakra earlier in this section. With a single candle designate the right side of the candle to mean 'yes' and the left side to mean 'no.' Ask a yes or no question, light the wick and then watch the candle. If the wax drips more onto the left side the answer is no, if it drips more on the right said the answer is yes and if it drips about equally it means that an answer cannot be revealed at this time. If using more than one candle, designate each candle as a potential answer. The candle that drips cleanly and evenly is the answer. If none of the candles burn cleanly or evenly then either the question was unclear or an answer is not available at this time.

My favorite new divination method that I have yet to try, and would be a good one to use for children since it is a visible form of magick, involves the use of lemon juice. Take a toothpick and dip it into lemon juice, either squeezed from a real lemon or the bottled juice, and on two separate pieces of regular or parchment paper write either 'yes' or 'no' or a possible future outcome such as "quit job" or "don't quit." Light a candle and concentrate on the question. Set the pieces on a table and mix them up so that it is not known which answer is on which paper (the lemon juice will not show up until held over heat, so the papers will appear blank). Pick a paper at random and hold it over the flame close enough that it heats it up but not catches fire. The heat makes the lemon juice scorch the paper and the message will be revealed.

Fire Gazing

For simple fire-gazing all that is needed is to sit in front of a roaring fire and ask a question (either verbally or mentally). Gaze into the flames and observe what it is doing. Images may appear in the flames or the coals and can be interpreted symbolically like dream or other divination symbols. If no images come to mind or the eyes grow tired, stop trying to divine and try again later. Fire gazing is best used for meditation in which the subconscious brings forth images, thoughts or feelings to the person.

Magick for the Fire Witch
Section VI

Ashes and Smoke

Ashes and smoke are the by-products of fire, one becomes the earth element and one is of the air element and both can be used in spells, rituals and divination. In the ancient art of alchemy ashes are also considered to be earth because fire is hot and dry whereas ashes are cold and dry, which are qualities of earth. However, in magickal practices, ashes can still be considered of the fire because they were made from the fire. Something had to burn and turn to char in order to create the ashes. They are a direct link to the fire element such as flames, but in a different form. Ashes can be used to empower charm bags or for divination and the charred and ashy end of a stick can be used in magickal writings.

The smoke is also a result of fire and can be considered of the fire element. It is also of the air element because it wafts in the air, this is why incense is considered an air tool. The flame of incense is extinguished to the point where the stick or cone only smolders, thus being of the air. Smoke can be used for scrying, divination and for carrying messages to the Gods. It is also a purifier and objects can be passed through smoke to cleanse them. I include it in the fire section because of the old adage "where there is smoke, there is fire"; without fire we would not have smoke or ashes.

Ashes

Ashes are symbolic of transformation, regeneration and fertility, in part because of the myth of the Phoenix and in part because fire is thought to cleanse objects and make them like new. Despite a fire's destructive force it is an essential part of nature and often used either by nature or man to replenish a forested area. There are even certain fir trees that cannot release their seed unless the air reaches a temperature only the fires can bring. Because of this concept, comes the idea that sprinkling ashes over a field ensures a successful crop for that year. Ashes have long been believed to enrich the soil and are still used by gardeners today. It is certainly an alternative to burning a field or garden after crops have been harvested in order to replenish it for the next year.

Superstitions abound from France where ashes are scattered around a home as protection from storms to the South American belief that ashes can be tossed in the air to make the rain fall. At Yule (December 21st or Winter Solstice) ashes can be mixed with corn seed to improve the harvest or given in food to livestock to promote their health. Today, a practitioner could use ashes in a charm bag, to set on an altar, in an amulet or scatter them after a spell or ritual to help spread the magick and give the energy back to the earth.

The ashes of the deceased are believed to possess magickal qualities because they are symbolic of the person's rite of passage from one life to next. In Ancient Egypt the ashes of a red-haired and deceased person were spread over the fields to ensure good crops; red-haired people were thought to be lucky (unlike some superstitions in other cultures that state red-hair is unlucky). In Africa the deceased's ashes were eaten with food so that the survivors would receive the deceased person's good qualities.

Ashes are often held sacred throughout the various cultures and belief systems of the world. Cremation has become a popular and cheaper version to underground burial and ashes are either scattered over a person's favored spot or held sacred in a decorative urn. A friend of mine said that when her friend's young son died in a car accident the ashes were divided up, placed in small bottles and given to his closest friends.

In Catholicism the use of ashes holds significance on the 1st day of Lent, which is known as Ash Wednesday. The ashes are symbolic of repenting sins and the season of Lent is one of penance, reflection, fasting and preparing one for Christ's resurrection on Easter Sunday. This custom is in honor of the Ninevites (citizens of Ninevah of Biblical lore) who did penance in sack-cloth clothing and ashes rubbed on their forehead.

The Ninevites foreheads were marked with ashes to humble their hearts and remind them that life passes away on earth. The ashes, traditionally speaking, should be made from the blessed palm trees in the Palm Sunday celebration of the previous year. They are christened with Holy Water and scented by being exposed to incense. The tradition of anointing foreheads with ashes continues today in Catholicism, but the sack-cloth clothing has disappeared and there does not appear to be a standard form of dress for this rite.

In pagan rituals ashes might also be mixed with either blessed water or scented with incense ashes or oils. Instead of a cross marked on the forehead, as Catholics do, a pentacle or other sacred symbol could be drawn in the center of the forehead, right over the metaphysical third eye.

In both cases, it would be fitting to recite the popular Anglican burial litany of "Ashes to ashes; dust to dust" or the Biblical phrases of either "Dust thou art, and unto dust thou shall return" (Genesis 3:19) or "I will bring thee to ashes upon the earth in sight of all them that behold thee" (Ezekiel 28:18). Neither one specifically mentions a religion or god and can easily be adapted to pagan practices.

The Boy Scouts of America (an all-male youth group) have a tradition involving ashes that goes back many generations (at least to the 1930's). After a campfire, the ashes are collected and either taken to the next camping event to be placed in the fire pit prior to lighting a new fire. Sometimes they are handed down to future generations or troops as a sign of friendship, good luck or prosperity. Some ashes even travel the world and have been a part of thousands of Boy Scouting events or celebrations. The ashes are sometimes referred to as Campfire Ashes, Ashes of Friendship, Trail of Ashes, or Spirit Ashes.

Boy Scouts teach community skills but mainly focus on life and survival skills. There are different levels or 'orders' to the boy scouts that take their knowledge and skills from a variety of sources or traditions often comprised of Native American beliefs, where it is said that this tradition is derived from. On the website "The Boy Scout Campfire Ashes" (see Bibliography for website address) there is this wonderful quote: "We carry our friendship with us in these ashes from other campfires with other comrades in other lands. May the joining of the dead fires with the leaping flames symbolize once more the unbroken chain that binds scouts and guides". Also on the website is a listing of years and places that the campfire ashes have seen. It is very fascinating and I recommend taking a look at it, and starting a personal or group log of fires, purpose or event, and where the ashes went after that.

Smoke

Smoke signals are one of the oldest forms of communication, and while patterns such as puffs or long draws of the smoke (think of dots and dashes in Morse code) could be used, smoke was mainly used to notify others of a people's presence, such as the Australian Aborigines do when entering lands not their own. In ancient China, soldiers that were stationed on the Great Wall would use a system of smoke signals to communicate to the next tower or station that there was an impending enemy attack. In only a few hours, they could send a message a distance of 300 miles. In 150 BCE the Greek historian Polybius devised a more complex system of alphabetical and numerical smoke signals. Known as the "Polybius Square" his system enabled messages to be sent via a pair of torches and a version of this system was used as recent as the First World War.

Smoke signals are perhaps associated more frequently with the Native Americans in which each tribe had a specific system of smoke signals. Typically, fires for smoke signals were built at higher elevations, such as hills, and started with damp grasses which would make a large and thick column of smoke rise up into the air. Wet grass would continue to be added until the message had been delivered. The location of the fire also had meaning and if built halfway up a hill it meant that all was well but on top of the hill could mean danger.

Smoke signals are still used today in some aspects. To signify the selection of a new Pope the College of Cardinals in Rome, Italy, conduct a secret ballot and the ballots are burned after each vote. Black smoke indicates a failed ballot and white means a new Pope has been elected. In a non-intentional message, the cliché "where there's smoke, there's fire" lends to us a warning system that when we see smoke we look for the fire and, if necessary, call the appropriate authorities.

Spells and Rituals

Pagan Campfire Ashes

Borrowing slightly from the Boy Scout saying, this can be adapted to pagan practices try reciting this verse either as the ashes are collected or as they are dumped into the next fire:

> *With these ashes we carry the friendships and beliefs of other ritual fires*
>
> *and other kindred souls with the intent of joining the cold ashes*
>
> *to that of the leaping flames in symbolism of our powers and desires.*
>
> *From the fire to the earth, from dust to dust, and from ashes to ashes*
>
> *We pass along our knowledge and friendship. So mote it be.*

Add the ashes to the new fire, and don't forget that after this new fire has gone cold the ashes need to be re-collected and stored until the next fire.

Beltaine/Samhain fires

From superstition we also get that ashes from a May Day fire (Beltaine in the northern hemisphere and Samhain in the southern hemisphere, typically held on May 1st) are also said to protect against evil or ill-intent magick (Britain and America) and the ashes from these Sabbat fires were often placed in the snows to protect from misfortune (Wales). To turn this into a spell, gather some ashes the next morning after a Beltaine or Samhain fire. As they are gathered recite:

> *Ashes from the Beltaine (or Samhain) fire;*
>
> *Protect me from the situations that are dire.*

Place the ashes in a charm bag, amulet locket or bottle or set on an altar.

Smoke Communication

To use in communication today, meditate on the smoke of a fire and concentrate on a message that needs to be sent. Visualize the recipient of the message and that the message is being taken in by the smoke and drifting upwards with it. As the smoke rises and disperses into the air it will release the message and deliver it to the person who needs to receive it.

Divination, Meditation, Scrying

Divining with Ashes

There are several ways to divine with ashes: Tuphramancy (general divination), Tephramancy (ashes of burned tree bark), and Tephromancy (ashes from burned sacrifices), Ceneromancy (ashes from a ritual fire or fire burned specifically for divination). Keep in mind, Tephromancy is not recommended because no living thing should be harmed in magick, but if the 'sacrifice' is an inanimate object made or used specifically for the purpose (such as in the example of the hazel nut mentioned later on) then it not going against the laws of magick as practiced today.

In dream divination to dream of ashes means that it is time to reconsider certain aspects of life (transformation). Further symbolism in the dream will help to aid in what aspects need to be revamped. For example, if the dream has work-related symbols in it as well as the ashes then it could mean a change in a career is needed, or time to find a job or career if currently not working.

In the past, divination did involve the ashes of a burned object and determining the future by the patterns seen in the ashes. In Scotland on Samhain it was popular for fortune-tellers to recommend that a maiden name one hazel nut for each of her suitors and toss them into the fire. The nut that burned to ashes completely would prophecy the name of her husband. For example, if she named one nut Charlie and the other Scotty and the one named Scotty burns completely to ashes that would be the name of her suitor she would end up marrying.

This can be modernized by naming one nut 'yes' and one 'no' and tossing in the fire. It might be simpler if each nut is placed in a specific part of the fire to make it easy to remember which nut is which. Think of a yes or no question and meditate on the fire. The nut that has burned completely is the answer.

To divine with ashes from a fire, collect a handful of ash from a cold fire or fire place and scatter the ashes in a rectangular shape on the ground. This needs to be done where the breezes can flow easily, and make sure there is a good depth to the ash pile. Ask a question and then use a finger to write 'yes' on one side of the rectangle and 'no' on the other side (in the ashes). Leave them undisturbed overnight and in the morning, check on the ashes. If both of the words are still legible or both are completely illegible then there is no possible answer at this time. If one has been erased in any natural form (animal tracks, wind, rain, etc) then the word that remains is the answer to the question. For example, if the word 'yes' is wiped out then the answer is 'no.'

In Yorkshire, ashes spread over a hearth on New Year's Eve or St. Mark's Eve can give a hint to what the next twelve months will bring. If the foot prints in the ashes led to the front door it prophesied a death in the household (going out) but if they led away from the front door it meant a birth (coming in). Incidentally, St. Mark's Eve has its own fortune-telling superstition. Held on April 24th it is the eve before St. Mark's feast in which it was customary in the 17th-19th centuries to sit on the porch between 11 pm and 3 am in order to see the apparitions of those due to die during the year.

Divining with Smoke

To use smoke in divining is called either Libanomancy (burning incense) or Capnomancy (specifically if the smoke comes from an altar or sacred fire) or in easier-to-remember terms, "smoke reading." The most obvious way of divining with smoke is similar to fire gazing in that a person divines messages and symbols by patterns in the smoke. However, there are other methods such as watching smoke from a fire and concentrating on a yes or no question. If the smoke rises straight up and is thin and light the answer is positive. If the smoke hangs heavily and thick near the area or around the fire then the answer is negative.

Another way is to light a candle and pass a plain white card (like an index card) quickly through the flames three times while asking a question. Then interpret the carbon deposits left on the underside of the card by symbol divination. The card must be passed quickly through the flame so as not to catch it on fire. Symbols or patterns can be interpreted according to intuition, personal meaning in symbols or from basic dream or symbol dictionaries.

Magick for the Fire Witch
Section VII

Fire in the Skies

Most people won't think of fire as being in skies but the sun, lightning, and meteorites all come from skies and are of the fire element. Even though they cannot be stored in jars or harnessed in a physical way, there are methods to using the natural powers that the sky-fires give to us. Keep in mind that these are powerful forces and common sense in safety should be adhered to at all times. It is better to use these objects in quick spells, for charging objects or to harness the power by focusing on their energy and magickal properties.

Meteors and Meteorites

Meteors and meteorites are any part of a meteoroid that has made it through Earth's atmosphere. Meteor showers occur more frequently then we realize but a person's position on earth, weather conditions and times of the showers are all contributing factors in whether a shower is seen and it is not as easy to obtain pieces of meteorites as it is other stones, but are excellent stones to ad to any magickal collection if they can be obtained.

In some cultures, especially remote tribes, meteorites were believed to be either messages from the Gods or omens of things yet to come. They held powers of fertility and Shamans or tribal wise men called them "seeds from Heaven." Fragments found on earth would be shaped into fertility objects and were carried as a charm or amulet.

Today, meteorites are believed to hold healing properties due to their magnetic qualities. Magnets have long been thought to enhance circulation, improve memory, and clean the blood. Magnetic therapy is a metaphysical treatment for many different ailments and even though it is not as widely known as acupuncture, Reiki or reflexology, those who use it swear by its affects. I have a copper bracelet with magnetic ends and when I am feeling ill or just out of sorts I wear it, making sure that the magnets touch my wrist, and I always feel better within a couple of hours.

Sun

Believed to be the source of fire used by mankind, the sun has a long history in superstition, folklore and mythology. Sol is the personification of the sun and comes to us from Roman mythology where he is the God of the Sun (Greek equivalent is Helios). It is believed that the bonfires lit on Beltane and Litha (June 21) are to celebrate the sun and are a form of sun worship. Lighting these bonfires can be used for cleansing crops or livestock, bringing luck to local communities and promoting fertility. The sun is also representative of the God in Wiccan-based paganism and is shown on an altar by a gold candle.

The sun can be used to banish unwanted or negative energies, and is believed to kill off most nighttime creatures such as the folkloric vampires. It can also be used to cleanse stones or other magickal tools if they are left out in the direct sunlight. In folkloric times to turn, move or cast a circle in deosil fashion (clockwise or sunwise) was believed to be done by someone practicing 'good magick' whereas going widdershins (anti-sunwise or counterclockwise) was done to perform 'bad magick'. Today deosil is used to invoke, cast a circle or bring something to the practitioner and widdershins is used to banish, uncast a circle or to remove something.

Stars

Stars have always thought to be magickal in some fashion and superstitions abound regarding these celestial bodies whether they are shooting across the sky or staying put. Some beliefs say that shooting stars are souls falling to Earth to bring life to newborn babies. In pre-Christian beliefs the stars were said to be the home of the Gods but early Christians changed this belief and the star simply being pesky rocks that deterred people from entering Heaven by artificial means. Presumably, souls were attracted by the light of the stars and went towards them instead of to Heaven.

The stars were so revered that many cultures created legends and shapes out of their alignment in the skies. Various cultures had their own stories and constellations but today there is one global 'mapping' of the constellations that is based on Greek mythologies. There are 88 constellations in all, and it is said that every star is part of some constellation.

In Christian mythology with the story of Christ's birth there is a star that plays a prominent role in announcing his birth and leading three wise men to his birthplace. The wise men are described as being Magi or Kings (as in the Christmas carol "We Three Kings"). A few have even dared to say that the wise men were early astrologers because they followed the star in order to find the place where the savior was born. Because of its Christian tie-in with a December holiday stars have become objects of decoration on Christmas paper, tree-toppers, tree-ornaments and an array of other winter decorations.

Today, there is still some superstition surrounding the stars in the sky and there is a thrill at seeing the first star of the evening or picking out constellations. There is a common nursery rhyme that children often recite and can be used as wish spell by anyone.

Starlight, starbright,

First star I see tonight

Wish I may, wish I might

Have this wish I wish tonight.

Common belief, like with other wish-making opportunities, is that it is bad luck to tell anyone the wish once its made.

Lightning

Lightning is one of those natural phenomena that is rife with superstition and lore in many cultures and beliefs worldwide. Even today, people are either fascinated by it or frightened of it and the popular 1980's movie "Poltergeist" made us all afraid of lightning-struck trees that would break in the window and eat us. This fun horror movie also taught us to count the seconds as one one-thousand, two one-thousand, and so on in between a lightning strike and thunder; each second equals one mile of distance between us and the storm. In Dragon Magick it is of the air element since it comes from the skies.

Sometimes it was viewed as a blessing but most often it was seen as a sign of wrath or vengeance from the gods. Lightning is viewed as a vengeful act with the victims being ostracized in either life or death because they are viewed as one who angered the gods. This is even seen in Christian lore with the idea that anyone committing blasphemy will be struck down by God. It would be considered unlucky to be seen associating with a person who was struck by lightning and lived or honoring one who died of a lightning strike for fear of offending the god who did the smiting.

Within the Zulu tribe of South Africa any animal, person or tree that is struck by lightning is considered to have been struck because the spirits wished it so. This made the object tainted and would be condemned by the tribe. People were not mourned nor buried with a ceremony; animals were buried but never eaten; and any tree felled by a lightning strike would not have been used for any purpose. A Zulu male can attempt to counteract impending lightning by going out to where the cattle are kept, beat a shield, burn herbs and implore the spirits to protect the cattle.

Zeus, of Greek lore, is another god attributed with powers of lightning and is said to have lightning bolts as weapons. They were invented by Minvera, Goddess of Wisdom, and given to Zeus as a gift. The Greeks and Romans considered any area struck by lightning as sacred and often built their temples at those sites. In Scandinavian lore we see Thor who is often depicted with a hammer and a lightning bolt in hand and on his helmet. Thor is said to throw bolts at his enemies and he is where we get the name Thursday in our days of the week (Thor's Day).

Other cultural gods include Indra (Hindu) as the god of the heavens, lightning, rain, storms and thunder; the Maruts (Hindu storm deities) used the thunderbolts as weapons; the Umpundulo is a lightning bird-like god of the Bantu tribe in Africa; Tinia, an Etruscan god (of the tribe Estruria circa 800-300 BCE); Adad the Babylonian God of thunder, lightning and prophecy; and many Native American tribes often viewed the lord of lightning as a Thunderbird (Navajo). The Thunderbird, believed to produce thunder or lightning, is commonly seen in Native American art or on totem poles and is shown with a lightning bolt as a twinkle in its eye.

Another popular myth that is not often considered under the category of lighting is one see with the advent of Christmas and the mythical character Santa Claus. Two of his flying reindeer are named after these stormy phenomena: Donner (thunder) and Blitzen (lightning). In Catholicism there is even a saint for lightning. Saint Barbara (circa 306 CE) is the patron saint of lightning and has become a symbol of martyrdom. Her father was killed when lightning struck him and she has become somewhat of a martyr for her pain and loss. In more modern times she has become the patroness of artillerymen and all workings with explosives (the connection the lightning being the loud sounds made).

Superstitions and myths regarding weather exist today from the ever-popular "lightning never strikes the same place twice" (which is a complete myth as it strikes lightning rods and tall buildings repeatedly) to more obscure myths. Weather lore tells us that lightning from the East is considered a good omen while coming from the West is considered ominous. Some cultures made medicines from stones that were thought to be struck by lightning and in Roman, Hindu and Mayan myths it was said that mushrooms grew from where lightning had struck the ground.

Lightning charges the air with its energy and that can be used to empower spell work. Incidentally, since spirits are said to use energy to manifest there is a popular belief among paranormal groups that contact with the other side can be made easier during a storm where lightning is present. Lighting is often associated with wind, rain and crop growth and in Native American tribes the power of lightning has great power in their heat rituals. Try using the energies in the air to aid in either personal growth or prosperity, for agricultural growth, for healing or for communication with ancestors and spirits (for ancestral worship or spell work, not just in paranormal investigating). Spells that are empowered with lightning will be like the lightning: quick, strong and powerful.

Just doing a spell during a storm can help empower it, but there are ways to try and harness the energy created by lightning. Remember, it is never wise to go outside in a storm or to carry metal outside during a storm; keep in mind that lightning is electricity and electricity is a very dangerous thing. Using lightning for magick means to do a spell indoors, to charge objects with the lightning or to use lightning struck objects but never to try and directly harness electricity.

Spells and Rituals

Use the powers of the sun for energy or for cleansing gemstones or magickal objects by placing them out in full sunlight, quite often objects are placed outside for twenty-four hours where they get both moon and sunlight. The previously mentioned nursery rhyme for stars can also be used to make a wish on the first star of the evening (the wish is the same as intent in spell work).

Lightning Struck Objects

If lightning strikes a tree take a branch from it and powder it (use sandpaper or a nail file for hard wood or soft woods may be crushed in a mortar and pestle) and use the powder to empower spells. A decent sized twig could also be used as a wand or other magickal items can be carved out of wood from a tree struck with lightning. Stones and water can also be collected after a lightning storm and used in spell work or the stones can be used as amulets. These items have become charged by the lightning and can be used as safe ways to harness its power. I have also included another star spell as well as some little-known lightning spells. Not very many people use lightning or the power of storms in spells, but the energy in a storm cannot be denied and can be a very powerful component, as we have already seen in Magick for the Air Witch.

Stars and Mirrors

Go outside with a hand held mirror, preferably the kind with a handle, and stand where the starts can be clearly seen. Position the mirror so that seven stars are reflected in it. Make a wish on each of the seven stars. If this can be done at a time that the moon is waxing (getting more full, within 1-3 days of being full) it will be even more effective and as the moon waxes into full the magick will come to completion. Since mirrors are believed to reflect a person's soul, so too is the essence of the stars being reflected and absorbed in the mirror.

On the reverse side, hold the mirror so that only three stars are reflected in the mirror and when the moon is waning (going from full to crescent) name each reflected star with three things to banish such: smoking, biting nails, negative thoughts. As the moon wanes, the negative traits will also wane. Of course, it takes a lot of effort on the part of the person doing the spell. No one will wake up no craving cigarettes or having the urge to stop biting nails, it must be worked at, but the spell can help to ease the desires.

Wish Spell

When it is lightning out, visualize intent and each time that the lightning flashes imagine the wish or desire being sent out on the bolts of lightning. As the lightning flashes, recite the following verse to further the intent:

> *Lightning bolts fast and briskly,*
>
> *carry my desires forth quickly;*
>
> *of the skies and the earth below,*
>
> *allow thine magick to grow.*

It is not necessary to continue this throughout a storm's duration, since they can last for hours, but try it for the space of at least three lightning flashes. Odd numbers are considered spiritual numbers, usually between the numbers of three and nine, so pick one of those for the number of times repeating the verse and visualizing the intent.

Divination, Meditation, Scrying

Ceraunscopy

Ceraunscopy is the term applied to divining with thunder and lightning, and while it does not see to be so common today, in the past people would divine with it based on the directions the bolts came from, similar to divining with the wind's directions. Bolts from the east meant favorable conditions coming soon and bolts from the west were bad omens. Those from the north were the worst and the northwest meant very bad news was on its way. In the Middle Ages, Europeans believed that thunder and lightning were omens of impending war, natural disasters or death.

Magick for the Fire Witch
Section VIII

Fire Mythology

As stated earlier, fire has been around for centuries with an indeterminable date as to when men first started to harness and use it. At some point, we did and each culture or belief system has its own theory as to who brought fire to the mortal man, but all tend to agree that it was either brought from the sun or the underworld and that the gods had access to it first.

Fire Creation

One particularly neat fire creation story comes from the islands of the Pacific Ocean. Before man knew how to make fire only the gods of the underworld knew the secret, and they guarded it closely. Their belief in it being of the underworld was proven by the smoke that rose up out of the ground and out the tops of mountains (volcanoes). A young boy, Maui, lived in the upper world with the mortals but his parents were both of the underworld. They came to the upper world on errands of the gods of the underworld.

Maui's mother, Buaratanga, came to see him quite often and they would go on picnics. However, she never ate with him but went off on her own to eat. Maui decided to follow her and see why she always ate alone. She had fallen asleep and Maui peeked into her basket, the food looked a lot better then what he was used to and when he sampled it tasted better than the food he was used to. He knew that the gods had fire and he figured out that the reason her food tasted better was because it was cooked. Wanting to share cooked food with the mortals he followed Buaratanga when she returned to the underworld.

He had to slip through many gates and it took him a long time to sneak past all of the guards but eventually he wound up at his mother's house and he asked her for the secret to making fire. She did not know but explained that she goes to his father, Bu, and his father goes to the Fire God. She tried to persuade Maui to return to the upper world. When he adamantly refused she gave him one last warning "Beware, the Fire God is very powerful and can be very angry."

Maui asked for a firebrand to take to the mortal world but was refused because he said if man learned the secret they would be too powerful and might consider them selves as gods. Maui hid in a banana tree to watch and see if he could learn the secret himself. The houses in the underworld were built with holes in the roofs to let the smoke out from the fires. Maui could look straight down into the roof of the fire god's home. Chance happened along and it rained in the upper world, the water ran down into the underworld and straight into the hole of the Fire God's roof. The rain fell so fast and in such a quantity that it put the Fire God's fire out. He then grabbed coconut fibers, some sticks of banana tree and a hard block of wood with a hollow center. He put the stick down on the center of the wood and begins to twirl it fast until the friction caused the coconut fibers to catch fire. As he twirled the stick he sang:

Give, o give me, thy hidden fire, thou banana tree!

Kindle a fire for me from thy splinters, thou banana tree!

Maui returned to the upper world, collected the necessary items, and showed the tribe elders how he could call the fire out from the wood. We can use the above saying as a chant or rhyme prior to any fire work or when lighting candles or fires.

Elementals

Salamanders

In the fire element Salamanders are made of the fire and are thought to be seen in the glowing embers or the flames of a fire. Similar to undines and sylphs, salamanders are believed to be made up of fire and not just living in it. It has even been said that the balls of light seen over marshes and swamps, frequently known as St. Elmo's fire and sometimes seen as paranormal evidence, are actually salamanders. In some myths it is believed that the salamanders taught mankind how to use fire. The amphibious creatures we normally associated with this word were named after the elemental, not the other way around. But, elemental salamanders are depicted as looking like lizards and often described as being partly human.

Iron

Iron is considered a magical metal because it is able to withstand fire and it is stronger than most metals. Believed to have originated in prehistoric times, it has long been used as a charm against evil spirits. Iron is a projective stone that is ruled by the planet Mars and corresponds to fire, the goddess Selene (Greek moon goddess; Roman equivalent is Luna) and the male gender. It can be used for protection, healing and strength.

The purest form is found only in meteorites and can be used in defense magick to repel negativity and ill-intent. It also stops the flow of psychic energy or can be used to heal the self when emotionally wrought or when under a psychic attack. Inscribe the symbol for Mars on a piece of iron and wear an amulet for protective and defensive magick or take iron nails and insert them into blue or white candles for protection. A talisman of iron is believed to increase physical strength and visualizing a large iron gate while doing a spell of protection will help keep negativity away.

Viewed as a magickal metal because it is found in meteors, in ancient Egypt it was called "metal from the skies" and in the Aztec civilization it was known as "a gift from the heavens." A specialist was needed to fashion the metal into shapes (blacksmiths) who then became magickal in their own right because of what they could do with metal. Weapons and horseshoes were the most common tools fashioned from iron and because of the lore with the metal and blacksmiths, horseshoes became a symbol of good luck that exists today.

Horseshoes

Horseshoes are considered good luck if hung in the homes or over doorways. These simple charms were also considered lucky because traditionally they have seven nail holes with which to affix the shoe to the horse. The number seven is considered a lucky, magickal or powerful number and is steeped with its own legends and superstitions in a wide variety of religions, belief systems and cultures.

Being made of iron and with seven holes, horseshoes make for a powerful combination as a protective amulet. I also have to wonder if the fact that it is an item belonging to a horse has any merit as well. Horses were a mode of transportation as well as an extra worker on the farm: they helped to carry goods, plow fields, and with grazing were natural lawn mowers. Prior to modern times and the advent of 'iron horses,' every family needed a horse for civilized living.

There is some contradiction as to whether it should be hung pointing up like a cup (right-side up) or if it should be hung pointing down (upside down), like an upside down U. Some legends say that when it is pointing up it acts like a cup and fills with good luck and fortune. Others say that upside down, especially if over a doorway, it allows the good luck to roll over the bottom of the U and flow down the stems to surround the doorway and prevent evil from entering the home.

Horseshoes are such a common superstitious lucky item that the American poet, James T. Fields (1817-1881) wrote a poem titled "The Lucky Horseshoe" which is a light-hearted and whimsical tale about the bad luck that befalls one farmer who found this lucky item on the road but mistakenly hung it upside down. Everything on his farm failed and when a stranger chanced upon the farm he asked to see the lucky shoe. At seeing it upside down he states:

"No wonder skies upon you frown—
You've nailed the horseshoe upside down!
Just turn it round, and soon you'll see
How you and Fortune will agree."

To read the full poem, or for more information about James T. Fields, head over to the website http://seacoastnh.com/poems/theluckyhorseshoe.html.

If planning on using a horseshoe for magickal purposes it can be hung over doorways, on fence posts, near or on a gate, or even on altars for spell work involving prosperity and money. Small charms that are shaped like horseshoes can be worn as jewelry or placed in a charm bag to increase prosperity. Its image can also be inscribed on a candle for spell work involving prosperity, good fortune and money.

It really depends on each person if they believe it should be portrayed upside down or right-side up, just so it makes sense on why it has to be that way. For myself, I would probably inscribe it on wax, draw it, or place it on an altar right-side up like a U so that the symbolism is there for the cup-shape to fill up with the good tidings. But, I like the idea of the inverted U over a doorway so that the good luck flows over the bottom hump and down around the door like a protective veil or coating. Either way, try these charms to further enchant the spell:

Right-Side Up

I place (or draw) this horseshoe facing up

so that good fortune will runneth over thy cup.

Upside Down

Turn the horseshoe upside down

And good fortune will flow all around.

Regardless of how it is placed, a horseshoe is one of the luckiest charms to have in or around the home and a great way to represent fire since it is forged in the heat of the element of fire.

Blacksmiths

Horseshoes were also considered a lucky item because they were made by blacksmiths, which was a very prestigious trade and the smithies were thought to be imbued with special powers. A blacksmith creates objects from iron or steel by forging the metal and the objects made were useful and necessary. More frequently, the items were weapons, tools or horseshoes but can be anything that can be made of iron or steel. Because they work with fire and iron (believed to be magickal) they were thought to have powers of healing the sick and if married by a blacksmith it would ensure that it would be a long and happy marriage.

A renowned profession, blacksmiths have a lore and superstitions surrounding them as well as their own Gods. Hephaestus is the Greek God of fire and fire-based arts such as metal work and is the son of Hera and Zeus (his Roman counterpart is Vulcan). He was a skilled artisan whose forge was a volcano and it is said he made most of the weapons of the Gods.

In other cultures we see Goibhniu, a Celtic God of blacksmith, as featured in myth of the Tuatha De Danann (the name given to pre-Christian deities or fairies). He was one of a trio of artisans or workers (Luchta and Criedhne being the other two) who are said to be the child of Goddess Brigid and Tuireann. When Christianity came around his lore was transferred to that of Gobban Saer (Gobban the Joiner) who became the legendary builder of churches or cathedrals. His Welsh counterpart is Gofannon and he is featured in the Mabinogion (an anthology of medieval Welsh stories).

In Christian mythology Tubal Cain (not to be confused with Cain, the brother of Abel) in Genesis is labeled as the original smith and there is speculation that he is revered and symbolized to this day in Freemasonry, which got its start from the masonry workers. Considering masonry and blacksmithing may go hand-in-hand at times and were both prestigious professions, this may not be too far from the truth. Also in Catholic lore we get Saint Eloi who is the patron saint of metalworkers.

Anglo-Saxon and Germanic lore give way to Wayland Smith, or the Old Norse equivalent known as Volundr. Wayland Smith is seen in the epic story of Beowulf, he fashioned the mail shirt worn by Beowulf, and the Poetic Edda (a collection of ancient Norse poems). He is thought to have god-like powers and it is interesting to note that while he was a blacksmith, which is of the fire element, he was born by a mermaid, which is of the water element. Finish mythology has Seppo Ilmarinen, also known as the Eternal Hammerer, who is a blacksmith and inventor in the Kalevala (a Finnish epic poem).

Blacksmiths were also the makers of Witch Bottles; commonly produced in the 15th-19th centuries, these were bottles that were filled with items to ward off negativity or evil witchcraft and were often made of metal or earthenware.

Fire Creatures

A person might not typically think of birds as being part of fire folklore, but there are numerous birds that die in a blaze of smoke and fire and are rejuvenated in the ashes. Because of this, a few select mythological birds can correspond to the fire element. Dragons are a more poplar fire-creature because they all seem to have the ability to breath fire and are often seen as destroying entire villages with their fiery breath. While science says that these creatures were created by the ancients discovering dinosaur bones and creating their own stories about what creatures of these bones would look like, there are many who believe that dragons did indeed exist at one time.

Phoenix

The Phoenix is perhaps the best known of the fire creatures and its name has even come to modern languages to mean something or someone beautiful and unique or as a symbol of death and resurrection, giving birth to the popular phrase "rising like a Phoenix from the ashes." This mythical bird resembles an eagle and lived for 500 years before burning itself to death on a pyre. From its ashes arose another Phoenix.

It is said that the Phoenix has a lifespan of 500 to 1000 years (depending on the source) and that at the end of its cycle it always goes out in a fiery death by building a nest of myrrh twigs that it then ignites. In the ashes a new Phoenix, or sometimes the egg, is born. The new Phoenix will live as long as its predecessor and repeat the process.

The Phoenix is such a popular fire bird that its stories take place in Phoenician, Egyptian and later Greek mythologies. In Egyptian lore it states that the new bird will embalm the ashes of the old self and place them in an egg made of myrrh which is then deposited into the city of Heliopolis. The Phoenix has even found its way into Catholicism in the way of art, literature and as a symbol of Christ's resurrection, immortality and life-after-death. Various other cultures also have fire-birds similar to the Phoenix in that they perish themselves at the end of their lifespan through fire.

Incidentally, the eagle in the seal on the back of a one-dollar bill is rumored to be that of a Phoenix, and not an eagle at all. This is based on what "conspiracy theorists" say about the influence Freemasons have on our culture and society and that the symbols on the back can be decoded as secret messages by the Freemasons. Since the 2nd half of the seal represents the all-seeing eye (said to be of Osiris, and Egyptian God) and a pyramid (a structure that while seen in Mexico is more largely associated with Egypt) this makes sense: all of the symbols in the circular add up to Egyptology rather than a mix of cultures.

In some part of Persia (Iranian) lore has the Simurgh which lives 1700 years before being reborn. It is believed to be so old that it has seen the destruction of the world three times and that it possesses the knowledge of all the ages. In other parts of Persia (Arabic/Turkish) the Huma bird is likened to the Phoenix and perishes itself in fire after a few hundred years. It is said that it never rests but flies continuously. It is both male and female with one wing and one leg belonging to each gender. It is an auspicious bird and if its shadow flies over a person it is considered a good omen.

Zhar-Ptitsa

Slavic folklore tell of a fire bird, the zhar-ptitsa ('heat bird') whose plumage glows so brightly that one plucked feather will still glow and light up an entire room. This fire bird is seen mainly in folklore where there is a quest to capture the bird either due to a traveler finding a feather and being charmed by it or a knight on a quest for the king. It follows along the classic lines of a folk or fairy tale and has parallels to folktales in other cultures such as "The Golden Bird" by the Brothers Grimm.

Vermillion Bird

The Vermillion Bird, a mythical spirit creature, is associated with the Wu Xing discussed earlier and is one of the four symbols of Chinese constellations. It represents fire, the south and the season of summer, thusly giving it the longer title of 'Vermillion Bird of the South' in some areas. Known as Nán Fāng Zhū Què (Chinese), Suzaku (Japanese) and Jujak (Korean) the Vermillion Bird is a very noble bird elegant in both appearance and its behaviors. It is very selective in where it perches and what it eats and due to its reddish-orange feathers and the association with fire it is often associated with the mythical Phoenix of ancient mythologies.

Dragons

Dragons have long been associated with fire because of the idea that they breath fire, this was a defense and offense mechanism and the people of the times feared that dragons would and could destroy entire villages, regions or crops. To date, there have not been any living or non-living creature believed to actually be able to produce fire-breath but many do spit poison that when landing on the skin or eyes might feel and burn like fire. Dragons can also be associated with the other elements as well since there are air dragons, earth dragons, and water dragons (sea serpents). Dragons are so popularized that they occupy home decor, children's television, popular media, T-shirts, jewelry and even have their own path of magick.

Gods and Goddesses

Fire is thought to be a gift from the Gods, so most ancient and moderns religions of the world feature it in their rituals somehow. Fire is a flame from the Gods so it must be treated with respect. The Greeks believed that Prometheus was feeling sympathetic to mortals and brought fire down from Mount Olympus and gave it to the humans. Other legends say that the very first flame ever used by mankind was stolen from Sol, Roman God of the son and seen as the personification of the sun today, and he is jealous of all attempts at imitating his power. This has given birth to the superstition that a fire cannot be started in direct sunlight.

Pele

Pele is a Hawaiian Goddess thought to live in or be made of volcanoes and lava. She is the Goddess of fire, lightning, dance, volcanoes and violence. Her home is the Halema'uma'u crater in the volcano of Kilauea, one of earth's most and continuously active. Belief in the Hawaiian Gods survived longer than most other polytheistic beliefs but started seeing an end in 1819 when Chieftess Kapiolani defied Pele by eating sacred 'ohelo berries without offering them to Pele first or asking for her permission. The chieftess also threw stones into a lava pit in direct defiance of the polytheistic beliefs and when she was not harmed by Pele she told her people it was time to accept Christianity.

Pele, sometimes referred to as Madame Pele, is still highly respected in Hawaii (as are many other gods) by the locals whether they are Christian, Buddhist or Shinto. Pele garners a great deal of respect, perhaps because people see the awesome power of the volcanoes, and legends continue today about Pele's existence. In one tale she is thought to be an old lady in white who walks the roads with her little dog in Kilauea National Park and passersby will stop to offer her a ride. Similar to ghost and urban legends of other states or locales (Resurrection Mary or the Vanishing Hitchhiker) when the driver peeks in the rear view mirror, the backseat is always empty. Also, within the park that is considered her domain, it is believed that she is so protective of her home that it is advised to not take any rocks home. And, for those hapless souls who have, they report misfortune and mishaps befalling them and have been known to send the rocks back to the park via postal services with pleas to replace it. Photos taken within the park are reported to have her face appear in the smoke, rocks and eruptions.

To honor Pele and the element of fire make a loose incense of three parts frankincense, three parts dragon's blood, one part red sandalwood, two parts orange peel, one part cinnamon and a few drops of clove oil. Burn the incense on a charcoal disc in a fireproof container and meditate or reflect on what she means and what is hoped to be gained by honoring the fire element. Try reciting the verse:

Mistress Pele, Goddess of fire;

help me to obtain all I desire.

This type of spell can be walked away from so it is best to burn the incense on an altar. As it burns it will take the magick up and out in the smoke. When the incense has burned out, dismiss the elements called (if they were) and clean up the charred incense or disc. Thank Pele for her aid in this spell.

Prometheus

In Greek myths he was a Titan (rulers prior to the Gods) who felt sorry for the mortals and stole fire from the Gods and gave it to the humans. He became a hero amongst humankind but was punished by his fellow Gods for his good deed. There is some speculation as to who he stole the fire from and how he obtained it. Some legends tell of Prometheus stealing the fire from the heavens (skies), placing it in a hollow tube and returning to earth with it. Others say that he made a torch from an apple-bough, went to the heavens and lit it at the Chariot of the Sun. Since the chariot of the sun belonged to Helios, a Titan, this would have been a very grave crime in deed. Finally, there is a story that he stole the fire from Zeus who then punished Prometheus by binding him to a rock where a large eagle ate at his liver a little each day.

Helios

In Greek Mythology he is the equivalent to the Roman God Sol and is a God of the sun. He drives his golden chariot across the sky from the east and across to the western sky each day. The golden chariot is the sun, making this myth an explanation of how the sun travels across the sky. Remember this is still in a time when it was believed that the sun moved, not the earth. Helios was one of the Titans (creators of the Greek Gods) and is often described as handsome and crowned with a shining aureole (halo) of sun.

Hades

Hades, the Greek God of the Underworld and husband to Persephone, ruled over the kingdom inhabited by the souls of the dead. The term has become synonymous with a place similar to that of the Christian version of Hell. However, Hades was the name of the God and his domain was known as the Underworld. Hades might be thought of as the Greek version of Hell or Satan but in Greek myth the Christian versions were not yet around and Hades was not viewed as a demon or devil.

He was God with the misfortune of ruling a desolate and bleak kingdom. Hades, often misrepresented by modern people as the Grim Reaper, did not decide who came to his domain and did not try to use trickery to gain souls (other than gaining his wife Persephone, who was very much alive) but rather he ruled over the ones that came there. The Grim Reaper, however, is said to not only choose but often causes the death of his victims.

Hades is most known for abducting Persephone and keeping her with him in the underworld while agreeing to let her remain in the world of man for six months out of the year if she would remain with him for the other six months. Her mother was so distraught during the months that

Persephone was gone that, like in the story of Proserpina, spring leaves when Persephone does and returns when she returns to the mortal world.

Agni

Agni is the Hindu and Vedic God and his name is Sanskrit for fire. Agni has three forms: lighting, fire and the sun and is one of the most important Vedic Gods. He is known as the God of sacrifices because he is a messenger from and to other Gods so the people would sacrifice to him and he would deliver the message. He has eternal youth because fire is re-lit everyday.

Vulcan

The Roman God of Fire and a blacksmith to the gods; it was believed the volcano was the chimney of his forge and that the lava fragments and smoke erupting from it came from the thunderbolts that he made for Jupiter, king of the gods and Mars, God of War. There are many gods resembling blacksmiths in various belief systems and all of them seem to consider volcanoes as their forges and are able to control the fires of them.

Magick for the Spiritist Witch
Section I

The Spirit Element

In writing this book I debated on having Spirit as a section since it is an ethereal and not a physical element. However, the spirit is just as important as the other elements and deserves recognition. Spirit, the ether or the void are hard concepts to develop as an element because it is incorporeal and intangible. It is not something we can touch, smell, see, hear or feel but we have to just assume or have faith that it is there in us and that it will go on, in whatever fashion that may be.

People of pagan or alternative faiths often will say that they are not religious but they are spiritual. For some, this might be confusing. How can a person be one or the other and not be both? Simply put, the two terms define completely separate ideas.

Religion is defined as an institutionalized system of beliefs and opinions concerning the existence, nature and worship of a deity. There are usually codes, creeds, a doctrine, a bible, a leader of the church (such as the Pope over Catholicism) and a set of instructions and regulations on when, how, where and why to believe. In this manner, Wicca can be defined as a religion even though there is no assigned head of the religion and no formal doctrine. It does, however, have a creed and a set of regulations and philosophies with which to direct worship. It is still very flexible as far as religions go, but it can still be defined as one since it is one of the more organized forms of paganism and is acknowledged by the United States Government as being one.

Spirituality, or being spiritual, is defined as relating to the soul or spirit in contrast to material things. It relates to religion or sacred things rather than worldly things, but it is not a religion itself or connected with one specific religion. For those still searching or questioning paths they might indeed feel spiritual in their beliefs but they do not have a defined religious path or set of belief systems. This could be otherworldly things such as having a soul, afterlife, deities, and our purpose in life or it can be for worldly things such as emotions, feelings, morals and personal mottos. A person does not have to have a defined religion, the name of a God or a religious doctrine to feel spiritual. All a person needs is to have is a sense of inner self worth, a desire to achieve and to feel good about who they are, where they are and what they are doing.

Magick for the Spiritist Witch
Section II

Correspondences

Correspondences for spirit are hard to determine because it is incorporeal and cannot be relied upon by the five senses. It is also, as an element, intertwined with the soul in beliefs that it is not its own thing like the other elements. Most of the correspondences dealing with the spirit come from beliefs of the soul and its residence inside and outside of our physical planes. If pressed to give it specific characteristics I would say that its color would be indigo (the invisible color in a rainbow) or that it would be colorless, and that it would have no shape to it. I have created the concept of bringing the arms into the chest (fists near the heart) as a hand-sign to go along with the other hand-signs when in a ritual. Also, spirit could be said to be represented by a shape of the human form either in a picture, poppet, or stick drawing.

Please note that there are more correspondences here than in the other sections, I tried to show a variety of views of spirit as an ethereal void, as an element and also as an incorporeal entity. It is interesting to see all the differences and similarities in the cultures and may help a person to achieve their own views on what our spirit is and where it goes.

Traditional

Spirit is seen as the 5th element and is represented on a single point of the pentagram. In Wiccan or pagan traditions, the point it at the top signifying that the spirit, or soul, is above all materialism and in Satanism or sub-cultures of it, the point is at the bottom signifying that materialism comes before the soul. The center of an altar is also considered the directional point of spirit, in rituals the person representing spirit or the Ritual Leader my stand in the center of the circle. On a personal altar, the spirit can also be represented with a god and goddess statue or candles and for ancestral worship or altars; the spirits of the ancestors are the spirit element. For solitaire rituals the person performing the ritual makes up the 5th element of spirit.

Platonic (Plato) and Aristotle Thought

Platonic philosophy states that each person has three parts: Logus, Thymos and Eros. The Logus is the mind or reason; it corresponds to the charioteer and directs balance between thymos and eros. It is what drives us to acts of glory and bravery and if left unchecked it can lead to 'hubris;' one of the most fatal of flaws in the Greek Law (referring to ancient Greek legal system) otherwise known as pride in the Seven Deadly Sins of Christianity. Thymos is our emotions and personalities and Eros, much like the Greek God Eros (God of love), is our base needs such as food, social interaction, shelter and sexual appetites.

Aristotle included spirit as Aether in his system of the classic elements of Ionic philosophy. His reasoning was that the four elements of earth, air, water and fire tend to change but no change had been observed in the celestial regions. He determined that it had no qualities as it was neither hot nor cold, or wet nor dry and it was incapable of change. Spirit as the ethereal void is believed to be a material filling a region of the universe around the terrestrial sphere of the planets. It is the nothingness from which we sprung, the outer edge of creation and outer space.

Gullah

The Gullah culture is a group of people that are of African descent residing along the coasts of South Carolina, Georgia, and northern Florida and on their neighboring sea islands. Their language is similar to the Creole of Louisiana and is English with heavy influences of several West African languages. Their belief system is mainly of a monotheistic Christian version but similar to the Voodoo of Haitian-influenced areas, Gullah has a fair mix of West African religious beliefs tossed in.

Their magick mainly revolves around 'superstitious magick' for protection and warding off curses and hexes. A Gullah belief that is a favorite of mine is that the body has both a soul and a spirit. The soul goes on to either Heaven or Hell and the spirit stays in the earthly plains to act as a guide to those left behind. My brother and I further expounded on this theory by saying that if the soul went to Heaven then the remaining spirit would be seen as good by those still in the earthly realms and if it went to Hell it would a a bad spirit.

Hinduism and Buddhism

In the tattva it is symbolized by a black circle. Spirit, or as some pagans prefer to call it 'The Akashi' (Hindu word for spirit), is linked to Brihaspati, and otherwise known as Jupiter. The ancient Vedic culture believed the soul to be symbolized by the element of fire. (The Vedic belief system is of the Hindu religion relating to the Vedas, which are a collection of Aryan hymns dating around 6th century BCE.) Hindus also believe in reincarnation which means that a soul will inhabit many different physical hosts before moving on to the otherworld.

Buddhist believes revolve around the idea that all things in the universe are in a constant state of flux and ever-changing. They don't deny the existence of the soul but rather deny the existence of it as a permanent entity; such as a spirit, ghost or angelic being. The belief is that the soul moves fairly quickly onto other bodies or physical hosts after leaving its previous one.

Basic Christianity

There are many different sects of Christianity, literally hundreds, and it is nearly impossible to specifically define each of their beliefs of the soul and afterlife, but in general Christians have an ontological view in which the soul is a distinct form yet it is integrally connected with the physical body. People's souls are judged by God and then sentenced to either eternal paradise (Heaven) or eternal damnation (Hell) and there is no reincarnation but rather the soul ends up in one or the other.

Some sects don't believe in the existence of spirits or ghosts, such as Mormon beliefs, and that if a person does see an apparition it is only a trick of Satan; even if the apparition is a dearly departed family or friend and is very peaceful. Whereas other sects are more relaxed and may believe in apparitions, but limit it to only family or friends who can come back to warn or guide us but they may not believe in an actual haunting. Other groups, such as Catholics, believe that not only are they possible, but believe them to be demonic possession.

Islam

The Islamic religion is based on monotheism and the word of God as revealed to Muhammad in the 7th century. There are seven layers to Heaven and depending on the good deeds depends on how far a person ascends into Heaven. It is believed that the soul does not perish with the physical body but rather it is extracted from it and enters a suspended sleep known as Barzakh. It is in a parallel universe that the human mind cannot begin to comprehend and there it stays in a cold sleep until it is judged by Allah. Islamic believe also states that the soul is breathed into the embryo forty days after conception.

Sikh

In the Sikh faith, which is a division of the Hindu faith that broke away in the 16th century advocating a monotheistic doctrine but still incorporating aspects of Islamic beliefs, the soul (or atma) is part of the universal soul or God (parmatma). Based on this belief, we could say that the reason why man today is continuously searching for a God, a deity, a universal spirit or religion is because we are like lost children looking for our parent.

Remember the Random House book "Are You My Mother" by P.D Eastman and the little bird who hatched but its mother was nowhere around. He went to cows, dogs, and every other barnyard animal he could find looking for his mother. It can be said that we are like that bird, looking for our parent soul and searching each religion until we feel that connection.

Taoist

Taoists believe that the soul has two parts, a yin (Po) and a yang (Hun) and that Po is linked to the dead body and that Hun is linked to the ancestral tableau. This is similar to the Gullah belief mentioned earlier in which the soul goes onto the afterlife and the spirit resides on earth providing aid to descendants.

Egyptian

The Egyptians go farther than the Gullah and Taoist beliefs and state that the soul has five parts: the heart (Ib), the shadows (Sheut), the name (Ren), the individual personality (Ba) and the life force (Ka).

Magick for the Spiritist Witch
Section III

Tools of Spirit

Poppet

I have decided that poppets are perfect for the spirit element because they resemble the human form and therefore, take on the spirit of the person they are made for. Inanimate objects believed to have a soul or spirit is a form of animism. Poppets, or sometimes referred to as Voodoo dolls, are not to be confused with puppets, corn dollies, or kitchen witch dolls. Puppets are simply toys or for entertainment; corn dollies are made of corn husks and were used to ensure plentiful harvests; and kitchen witches are a folk art doll hung in homes to protect the house, the kitchen and its residents.

Poppets are instruments of magick that are used to cause something to occur to a particular person. This is a form of sympathetic magick, which means that the action by the practitioner resembles what they want the outcome to be. Sprinkling water outside resembles rain (maybe this is why it always rains after washing a car) and blowing on a clothesline resembles wanting the wind to blow as mentioned in Magick for the Air Witch earlier.

Often made of clay, cloth or wax a poppet is made to represent a specific person and made in that person's image. Even a single candle can be used if the practitioner puts forth intent into that candle to resemble a particular person, or carves an image of their likeness in the wax. Clay or wax poppets are often sculpted or formed by hand with items of a lock of hair or herbs being worked into the medium to further empower it. In Voodoo, blood or fingernail clippings from the person are often added. The wax or clay figure is then moved, melted, or stuck with pins to perform injury to the intended person.

Cloth poppets are usually made by cutting two pieces of cloth in a Gingerbread Man style, flipping them so the back side of the fabric is out and sew all around the edges, leaving a small corner for turning the material and stuffing the doll. The doll can be stuffed with herbs, feathers, natural fibers, and various items can be added such as personal objects or gemstones. The herbs and gemstones should correspond to the intent of the poppet.

After the doll has been created it can further be decorated with bits of cloth for clothing (especially clothing from that person), ribbons, and drawing or sewing on a face. Then, in a simple ritual it will be consecrated and named for that person by reciting words such as "by this figure and all that I do, I do unto (name)."

Most people associate poppets with Voodoo dolls, imagining a witch doctor somewhere poking pins into a stuffed doll, or with evil witchcraft that has intent to harm or control someone. But, poppets can be used for good. Cloth poppets are more popular today for healing purposes and are stuffed with herbs of healing or even a picture or memento of that person. Then, they could either perform Reiki on the doll or just focus healing energy onto it. If the intended person is afflicted only in one area, such as a broken leg, healing energy can be focused on that same part of the doll.

Also, it is common in the pagan community to say "I'll light a candle for you" when someone mentions a tragedy or hard times in their life. While the ritual is simpler and not as engaging as making a poppet, the candle still represents the person and by lighting it we are hoping to send our healing vibes and positive thoughts to the person who needs it. Candles used in this fashion can be anointed with the appropriate oils or the name of the person can be carved into it.

There is even an article in Llewellyn's Magickal Almanac 2009 titled "Magical You" by Paniteowl that describes how to make a personal poppet and add to it things that need to be gone or purged, such as bad habits; think of it as a New Year's resolution doll. One of the examples in the article included a person attaching a cigarette to the doll in an effort to stop smoking. Participants were required to carry the doll for six weeks and then at a Sabbat it was tossed into the fire. Burning objects with an intent of expunging bad habits is a form of banishing and was mentioned earlier in Magick for the Fire Witch. Keep in mind that poppets are a very serious form of magick and since they represent a human and should not be played with lightly.

Poppets have a long history dating back to at least 1100 BCE where records indicate that a treasury official and harem of Pharaoh Ramses III used a poppet to bring about his death. There are even indications as recent as the middle 1600's of poppets resembling notable figures being found soon after that person's untimely death. Poppets were so feared as instruments of Satan that in Puritan America (16th and 17th centuries) ordinary dolls were outlawed in most colonies because they were too close to poppets and anything with a human visage was sacrilegious. Dolls or poppets were often used against a person to proof their illegal activities involving witchcraft.

Pendulum

Pendulums are great tools to represent spirit since they are used to communicate with literal spirits (ghosts) and to connect with the spiritual world. A pendulum really just a fancy word for any weight on a string; more accurately, it is a weight hung from a fixed point so that the weight can swing freely back and forth under the influences of energy or gravity.

Pendulums are more commonly used to communicate with the otherworld (a form of divining or scrying) or for dowsing (using an object to find lost or hidden things) but they were also commonly used by early midwives to determine genders of unborn babies. Gendering with a pendulum was often the only way to determine the sex of a baby and people swore by its accuracy. To check the gender of unborn babies, hold the pendulum over the stomach and wait for it to swing. A circle means the baby is a girl and if it swings in a straight line it is a boy. A pendulum can also be used by writing the alphabet in an arc (not a circle) and asking it to spell out a word or name. The pendulum will swing to each letter of the word or phrase. This is time consuming and not suitable for wanting long answers, only if short words or phrases can be achieved.

Pendulums can be as simple as ring or key attached to a string or even any ordinary necklace. Metaphysical stores sell fancy ones ranging from quartz crystal or gemstones to metal or any other material that is weighted. Most pendulums have some sort of point at the end, this is not really necessary but it can make for easier divining. For awhile, prisms were a common household décor. They were simple quartz crystals cut or faceted and hung on a string with a hook or key ring attachment. Often placed in windows, they were meant to catch the sunlight and dance rainbows across the room. These are really just a form of a pendulum and would go unnoticed by non-pagans when hanging in the window.

There seems to be a 'debate' in the pagan community as to how to interpret the swing of a pendulum. Individually, everyone has their own opinion of how to use one, especially as to which way means 'yes' and which way of the swing means 'no' and are usually very adamant about it. However, I have dad pendulums swing in all sort of ways: clockwise, counter-clockwise, north to south, east to west, and even in diagonals. The best method is to ask the pendulum. This can be done in one of two ways: 1) ask the pendulum "show me yes" and then double-check it by asking it to show no, or 2) ask a question known to be true "is today Wednesday?" and then ask a question that is false "is today Friday?" In the book "Dowsing for Beginners," author Richard Webster goes into more detail about this and pendulum use in general.

Magick for the Spiritist Witch
Section IV

Working with Spirit

Working with spirit requires knowing thyself and knowing the deities that are being honored or worship. It requires a deep connection and for many people can be uncomfortable because inner demons may have to be recognized and dealt with. On an altar it can be represented by a statue of a God and Goddess or candles that represent them, usually gold is for the God (sun) and silver for the Goddess (moon). Spirit can also be represented by a pentagram because it represents all of the elements. As previously discussed, the top point is spirit and in paganism the point, or spirit, is always on the top to show that the spirit is greater and more important than all material things. A pentagram can be placed in the center of the altar or hanging on a wall behind it. However, the spirit is always present in every ritual or spell work because it is present in the practitioner.

The spirit is the soul or essence of a person; their behaviors, thoughts and personality. It is what make us unique and is an incorporeal, eternal occupant of our physical self. Working with spirit, in some cases, may also mean to work with deceased spirits or ancestral spirits. Spiritualism is a term applied to the belief and practice of communicating with the spirits of the deceased whether it is through necromancy, pendulums, spirit boards or séances.

When working with literal spirits, that is of ghosts, be as respectful and as polite as if communicating with a human, never call up anything that can't be controlled or banished, and never assume that only good spirits will come forth, even if that is all that is called on. When working with living things such as other people (in group rituals) or animals (as familiars) always adhere to the "harm ye none" creed and respect each living thing.

Indoor Spaces

Inside, spirit can be evident within the practitioner. If the other four elements are on the altar, the five elements are present because the practitioner is always there performing the spell or ritual. A person can also tap into their inner self, but this takes the proper visualization and a trance-like meditative state. It is basically allowing the subconscious mind to take over and send messages to or solve problems for the conscious mind.

Indoor spaces honoring the spirit might also include an ancestral altar, or one that honors household spirits, or just lighting a simple white candle. On an altar the God and Goddess candles can be lit during an invoking or calling of the other elements by inviting the God and Goddess to the "party" (either a solitaire or group ritual). Remember, High Magick is asking the gods to do the work and Low Magick is inviting them to the party but the practitioner is doing the work.

Outdoor Spaces

Many group rituals are done outside for the sake of having enough room and would be done in the same manner as the solitaire ritual inside in that the elements are all being called to the circle. The participants in the circle all represent spirit, but it could also be represented by statues or objects placed in the center of the circle. Some group rituals might have one person to represent spirit and he or she will stand in the center of the circle.

Spirit can also be represented outside by having fairy or spirit houses. These are small houses that are meant to be open invitations to beings of the spiritual and fairy realms. Often decorative, these houses make great yard or garden ornaments and are also a neat way to invite positive spirits to the home.

Rituals and Spell work

In working with spirit when defined as the God and Goddess, High Magick is used. This is for serious issues that take an effort greater than what the practitioner can give with a simple spell. In my group, we did a High Magick ritual to aid us in being recognized as a non-profit group. Naturally, we still have to apply for the proper permits and tax exemptions, but we felt we needed some divine assistance to aid us in being accepted in the community and letting our efforts run smoothly. Most often, invoking the God or Goddess is done at Sabbats, group rituals or during full and new moons.

Full and New moons rituals are called either "Drawing down the Sun" or "Drawing down the Moon". In the "Drawing down the Sun" the God is invoked and his energies are drawn down into the High Priest, who has entered a trance-like state. In the "Drawing down the Moon" ritual the opposite happens; the energies of the Goddess are drawn down into the High Priestess. For more information on either ritual I recommend reading the works of Doreen Valiente or Gerald Gardner who both go into more detail on these rituals.

Altars

On an altar, the God commands the right side of the space and is represented by the color gold, a male gendered statue, or the sun. The Goddess is represented by the color silver, a female gendered statue or the moon and is on the left. Together, they can be represented by a mortar and pestle (with the pestle resting inside the mortar) or by placing an athame into a chalice. As an element all on its own, and not as a deity, it can be represented by either the pentagram or a white candle placed in the center of the altar. I have even placed offerings in the center to represent both the spirit and the intent.

The offering should represent the needs such as grains or foods for prosperity or coins for money. Spirit can also be represented in the center of an altar with a white candle; white being the color of the spiritual world and also of protection. When calling on spirit remember to hold arms crossed and over the chest with hands in fists (like the sign for love), or place palms together in front of the heart like in a prayer pose. There does not seem to be a sign for spirit in rituals, so I have created this one as a way to show that spirit is either invited (in the form of the deities) or acknowledged as being present (in the practitioner).

Spirit Altar

Having a spirit altar is not going to be constructed in the same manner as other elemental altars. They will either serve a purpose of honoring ancestral spirits or to honor a specific deity, with that deity fitting intent such as love, protection, prosperity or money.

October 31st is a common time when we see ancestral altars or shrines in a variety of religions. Halloween has become a fun and festive time and the decorations that adorn houses and neighborhoods are not considered ancestral worship. But, there is resurgence in worshipping and honoring our ancestors with those who celebrate Samhain (Celtic version of Halloween).

Hispanic and Mexican cultures honor the dead in the graveyards for Dio de Los Muertos by having picnics near the grave of a loved one or decorating the grave. In churches or cathedrals a multitude of white candles are lit and people go to remember or hold vigils for their deceased for All Soul's Day (celebrated on November 1st).

In Voodoo and Catholicism, altars or shrines are set up with many white candles and quite often, more so in Voodoo, other artifacts or personal items are added to the altar. Shrines are defined as any holy place of worship associated with a person or event. Often we see public shrines that are set up at places where tragic events happened such as the collapse of the Twin Towers in New York, USA or for prominent people and celebrities. Two of the more recent and famous shrines were created in England when Princess Diana died in a car crash (1997) in which a shrine was created near Buckingham Palace and also in Australia for "Crocodile Hunter" Steve Irwin (2006) when he died suddenly while filming for his television series.

In a personal home, an altar can be set up to honor deceased family members by placing pictures or mementos of them on the altar and lighting a few candles. Or, an altar with white candles and a picture of the person can be set up to send healing vibes to someone suffering an illness or tragedy. Always ask the person (if possible) if they mind having an altar in their honor and when they no longer need blessings, respectfully take down the altar. Keeping an altar up for a living person can start to creep over the edge to stalking and might not be appreciated by the honoree.

An altar can also be set up to honor spirit by using its definition as a deity. Place the candles for God and Goddess on the appropriate sides of the altar. Pictures of the God and Goddess can be added as can any other object that corresponds to the deities.

Magick for the Spiritist Witch
Section V

The Incorporeal Soul

Debating what to include in this book seems to be a common theme and a section on spirits and ghosts was no exception. I have a very large curiosity and fascination with the paranormal realms, and in the end, inclusion of this chapter won out because I feel that to know the element of spirit is to know the soul within (and without) our physical bodies. As stated earlier, if standing at an altar, the practitioner is the spirit element. The spirit is also evident in our ancestors and in the deities.

Ancestral Worship
Ancestral worship is seen heavily in religions influenced by West-African cultures such as Voodoo, Native American and Gullah. It is a form of worship in which a practitioner will summon their ancestral guardians for guidance and protection or to honor their passing. All of the cultures mentioned highly respect the wisdom of not only their deceased ancestors but also of their living ancestors. Ancestral worship is to be used for serious inquiries only as it can take a lot of energy out of the practitioner as well as the spirits called upon; definitely not a ritual to use to ask what color shirt to wear (read more about this further on). The ashes of the deceased also have an important part in ancient or tribal cultures, but are not often used by pagans of today.

As learned earlier, Shu is the Egyptian God of Air and holder of the sky and he can lift up the spirits of the dead so that they might rise up to heaven. For recently deceased friends or family, try a simple ritual such as lighting a white candle and asking that Shu take them on up gently. This can be done at anytime, but there is a tradition of lighting candles on Samhain in honor of the recently deceased.

Within the Pueblo Native Americans, ancestral spirits are known as Kachina and were believed to be the religious or wise men of the tribes that became these ancestral spirits to aid in guiding the descendants. Today, Kachinas are depicted as carved wooden dolls and often sold to tourists but traditionally they were religious icons in the homes of Hopi and Zuni Native Americans.

Ancestral Worship Ritual

To create a portal for contacting ancestral spirits, a person needs an altar dedicated to that spirit-person (such as a grandparent). A personal altar can be used if some alterations are made to it, I re-do my altars for every purpose or Sabbat, or a separate altar can be created just for this purpose. Most of us probably do not have the ashes of the deceased and may be leery of using ashes anyway, but a lock of hair, an object of value to them, or a small sample of dirt from their grave will work fine for placing on an altar.

Cast a protective circle by calling the elements and casting a circle. In the center of the altar, place a fireproof container and place a lit charcoal disc in it. When it is glowing red hot add dried lavender, cinnamon bark, and wormwood onto the disc. Call out to benevolent and loving ancestor spirits (remember there is no guarantee only benevolent spirits will answer) and recite the following verse:

Ancestors of my blood and spirits of ancestral love,

As it is from below and above,

Spirits of family who wish me only well,

Be welcomed to the circle at the sound of the bell.

Ring a bell three times and welcome the ancestor's spirit. Ask the question either verbally or mentally and focus on it until an answer has been received. When the communication feels complete, or has been

broken, ask for them to return to their world with this verse:
> *Ancestors of my blood and spirits that ebb and flow*
> *As it is from above and below,*
> *Spirits of family, who advised me well,*
> *Return to the otherworld at the sound of the bell*

Ring the bell three times to send them back, then open the circle and dismiss the elements. In most rituals, a person walks away from an altar (after cutting a symbolic door) and has a bit of food and drink to keep the energy up. But, at an ancestral altar this is not advisable as the spirits of the ancestors (and others) can come through and the longer a portal is open the better chance they have of coming through, and sticking around once the portal is closed.

Sabbats or Holidays of the Dead

Halloween

If thinking of a "day of the dead" most people will associate the holiday of Halloween on October 31st. This is the modernized and traditional holiday for both the Celtic Samhain and Catholic All Hallows Eve. In fact, Halloween is a condensed word for Hallow's E'en (Hallows Evening). Today, it is thought of more as a children's holiday, a time to wear costumes and for parties. Costumes range from the scary to unusual to celebrities and characters from popular media. Children visit neighborhood houses, ring the doorbells and cries of "trick or treat" are heard throughout the land as children ask for candy. Adults hit up the bars, clubs and parties hoping to have some fun and win a costume contest.

Beltaine and Samhain

These are two of the major Sabbats in which the veils are the thinnest between the two worlds. Beltaine is on May 1st but usually celebrated at 12 midnight on April 30th, which is also known as Walpurgis Nacht (night) in Germanic lore. Samhain (pronounced SOW-ain) is October 31st, of what is traditionally called Halloween or the Catholic version of "All Hallow's Eve." In the southern hemisphere both these dates are reversed with Samhain on May 1st and Beltaine on October 31st. Both are a time when the spirits can cross back and forth with greater ease, but usually only Samhain is honored as a festival to the dead and Beltaine with more frivolity and honoring summer. But, because of the thinner veil, this is the ideal time to practice ancestral worship or spirit communication.

An altar should be set up and all prepared prior to the magickal workings so that the practitioner can be calling upon the ancestor's at the stroke of midnight. This can be set up in the ways previously mentioned or simply by placing an extra plate of food out for ancestors. Another tradition that has become quite common among pagans on Samhain is to light one white candle for each person that has died in the past year (from October to October). A large tray or bucket can be filled up with sand and then each person can light a tea light candle and say a quick prayer or blessing. The belief is that the prayers or messages will travel with the smoke and go to the deceased's spirit.

Dio de Los Muertos

Having lived in New Mexico, I learned of this Hispanic holiday and while I have never celebrated it, I love the customs behind it. It is like a combination of Halloween and the "All Soul's Day" and is celebrated on November 1st. This is a time to gather family and friends together to honor and remember the deceased. Families often build private altars in their homes, on graves or have picnics in graveyards. Candy in the form of skulls and skeletons are made and given to the children as a treat and the decorations are usually of skulls and skeletons. It is a celebration of the person's life rather than a mourning of their death.

Ancient Aztec's had a similar feast that was dedicated to the "Lady of the Dead", otherwise known as Goddess Mictecacihuatl. She is usually depicted as having a skull face and a skirt made from serpents; her only purpose is to guard the bones of the dead. It is believed that the bones of past world were used to make the first humans of this world and, in turn, our bones will be used to make the beings of some future world. Therefore, the bones had to be guarded to ensure that future generations would exist.

In Portugal and Spain All Saint's Day coincides with the "Dio de los innocents" or "Day of the Innocents" and is the first of the "Day of the Dead" celebrations and one in which deceased children and infants are honored. Flowers and trinkets are placed on graves and feasts are usually had by family members.

All Saint's Day and All Souls' Day

All of the holidays or celebrations that take place around October 31st tend to merge into one another in their customs and beliefs. Halloween, as mentioned in the Samhain section, is an Americanized version of a celebration of the dead. The word itself is derived from Hallow's Eve, which is another term for All Saints Day. Hallow simply means something or someone that is considered holy or sacred. The evening, therefore, was considered sacred. Today, the traditions of trick-or-treating, parties, and costumes resemble very little of the original traditions.

All Saint's Day is celebrated on November 1st in Western Christianity and the first Sunday after Pentecost in Eastern Christianity. It is in honor of all of the Saints of the Catholic Church, both the unknown and known. It is a commemoration of all who have attained their beatific vision whereas All Soul's Day is in honor of those who haven't yet been purified or reached Heaven.

In the United Methodist Church, All Saint's Day has been changed to honoring members of the local congregations that have passed away in the previous year. A candle is lit by the Acolyte (assistant) and the person's name is called. A liturgical prayer is then offered up to all the souls. This is similar to the Samhain tradition of lighting one candle for every family member or close friend that has passed away in the previous year.

All Soul's Day is a Roman Catholic celebration based on the simple doctrine that the souls of the faithful that have not been cleansed of venial or fully atoned sins, or cannot gain the beatific vision may be helped along by prayer from the living. This relates loosely to the Day of the Dead celebration in that people are honoring those that they knew in life rather than long-dead Saints and one in which its origins are related to the ancestral worship of both Asians and Native Americans. In Brittany people would go to cemeteries at night to kneel bareheaded at the graves of their loved ones. They would also anoint the tombstones with holy water or pour libations of milk on them.

Ethereal Beings

The word 'apparition' is a generic term for more ghosts, spirits, angels or demons. Apparitions can take the form of mists, ectoplasm, orbs, vortexes, disembodied sounds, full-body apparitions, or EVP's and even include guardian spirits, angels or spirit familiars.

Ghosts and Spirits

There is much debate on which term is correct with some ideas leaning towards the term 'spirit' being more politically correct. I heard a psychic on television once state that she believed ghosts were the souls who had not crossed-over and were haunting a place or person and that spirits were the souls who had crossed-over but were allowed to return to earth in order to communicate to their descendants as a way of reassurance to them, to give advice, or to warn them of dangers. The term "spirit-person" has become widely accepted and popular among paranormal investigators largely due to the television show "Most Haunted" out of the UK in which paranormal investigators film real investigations of haunting.

There are endless myths, superstitions, movies or television shows, and ghost stories to appeal to any paranormal fan. Some of the superstitions range from the bizarre such as covering one's mouth during a yawn to keep spirits from entering the body, to the cute superstition of not slamming doors as it can catch spirits and cause them harm. There are ideas about how to get rid of them such as carrying a cross made of Rowan to making noise and opening all the doors on New Year's Eve to chase them away.

There are two types of haunting accepted by most paranormal investigations: residual and intelligent. Residual haunting are described a "echoes of the past" in which memories or feelings are imprinted within the energy and life force of a home or area and can replay a certain scene at certain times. The times might vary from occurring every night, to once a year or even longer, but they are incapable of interacting with the living or current events. Intelligent haunting are spirits that are aware of the living and can communicate with them. Whether they know they are dead or not will depend on the specific entity, but they are capable of interaction and are more frightening because of this.

Ghosts can also take the form of disembodied voices, full-figure apparitions, orbs, and streaks of light, shadows, or just a particular body part (often a face). Orbs are balls or pockets of energy and can be ghosts or other paranormal energies in an isolated spot. They are often the most misdiagnosed in photography since bugs, water droplets and a number of other things can create orbs.

Ghosts or spirits can be evil or good, helpful or harmful. Much skepticism still exists about the existence of ghosts and paranormal investigators and despite some awesome equipment and evidence; skeptics will say that if they existed science would prove it. But, skeptics ignore that science already is starting to prove their existence with EVP's (electric voice phenomenon), video and picture footage, EMF detectors (electromagnetic fields) and thermal image cameras. Eventually, they may be proven without a shadow of a doubt. At one time controlling fire was paranormal until man learned how to do it and harnessing electricity was impossibility until Ben Franklin proved it could be done. All of the technology we have today would have been "paranormal" to those of the past or believed impossible until science figured out how to do it and we are far from having discovered or invented everything. Just because science hasn't proven the paranormal world yet, doesn't mean it won't.

Angels and Demons

Over 50% of the world's population believes in angels and the earliest record of angel sightings is 10,000 years old. They frequently in many prominent Biblical stories such as Gabriel heralding the birth of Christ, but have also worked their way into home décor, popular media, and other belief systems have some form of guardian or benevolent spirits. Folklore has angels depicted as playing harps or trumpets, wearing white gowns with white feathered wings and always playing on tufts of clouds.

Angels mainly take place in Judeo-Christian or monotheistic beliefs systems, but are not limited to monotheism. Angels are thought to be either divine beings who act as messengers to God (monotheism beliefs) or as guardian angels or spirit guardians (many pagan beliefs acknowledge spirit guardians). Guardians are believed to be a spirit or angel who has come down from the Heavens to give aid to humans. They are accredited with saving lives or bringing vital information to those still in the earthly plane and many people believe that their family members or friends have become their personal guardian angel. Sometimes, a spirit guardian takes the form of a beloved pet.

Cherubs are a depiction of 'baby angels' with a chubby face, wearing a diaper, and often with a harp or bow and arrows. Cupid is an icon of the American version of St. Valentine's Day and he is said to be a cherub, but pagans know him as the Roman God of Love, Eros is his Greek counterpart. In the ancient mythologies the god is in adult form but still with wings and believed to be able to cause two people to fall in love. Cupid is the son of Venus and Eros is the son of Aphrodite, both are goddesses of love. However, in true Christianity, a cherub is the eighth-highest of the medieval hierarchy of the angels. The orders in least to greatest are as follows: angels, archangels, principalities, powers, virtues, dominions, thrones, cherubim and seraphim.

Angels are often seen just before or during a tragic event and give people a calming feeling that aids them in surviving the tragedy. Angels can also come in dreams to people and either act as a warning or to bring a message. In the dream world, they may not resemble the image we think of when we hear the word 'angel.'

For example, I am still trying to figure out if a dream I had was about angels, or maybe it was a result of writing this section. Anyway, in it, I was living in a big house and hanging out with Steven Tyler, lead singer of Aerosmith and David Boreanaz, actor. What do these men have to do with angels? The band Aerosmith had a hit song titled "Angel" and the band logo has wings around the name. Boreanaz played a character on television named "Angel" of both the "Buffy the Vampire" series and its spin-off "Angel." Remember, angels in dreams can come in many forms so be on the look-out for obscure symbolism.

Demons are a Christian conception of evil (even though there are evil entities in other belief systems) and are often said to be minions of the Devil. They were angels that fell from grace and are now viewed as evil beings set out to carry on the deeds or orders of their new master. In the Mormon belief there is no acknowledgement of ghosts or spirits whether good or bad, all spirits are the product of the devil and are demons. They are his way of tricking people away from God.

Demons are said to be able to possess people and the Catholic Church still acknowledges and approves exorcisms each year. They are featured more prominently in Catholicism than any other religion and are a thing to be feared. Horror movies, such as "The Exorcist" (1973), play upon people's fear of demons and possession. They enter a person's body and can cause drastic physical, mental and emotional changes to them.

Demons are usually depicted having horns on their head or as hideous beings and there seems to be a wide variety of them. So-called 'experts' have tried to count the number of demons in existence. In 1467 Alphonse de Spina predicted that since there were 400 million angels, at least one-third of them had fallen from grace. This calculated to 1,333,316,666 demons in existence. However, in 1583 Johann Weyer estimated that there were 666 legions of demons with 6,666 demons in each legion and each one ruled by 66 hellish dukes, princes or kings. This brought his total to over 4 million demons.

Demons are also believed to be capable of procreation, so within the past 500 years since the last demon census, the total now must be insurmountable. It was also deemed at one time that all of the pagan deities were also demons. Hindusim has at least 10,000 various deities and the Egyptians have just about as many. Also, factor in all of the other pre-Christian beliefs systems and by now Hell must be a very crowded place indeed!

Household Spirits

These are spirits that dwell within each home, whether they are considered spirits of the dead, earthly beings such as elves or fairies, pets, or an incorporeal form of the house itself, they can be honored to ensure protection, prosperity and happiness comes to those residing in the home.

To honor household spirits of any form, place small offerings to them similar to placing offerings to the God and Goddess on an altar. The traditional foods of choice are any form of grain (pure grain, muffins or breads), milk, fruit and wine. Incense can also be burned as a way to honor them as can white candles or placing little trinkets near where it is believed that they reside. If an area is not easily discernible, then place coins or trinkets on an altar with some white candles, incense and foods. Hanging dried herbs or setting potted plants near the front door will also honor or attract household spirits: bittersweet (healing and protection); corn (luck and fertility); ferns (a favorite of fairies); goldenrod (prosperity and health); pine (the ancients believed it represented life force); and garlic (protection).

Spells and Rituals

There are a number of spells to conjure up spirits and most of them tend to take on a horror movie Hollywood affect. It is not wise to conjure up anything that cannot be controlled or banish, and there are never guarantees as to what or who will come forth (I know I've said this, but it bears repeating). No one invites a questionable stranger into their home or gives out personal information over the internet so don't invite paranormal trouble into a home or spiritual life. Instead, here are a couple of recipes for seeing spirits that already exist in a place and a couple for banishing unwanted energies or entities.

Spirit Oil

This spirit oil can be used for anointing candles in exorcisms, séances, to counter spells, increase clairvoyance or to purify and protect against evil intentions. Mix one tablespoon of each: powdered Orris root, dried Solomon's seal, dried rosemary, and a small pinch of powdered jade or turquoise (gemstones can be powdered by rubbing the stone on a metal nail file). Add in three drops sandalwood oil and mint oil and fill the rest of the bottle with a safflower oil base. Store in an airtight container for three weeks in a cool, dark place and then strain the mixture through cheesecloth.

Spirit or Apparition Incense

Both of the following incenses are for making spirits appear and would be good to burn during an ancestral altar or at Beltaine or Samhain.

Mix equal parts of anise, coriander, cardamom, lavender, sandalwood and willow bark or, mix three parts wood aloe, two parts coriander, one part camphor, one part mugwort, one part flax, one part cardamom, one part chicory and one part hemp. Burn either incense on a charcoal disc.

Negativity and Demon Trap

On a piece of white paper write the following words in a spiral, starting on the outside of the spiral and working in:

> *Spirits of disruption and disharmony, into this trap you are drawn.*
>
> *From its center you must return to your original domain.*

Place the paper under a rug by the front door. If anyone enters with a demon in their wake it will be trapped at the front door. This could also be done by placing the paper under a spirit board to aid in keeping negative entities from communicating.

Banishment and Cleansing

Point an athame at the sky, then towards the earth and finally straight out while turning in a 360 degree circle and reciting the following verse:

> *Spirits of evil, unfriendly beings, unwanted guests go home!*
>
> *Leave this place and be cast into the outer realm.*
>
> *By the powers of the God and Goddess and of my will,*
>
> *You are banished until all of eternity grows still.*

Sprinkle the house, area, or person with blessed water and light white candles and sage to further banish negative energies. The doors and windows can also be opened and as the smoke drifts outward it will take the negativity with it.

Spell to Banish Bothersome Spirits

This is a simpler banishment that can be done anywhere and is especially good for paranormal investigations where herbs, athames, or other tools of magick might not be nearby. Place a hand extended outwards to start the flow of energy and envision a bluish white light emanating from the palm and fingertips. Fill the room or area with the light and recite:

> *What once was dark is now filled with light,*
>
> *And this spirit is removed from my sight.*

This can be done as often as need, but may take energy from the person performing it so if feelings of tiredness, dizziness, confusion or fatigue remain after doing the spell drink some water or get something to eat and rest for a few minutes.

Incense to Ward of Spirits

Just as there are incenses to increase the ability to see spirits there are incenses to keep them away. Mix three ounces of juniper leaves, four tablespoons of dried rosemary, two ounces of fennel seeds, two teaspoons of both basil and angelica, three teaspoons of linden flower, and a pinch of salt. Burn the incense on a charcoal disc to rid a home of paranormal presences.

Divination, Meditation, Scrying

Necromancy

In the Middle Ages there was a belief that the spirits of the deceased were privy to all of the knowledge of future events and could communicate back to the living to inform them of these events. Necromancy is a form of scrying or divining through the use of communication with these spirits. In the Middle Ages it was believed that to communicate with the dead meant raising the dead and asking them questions. We see this in popular fiction today with Laura K. Hamilton's series about the Necromancer/vampire hunter Anita Blake. The character of Anita can animate the dead long enough to ask questions but rather than focus on future events it is used for unanswered questions such as who murdered them or where did they leave information about the will.

Raising the dead is not practiced today but there are forms of communicating with spirits such as pendulums, spirit boards and séances (see more about spirit boards further on). In Voodoo, there is a belief of raising the dead to turn them in zombies and the person performing the ritual can use that deceased's physical body to perform tasks. The zombified person rarely even has cognitive thought let alone being able to predict the future. Zombies also take place in popular horror movie fiction but are usually the result of catastrophic events such as comets, illness or apocalyptic conditions.

There is a myth about a book called "The Necronomicon" that is said to "be the most evil book in the world" and is thought to include raising the dead as a ritual, among other things. However, the original Necronomicon book, and its reputation, was created from the mind of H.P. Lovecraft. No such 'real' book exists. There are copies that have been printed in which the authors or publishers claim it is from the original text of centuries ago, including translations from supposed texts dating back to 735 CE, 950 CE and 1228 CE. However, all are fakes because there is no original book. It was a fabrication of Lovecraft's for his books and stories; the first of which it is referenced in is "The Hound" publishing in 1922.

Spirit Boards

A spirit board is any board with letters, numbers and often a few key words such as hello, goodbye, yes and no written on it. It has a device known as a planchette and the idea is that two or more people will place their fingers on the planchette and ask questions as a way of communicating with the dead.

The Victorian age brought the popularity of spirit boards back to the mainstream with it being used almost as a parlor game. The great escape artist, Houdini, and his wife promised that when one died the other would try to communicate with them in a spirit board. Even though there were many attempts, his wife was never able to successfully communicate with him. Sarah Winchester, heiress to the Winchester Rifle fortune, also used a spirit board.

When her husband and infant daughter died close together a psychic told her it was a result of the spirits of those who were killed by the rifle. To keep the spirits away from her she had to keep them confused. She did this by hiring men to work on her house 24 hours a day and 7 days a week for the next 30 years (she died in her 80's). She drew up plans for the house, now known as the Winchester Mystery House, through instructions given to her in her nightly spirit board sessions.

Many tales have been told of spirits inhabiting a house after improper use of an Ouija board so it is important that I state that the board itself is not evil and it is not a tool when not in use, no more so than a hammer is a tool if not being wielded. The hammer does not hammer by itself and the board does not open doorways by itself. As it sits on shelf it is not a portal to spirits and does not collect anything more than dust.

The portal was created when the practitioners used it, and the spirits entered during the use of the board, not as it sat in the closet. If not closed properly they the spirits might not leave, but if properly closed the board does not act as an open doorway between the worlds anymore than a locked door is letting in strangers to a home. We hold the key to opening the locked Ouija, so use the key to lock it back when done.

The term 'Ouija' is also just a brand name created by Parker Brothers. It may be a combination of 'oui' and 'ja', one of which is French and the other Scandinavian for the word 'yes.' However, the term itself is just a product name. The board is a spirit board, talking board, or angle board (produced and used by Christians). It is also called a "Psychic Circle" which is another product name and a mass-produced item.

Magick for the Spiritist Witch
Section VI

Animism

Animism is a widely accepted belief system that follows a doctrine that everything in nature, either animate or inanimate, has a consciousness or soul. This is considered to be true for natural items such rocks, trees and animals but can also go further to include bodies of waters, anything made from natural materials, and all inanimate objects. In Alchemy, this belief is described as everything in nature being alive and having a divine spark or vital force within it. This vital force is called 'pneuma' which literally translates to breath (breath of life). The soul of all of nature was called 'anima mundi' or the 'spirit of the earth.'

It can also be defined as a belief that a supernatural force not only animates, but also organizes all of the events or occurrences within the universe. In layman's terms, this might simply be described as fate, which is an occurrence of unknown forces predetermining events or destinies with far-reaching consequences on a person or group of people. Fate or destiny cannot be predicted or controlled, however it can be assisted. Fate might have led two people together, but they must now initiate and keep up the contact. Fate may have brought an opening at a dream job, but the job-hunter must apply for the job. To quote the character of DaVinci as portrayed in the 1998 movie "Everafter" fate is real "but sometimes she needs a hand."

A third definition is that it is a belief in which the spirits or souls of people can exist separately from their bodies. This would coincide with Astral Projection or Out-of-Body-Experiences (OBE) in that the spirit can walk in other planes while the body is in a sleep or trance state. There is a belief that coma victims are the result of the spirits or souls being lost on other planes and cannot find their sleeping body. This definition also would indicate a belief in an afterlife in which the soul exists without a physical body.

The term first came to use by Sir Edward Burnett Taylor who used it to describe a theory that primitive people believed in two parts of humankind: the physical (our waking and living world) and the phantom (dreams or trance-like states). Today it has come to mean that all objects have a soul or spirit that can survive the destruction of its host and ties heavily in with ancestral and nature worship.

Most primitive religions seem to be a form of animism in that everything around them was believed to have a soul or life force. Indeed, in an age where there were no synthetic materials and they had to make their own tools the religion of animism was probably more vital then today with our synthetic, store-bought and materialistic world.

This goes back to what I was saying earlier that I believe the primitives worshipped the items they could see: water, fire, animals, the sky, the ground and shelter. There were no names for gods or deities in that time and they had a very rudimentary idea of religion, maybe not even being able to put it in defined terms. But, they knew that they needed the basic elements of earth for shelter and food, water to drink and for washing, fire for warmth and cooking and air to breathe. Animism at this stage was probably the most pure of any religion today or in the modern past.

Spells and Rituals

In many Native American beliefs and those of Indonesia or Indo-China, animism was a very strong belief that was acknowledged through the use of spirit houses or totem poles. A pagan practitioner today could adapt these to their beliefs and create a personal totem pole or spirit house. These items can decorate yards or altars, be used for meditating on, or be used as a craft or activity in a group gathering. Try searching craft books or the internet for some neat ideas on how to create totem poles or spirit houses.

Totem Poles

These intricately carved and painted poles are the result of the tribes of the Pacific Northwest coast (including parts of Canada) and some Alaskan tribes. Contrary to popular belief, these poles were never designed as idol worship and did not represent gods. This concept came from Christian missionaries who viewed the Shamanic religion as a cult and the totems as god representations. With Christian religions teaching not to worship false idols, these totems were declared god-worship and viewed in a negative light.

Totem poles actually served two purposes to the people who created them: 1) to celebrate cultural significance such as legends, notable events or clan lineage, and 2) as artistic representations of a person or group of people. Usually carved out of cedar wood (a very hard wood with a pleasing scent often believed to be a protective wood) they were painted with dyes made from local plants and erected at significant points in the village. On the poles, various animals or scenery would be depicted that related to the events or purpose of the pole.

Personal totem poles could be carved in wood or sculpted with clay and then painted. The type of wood, paintings and designs should all fit with personal beliefs or significance such as a spirit animal, a patron god, a favorite symbol, or even name initials. Charge the totem pole with personal powers and energies the same as charging any other object. There are also easy and printable instructions for the less artistic at the site "Animal Tribe" (see Bibliography for address)

Spirit Houses

Spirit houses are often highly decorative and not much bigger than traditional bird or doll houses. They seem to dominate Asian cultures with beliefs in Animism, Hinduism and Buddhism. In Thailand (where Spirit Houses are commonly seen near offices, houses, businesses and roadsides) there is a belief in 'nagas' (mythical water snakes), land gods, wayward ghosts, and tree nymphs (among a wide range of gods and deities). The belief is that all of these spirits or deities can affect the daily lives of the mortal world are also affected by it. The spirit houses are a way of honoring that entity and keeping it happy.

This is especially true in the advent of new buildings being erected. The resident spirits of the area will lose their homes when the new buildings are built, and if the spirits are left to remain homeless they can turn quite nasty. Spirit houses are built with each new construction so that the spirits will have a place to live and quite often they mimic the real building as intricately and decorated, but with no furnishings inside.

In pagan practices fairy houses are often constructed with a similar observance: to give the fairies a home. This has been done by making a structure out of twigs, leaves, stones or moss; old terra cotta pots; or decorated bird houses. Instead of appealing to the spirits, fairy houses appeal to the fairies and their kin in the hopes that they will not play mischievous pranks on the mortal residents and also for protection or aid in gardens.

Either kind of house can be made in a variety of ways from the very clever and crafty to simply decorating a pre-built birdhouse. This would make a great family project and there are many ideas online for decorations and materials. Spirit houses should be as decorated and intricate as possible whereas fairy houses should remain more natural. Fairies want something that resembles their natural habitat and is not lavishly decorated. I have a small bird house in which the only decorations are bark glued to the roof and the house is painted in natural colors. Spirit houses can be created for housing household spirits, animal spirits, or guardians and guides. If working with a spirit familiar, it is still important for them to have their own space to go to when the magick is done. This does not have to be a large space; a small spirit house can sit on an altar, outside or anywhere else in the home.

Effigies or Fetishes

Effigies or fetishes are small sculptures that usually depict animals, people or gods. Both are inanimate objects that are revered or worshiped and believed to have magical powers or be animated by a spirit. Fetishes usually depict animals and are worn by practitioners to represent their totem or spirit animal. Effigies usually take the shape of a man or god and are basically defined as a dummy created in a rough fashion and meant to insult or injure someone. They can be a hand-held size, such as a poppet or Voodoo Doll, or life-size. The infamous Wicker Man is an example of a large-scale effigy. Often the product of movies (including the controversial 2006 "The Wicker Man" starring Nicholas Cage) the Wicker Man was actually used by ancient people; such as the Gaul civilization which is a mixed race of ancient Roman, Celt and French cultures (circa 5th century BCE.)

Currently, in my house, we have and Effigy Man and Effigy Woman just for fun. My husband found a chunk of wood that looked like a face with indented eyes and a long twig-stump resembling a long and crooked nose. He made a human figure out of it with some more twigs and a few eye-hook links; we affectionately dubbed him "Effigy Man." Then, when I 'inherited' a ton of wooden spools from my mom I attempted to make a doll from them. She became Effigy Woman and she hangs near her man. (They are decoration only and have not been used against or for anyone.)

Fetishes are more common among pagan practitioners and usually made of gemstones or wood and available in metaphysical shops. A person will purchase (or carve one) that fits with their animal familiars, which are real animals or spirit animals that assist a person in their magickal workings. In superstitious times, it was believed that all black cats were familiars of witches and were used as evidence against women accused of witchery and often killed along with the accused. Today, practitioners are not limited to just one type of spirit animal or familiar.

Spirit animals are sometimes defined as familiars, but in another sense they can be the animal-spirit of the person and are not thought of as a separate creature, sort of like a were-creature in that the person can transform into the beast but in spiritual, and not physical, form. This goes back to Native American lore in which each person was believed to have the spirit of an animal within them such as an eagle, a deer, wolves, a snake, bears or wild cats. This could be determined either by the first animal the mother sees upon the birth of the child (the animal often being incorporated in to the name, such as Running-Deer) or through trances done in sweat lodges or by smoking peace pipes. Often the person would wear skins or feathers of their spirit animal to show their connection. The spirit animal can be called upon for wisdom, protection, or for the person to be able to see through its eyes. For example, a person with the spirit animal of an eagle can connect with an eagle in the sky and get a bird's-eye view of things.

Spirit or totem animals can be used by thinking of that animal, its characteristics and how it would get out of a situation. A variety of animals could be used by one practitioner depending on the situation. For example, does this situation call for the wily cunning of a fox or for the strength of a bear? To use spirit animals learn as much as possible about a variety of animals and what their skills, attributes, quirks, weaknesses and strengths are.

To honor or connect with the animal other items besides effigies and fetishes can be carried or worn such as a feather, horn, claw, talon jewelry pendant, or picture. Effigies or objects can be worn, placed on altars, carried as charms, or held during meditations or rituals. Images of that animal can also be painted or carved onto magickal tools to empower them with the spirit of that animal. The books "Animal Speak" by Ted Andrews and "The Once Unknown Familiar" by Timothy Roderick are wonderful books to get anyone started on finding either their spirit animal or the meanings behind animals.

Divination, Meditation, Scrying

There really isn't a way to divine or scry with the concept of Animism since it is not a concept and not a specific object. But, since it is the belief that all objects have a soul any scrying device can be considered a part of animism because the practitioner is drawing on the energies of the object being used. Meditation can also be achieved through the belief of animism if acknowledging the object as having a life force and using that to empower the subconscious, such as sitting in a forest or by a stream. Often we seek the solitude of nature for thinking or relaxing, and this can be said to be a meditative form of animism since we are using nature to help us quiet our thoughts or put them in order.

Any natural object such as a rock or tree can be used for meditating or to connect with the life force inside of it by placing hands on the object and feeling its life force or energy. Allow the mind to drift or go blank and let the subconscious mind do its work. In a way, meditating with objects in this manner is a little like psychometry, which is a form of divination achieved by touching an object and receiving images related to a person or event. This is often used in paranormal investigations by psychics who touch an object and see images of events surrounding the object or its previous owners.

Try this at home by picking up an object and feeling its every angle, texture, and feature. It will work best to sit in a quiet room with eyes closed as the eyes will pick up their own observations and a person might end up focusing only on the visual and not the other senses. Utilize the senses of sound, touch, taste and smell before opening eyes and using the visual sense. Try to understand how the object was made or how it works and try to pick up images of who may have owned it first, or what was the person like who made it, etc.

For natural items, such as rock, there probably won't be any personal experiences surrounding it but it will still have seen rainstorms, been covered with dirt, been kicked around or broken off from a larger rock. Try to feel what the object has gone through and seen. Determine if the energy is a low vibe or a high vibe for that object. Earlier we learned how to determine vibes in stones, and this can be done with any other object that a person owns.

In a quicker and simpler form this could be done in stores to help pick out an object to purchase. This is not or ordinary items like clothing or food, but for the magickal items. It is a common idea in the pagan community that a person should choose an item based on one that seems to call out to them. This is done with tools, gemstones, Tarot cards, altar cloths and a wide array of other magickal supplies. In way, this is practicing a form of animism because the person is feeling the energies, or soul, of the object before choosing it. This is a similar concept to why certain people are friends; we don't make friends with everyone we see or meet but only with those people that call to us. Their personality, their essence, their soul is what makes us like or dislike someone and we choose friends based on vibes we connect with.

Magick for the Spiritist Witch
Section VII

The Hidden Realms

The Hidden Realms, sometimes called the Otherworld, means different things to different cultures and there is no end to the number of paranormal, supernatural, or ethereal creatures that exist and each religion or culture has its own lore and legends. But, a basic definition of the realms is the belief in the existence of other realms (dimensions or planes) and that the creatures of lore such as fairies, dragons and unicorns, may actually live in these realms. It is believed by some that these realms can be visited now only through deep meditation, dreams, or astral projection.

Beliefs further state that perhaps at one time the veils or doorways were thinner between the realms and it was easier to travel between the two. Today, the veils are very thick and if people slip over to the other realm they often don't seem to return and it is usually done accidentally (as in missing persons, especially those connected with the Bermuda's Triangle.) Traveling between these realms is what gave the ancients knowledge of supernatural creatures came from, but in time skepticism and science caused the veils to become thicker until it was impossible to traverse in physical form.

Expanding further on the belief of missing persons, comatose patients might also have gone into these other realms, either accidentally of on purpose, and have lost their way to returning home (similar to being lost during Astral Projection as mentioned earlier). The Bermuda Triangle is often believed to be a doorway to another realm, perhaps where Atlantis now exists. It is even said that the unknown creatures classified under cryptozoology are from these other realms and, like missing or comatose people, have slipped into out realms and cannot return home. Perhaps there is a Bigfoot lying in a coma or gone missing in a realm where all of society is made up of these large primates. Maybe there are sightings in other realms that report a "mostly-hairless, wingless, and bi-pedal creature".

Science will say that the dragons were just bones of dinosaurs discovered by ancient man, that led to tales of mythical proportions and that fairies may have been insects such as dragonflies or lightning bugs that resemble fairy-like creatures. Dragonflies, with their luminescent colors, large wings and intelligent eyes definitely look like a product of the fairy world. The lightning bugs' ability to light up at night must certainly have been thought of as supernatural before science explained it. Butterflies are very intricate and beautiful and often fairies in modern art are depicted with butterfly wings, could they also have been believed to be fairies?

At this point, it is impossible to say whether these creatures existed at all or not or still exist on some supernatural, otherworldly plain. Science hasn't proven they exist but neither has it proven that they don't. Either way, there are several traditions of magick that rely on belief in supernatural creatures such as Dragon Magick and Fairy Magick.

For the purposes of this book I am only discussing three basic Hidden Realm creatures. They are the three most common that are seen in a variety of cultures, they also have magickal belief systems based around them , and can be used in general terms encompassing a variety of creatures. Large beasts such as the Kraken, sea serpents, leviathans, and others can be lumped in with dragons. All sprites, nymphs, pixies, elves, brownies, gnomes and the like can be lumped in with fairies (even though fairies are often considered their own being). Unicorns are uniquely their own creature but could also encompass the winged horse known as Pegasus.

Dragon Magick

Dragon Magick has also been dubbed "Chaos Magick" because of the fifth element of chaos instead of spirit. Dragon Magick harbors the same belief of the four basic elements in that there is an earth dragon, air dragon, fire dragon, and water dragon. Each one lives primarily in its element and is usually the same color of the element it represents. To use that element the corresponding dragon would be called upon.

Dragon Magick, or the Draconic Path, also teaches a person to work in harmony with dragons and the power that they hold. They are not animal or spirit familiars and are not assistants, but rather should be viewed as equal partners in all spells and rituals. Dragon Magick can be incorporated into any path that a person already has designed for themselves. Most cultures tend to believe in dragons in some fashion (they are even mentioned in many Biblical passages) so they can be the perfect addition to any path.

There is a Draconic Code of Honor, moon phases, tools, symbols and divination similar to what other pagan practices have. The lunar phases are the same as what Wiccans or neo-pagans practice such as the full, new, and crescent moons. However, those on a Draconic Path also honor the void (when a moon is moving between Zodiac signs), lunar eclipses, the blue moon (when two full moons occur in one calendar month) and a black moon (when two new or dark moons occur in one calendar month).

For more information on Dragon Magick I recommend the site Fox Moon (see Bibliography for address) as it explains each of the aspects of this practice in clear detail with beautiful web artwork. On the site, there are divination methods involving Tarot, Runes and a way to divine for a magickal dragon name.

Fairy Magick

Fairies belong to a world that we don't live in, and probably will never get to see, so fairies give us a sense of mysticism, wonder and intrigue. The Celtic nations, especially Ireland, are known for their fairy lore and tend to be the most common. However, just as with the gods or deities, every culture has its own form of some type of supernatural being that is not of this world and yet not a god. Fairies are said to be in a realm similar to that of the elementals and, as said earlier, it can either mean its own race (called the Tuatha de Dannan in Celtic lore) or a term encompassing many different supernatural beings. There are also legends that say fairies were angels who refused to choose sides in the rebellion of Lucifer (Satan's angelic name) to the Christian God. By not choosing a side they were banished to another realm and lost most of their angelic powers.

In working with fairy magick there has to be a deep and inner connection to the earth or a pure and innocent soul, which makes it a perfect magick for children. When working with them in magick they are similar to dragons in that they should be considered an equal partner and not as a familiar or lackey. Fairies can be called upon to aid in all household or garden dwellings, for protection, and as a link to the other realms.

Fairies are common in folklore and fairy tales (commonly as fairy godmothers like in "Cinderella" and "Sleeping Beauty"). They are usually helpful and possess many magickal abilities; they come to us to give guidance or aid in some fashion. In "Cinderella," her fairy godmother helps her to get to the much anticipated Prince's ball, and in "Sleeping Beauty" they bless the child at her birth.

They adorn artwork, T-shirts, jewelry and are seen in popular media. Disney's Tinkerbell and the legendary Tooth Fairy are probably the most popular of the fairies, and not inclusive of children's entertainment only. Women are proud of Tinkerbell's duality of femininity and assertive independence and men are fascinated with her shapely curves and scanty outfit. The Tooth Fairy is a common legend told to children to encourage dental hygiene and be rewarded with money when the baby teeth fall out. There is a websites devoted to her (http://www.toothfairy.org/) that has hygiene tips, links and the going rate of a tooth!

Superstitions regarding fairies come to us from many cultures and fill up books about superstitions and folklore. In Irish lore when the stalks of flowers bend without a strong breeze blowing the flowers are bending in genuflection to the Fae Queen, who must be nearby. The fairies like offerings of wine and cookies and a person will gain their favors and friendships if leaving these out for them; they also like ginger and offerings should be placed near green plants or trees. Do not expect the food to be gone later, the fairies do not actually eat it but just absorb the essence from it.

For centuries, people have tried to see fairies and there have been many faked photos. The most famous these is the Cottingley fairies of the early 1900's in which two young girls made paper fairies and took photos of them. Today, there are still people who try to capture photos of fairies and more than one website boasting fairy photos. There are also spells written to aid practitioners in either seeing fairies or seeing into the fairy realms.

Without using any of the spells, the best time to try and see fairies is at any "in between time." These are any times where things are changing such as midnight or noon; dawn or dusk; from the last day of the month to the first day of the month; or even at New Year's. The eve of the New Year is said to be the most powerful since it is the changing of night to day (midnight), a change from the old year to the New Year, a change in the month, and a change in the day. It is a very auspicious time. Beltane and Halloween are also good times to try to see fairy folk, especially if at midnight, because those are the two times of the year that the veil is the thinnest.

Unicorn Magick

The unicorn is an ancient symbol and a favorite among fantasy and fairy-tale stories or movies. Unicorns are horses, almost always white, with one long horn in the center of its forehead which is said to be either gold or silver in color. In rare instances, unicorns have been depicted as goats. Some people speculate the horn is finely twisted and coiled hair while others say it is bone. Even though they resemble horses, unicorns have some distinguishing features (aside from the obvious horn) that separate them from their equine cousins. Unicorns are almost always depicted with a billy-goat style goatee, a tail like a lions and with cloven hooves. Horses do not have the cloven hooves that cows, pigs and goats have.

Contrary to popular belief, unicorns did not originate in myth. Over the course of centuries, they moved from the pages of historical texts to that of legends. First recorded as natural history in ancient Greece, the writers of these texts believed in the existence of unicorns claiming that they lived in India and they wrote about them as if they were real animals. Skeptics today tell us that unicorns were never real. They claim that what the people saw was misinterpreted, such as a double-horned animals, like antelopes, seen at such an angle that the second horn was hidden behind the first, appearing as if there was only one. Or perhaps, they found remains of two-horned animals but one horn was missing from predators scattering the bones. There is also speculation that animal's horns were mutated to form just one horn from what normally would have been two.

They are depicted in a very surreal way surrounded by a lot of magick and as very peaceful and almost untouchable creatures. Usually thought to be the most magickal of any animal they are sometimes portrayed as princesses cursed as a horse, or as sentient beings being able to feel emotions, exert free-will and speak. It is said that where unicorns play it is eternal summer and that the unicorn brings about a sense of gentleness, courage, healing and inner wisdom. They are also symbols of chastity, healing, divine love or sexuality and protection with its fabled horn also being composed of many powers. In medieval times and the powder of the horn was said to be used for detecting poison in foods or drinks given to Royalty. Since people of today say that unicorns are not real, there is no telling what people passed off as powdered unicorn horns, but those who used it believed it to be so.

Work with unicorn magick to heal emotional trauma to the heart and soul, to fill the body with a sense of love and peace, or for protection. Similar to guardian angels, a person can have a Guardian Unicorn and communicate with it through dreams or meditation. The horn acts like a wand in that it can direct energy and if working with Unicorn magick, a person can make or buy a wand that resembles a Unicorn's horn. Unicorns are shy, so in all magickal workings, be patient and quiet so as not to frighten off their spirit or essence. Since we cannot own real unicorns like we could a cat or dog, it is essential to have images of them in the form of jewelry, pictures of statuaries. A picture of a unicorn can also be carried as a reminder of its qualities and used for meditative purposes.

Pegasus is a winged horse that is often associated with the unicorn but there are no natural history texts claiming its existence and probably was not any animal mistaken for winged horse. They seem to come strictly from Greek mythology and do not even appear in other culture myths. Pegasus was the product of Poseidon and the Gorgon Medusa. Poseidon, along with being the god of the sea, was the god of horses and often took horse form to wander the mortal land. This is what he did when he coupled with Medusa. Poseidon's daughter, Clarissa, cared for Pegasus and from there, the tales of this winged beast are tossed around in various

Greek legends.

Today, the Pegasus is a constellation in the skies and adorns many logos, clothing, and occurs quite often in popular media such as the stop-go animation movie "Clash of the Titans" (1981). Working with Pegasus can be done in the same manner as working with unicorns since they are similar mythical beasts, however the Pegasus could be used in all air or earth magick since it can fly and yet lives on earth. It has no special powers like the Unicorn's horn but is generally accepted to symbolize similar aspects and does have the ability to fly and carry people on its back. Use Pegasus imagery in psychic travels or when needing to "reach for the clouds" with a life goal or dream. Wearing jewelry will remind a person that it's okay to fly to the clouds, but that we must always come back down to earth at some point, as the Pegasus does.

Spells and Rituals

Most of the spells that I have come across are for fairy magick, but slowly dragon spells are surfacing. There are some good ones at the site "Elements of the Dragon" (see Bibliography). Spells can also be adapted or written to coincide with dragon magick, or for someone studying that craft, the elemental dragons can be called upon when calling the quarters for an altar or ritual.

Dragon Spell of Cleansing

To cleanse an object, or even a person, use this spell and call upon the fiery breath of the dragons. Fire has long been associated with cleansing and general belief is that dragons can breath fire, a capability that no animals today (or in this existence) actually have. Light a candle of choice, and carve a simple image of a dragon in the wax. Set the object near the candle so that the light of the flame touches it, or if cleansing a person have them sit near enough that the light flickers on them and they feel the heat (but still a safe distance away). Then, recite the following words three times, increasing in cadence each time. (The actions of the spell are ones that I wrote, but the verse comes from the website "Elements of the Dragon").

"By mighty trees or Oak, Ash and Thorn
By all the oaths I have sworn,

I need the cleansing touch of fire
Touch this (name the object or person) with dragon's power!
— Dr. Els.

Pick up the object and pass it over the flame (be careful to not touch it to the fire) or have the person pass each hand over the flame, high enough to not get burned but low enough to feel the heat. Do not extinguish the flame of the candle in any fashion as this could be seen as an insult by dragons. It shows that we have greater power then them because we can extinguish their fire. Let the candle burn out of its own accord, so use a tea light or mini-taper candle so it doesn't take as long to burn out.

Fairy Sugar or Dust

Fairy sugar is simple to make and can be used as an offering to them, for adding to anointing oils, to aid in seeing fairies, or just as a fun thing for children to make for their own magickal supplies. To make fairy sugar, color some sugar with food coloring and add a few drops or rose oil, vanilla, or any flower-scented oil. Stir well and add more color or scent until the desired result is achieved. Let it air dry on a flat surface like a cookie sheet so that it won't clump. Once it is dry, store it in an air-tight jar in a cool and dry place.

To See the Fae

Anointing oils can be made with any base oil such as olive, jojoba or grape seed and by adding an herb to the oil. The most common and recommended is either rosemary or rose petals but any flowered plant can be added. Right before an in-between time visit a place where the fae are likely to visit and anoint the eyelids nine times each. Then, with an open mind and a pure intent look for the fairy folk, but be cautious it is said that they like to play tricks and try to entice people into their world.

Superstition and folklore also say that looking through any enclosed circle, such as a ring, will allow someone to see into fairy realms and that a circle of mushroom (known as a "Fairy Ring") is a doorway to their world. The fae dance within the circle of mushrooms and it is cautioned against standing inside of one, especially at an in-between time (for the same reason as stated above.)

Divination, Meditation, Scrying

To Dream of the Fae

A sachet can be made to aid one in dreaming of the fairy folk either for divination or to ask their help in magickal workings. Fill a mesh or cloth bag with rose petals, primrose, bay, lavender and milk pod tassels. Place the sachet underneath the pillow. This can also be hung in a prominent room of the house or a covered outdoor space such as a porch or patio in order to entice the fairies to come for a visit and bless the house.

Dreaming of the Fey can be a good way to connect with them spiritually, which is beneficial if using Fairy Magick, and also message can be passed along by them through dreams. If troubled by something try this method and maybe the fairies will answer the question, solve the dilemma or give some helpful advice.

Unicorn Meditation

This form of meditation is good for vision quests or to gain inner wisdom. This can be done at an altar or any sacred space by gathering together a favorite essential oil, a unicorn statue and a white ribbon. Anoint the ribbon with the oil and hold it in the receptive hand while visualizing walking in the woods where a unicorn might live, making the vision as detailed as possible. Visualize seeing a unicorn drinking water from a stream and walking up to it slowly. Remember that unicorns are shy, so walk easily and quietly. The white ribbon symbolizes being of a kindred spirit with the unicorn and it is in the receptive hand to show humility rather than dominance if held in the projective hand. Hold the ribbon out to the unicorn in the vision as well as holding out the hand that holds the ribbon in real life.

Now, visualize the unicorn looking up, acknowledging the ribbon and accepting the presence of a human in its domain. Tie the real ribbon to the statue while visualizing that it is being tied around a living unicorn. As the ribbon is being tied recite the verse:

> *Unicorn of legends, myths and tales of old*
>
> *May your youth and vitality fill me with the same.*
>
> *Unicorn of mystery, magic, and wisdom told*

May your peace and gentleness fill my soul.
Unicorn of purity, chastity, and innocent virtue
May your strength and endurance be with me.
Unicorn of inspiration, creativity and truth
May your wisdoms now engage my mind.

Meditate on the scene for as long as is comfortable or until the purpose of the meditation has been achieved. Thank the unicorn for its aid in the quest and quietly walk out of the woods, leaving it exactly the same as it was found. Come back to the physical self and record any feelings, visions, or answers that were gained in the meditation.

Magick for the Spiritist Witch
Section VIII

Mythology and Folklore

We wander around living our daily lives with nary a thought to the soul that resides in our physical self. Only when talking of the afterlife or when watching paranormal shows do we ever stop to consider what the soul is, where it goes, the affects our lives are having on it, or where it came from. When I started this book I wanted each chapter to have a flow, and in doing so I would need a section on the creation of spirit as I did for the creation or origin of the other elements. But, where does the soul come from? In all my discussions with people on theologies, life and the universe, or paranormal discussions I don't ever recall discussing where or how souls came into existence. It was generally assumed we all had a soul, and I've had numerous discussions on where the souls go when the physical body dies, but never on soul creation.

One might argue that souls are recycled, as we know, reincarnation is the belief that a soul goes through many physical bodies before ending up in an eternal afterlife. But, where did those souls come from to begin with? And, with the large population of people that we have it stands to reason that new souls are being created somewhere and by someone. Is there an assembly line somewhere in a factory that makes souls and stores them in a closet until needed? We will perhaps never know, but there are a few theories regarding soul creation and there are numerous superstitions regarding the safety of our souls.

Spirit Creation

There appears to be two main theories on soul creation: 1) deity creation (as in the Christian God) or, 2) propagation and recycling, like seeds. These theories are debated by both philosophers and theologians and referred to as "creationism versus traducianism". This debate is similar to debates of Earth's origin, creation versus the "Big-Bang Theory," and origin of man, creation versus evolution. In all of the cases, creation means to create something from nothing as a God is able to do, and the other side of the debate means that there were pre-existing conditions that led to the creation. Wrapped up in this debate of pre-existing conditions lies the scientific theory of Alchemy and its studiers, known as Alchemists, who are trying to find that one prime element that sparked all of life. Basically, it is the act of looking for that one-pre-existing material that all other materials were created from.

This whole debate is rather like the old stage magician's trick of pulling a rabbit out of a hat. One side of the audience believes that there was nothing in the hat and that by waving a wand or saying a few choice words the rabbit appears from nothingness and is pulled out of the hat (the magician is like a god and created something from nothing). On the other side is the group who knows that the rabbit is hidden in the hat or the table beneath. The magician did not create a rabbit where there was non e, but rather he produced the rabbit from pre-existing conditions (the rabbit, the hat, a trick table).

Creationism, as it relates to the soul, is the belief that a God or deity created all souls from nothing (the rabbit was never in the hat, but was conjured up). Gods have the power to create things from nothing, the Christian Bible tells of this in the first book of Genesis in which God created the skies, the heavens and the waters and then proceeded to fill the world with life of many kinds. All of these things were created without pre-existing materials.

Traducianism is the belief that souls are propagated, like seeds (the rabbit was placed in the hat prior to the spell). The propagation theory states that souls are first created from pre-existing materials and then recycled. Theories then veer off on different tangents as to where these pre-existing materials come from. Some believe that the soul is created from the father's soul only, that is to say that a piece of his soul goes into development of the new soul. Others say it is an equal mix of both father and mother and that a small piece of each soul goes into the new soul. This lends credence to the saying "my heart and soul" when parents refer to their children. This theory was developed because of the fact that the genes of both parents go into the genetic make-up of the child. Traducianism also ties into reincarnation beliefs because it is believed that souls are recycled. So, first a soul is created (either a hundred years ago or yesterday) and then it is recycled. This makes sense to those who describe people as having an old soul (seem to be years beyond their age) or a new soul (those lively, perky, and cheerful souls that seem exited by everything they see.)

As mentioned earlier, there are further debates as to when the soul actually enters the body, a conflict is basis for heated debates regarding abortion. Pro-lifers believe the soul is there at conception and Pro-choicers believe it enters later and in the Islamic religions it is believed that the soul goes into the embryo forty-days after conception and other theories that that soul does not enter until the child is being born.

No one will ever really know where souls come from or when they enter the body, perhaps in some far-flung futuristic setting these things will be proven without a doubt and humans will know the exact science behind soul-creation and the afterlife, but I doubt it is something we will see in our lifetimes. For now, we are left only to speculate.

Mirrors

This might seem like a drastic jump in topics, but mirrors have a lot to do with the soul, or rather of our preservation of it. Even though mirrors are indicative of the water element because of their illusion at having depth and for the reflective surfaces, they are also of the spirit element because it is believed that mirrors are a visual representation of a person's soul. Superstitions are endless when it comes to mirrors and they are often the subject of Urban Legends such as the "Bloody Mary" or "Mary Worth" stories in which a vindictive spirit can be called forth through the mirror.

As we know from earlier, Narcissus fell in love with his own reflection so much that it was the end of him and there is a superstition still around today that if one sees their reflection and the water ripples or break's up it is a bad omen (it has rippled or broken the soul). No good really ever comes from mirrors: they cause seven years bad luck if broken; if harm befalls the reflection harm will come to the person; in the house of the ill or dead spirits can take living souls to the other side; and vampires cannot be seen in mirrors because they have no soul.

However, there is hope for all of the bad luck. In a house of the ill or deceased, the mirrors can be covered up and broken mirror pieces can be tossed into a swift-flowing stream, buried, or put in a jar and placed in the window. Mirrors, especially black or dark mirrors, can be used for scrying the future (known as catoptromancy) and are often used by pagan practitioners. Caution needs to be heeded with scrying mirrors, however, because bad images or spirits can come through. Mirrors have long been associated with portals to otherworlds, or as portals into this one.

Crossroads

Crossroads are said to be a good place to see spirits and if creating an ancestral altar try to place it outside where two areas meet. If this is not possible, set an altar on a plus symbol drawn in the ground or place two sticks crossing each other on an altar. Crossroads doesn't necessarily mean any area that is in the shape of a plus or cross, but even "T" shaped intersection can be considered a crossroad. Where a person's driveway connects to the road is a crossroad and can be a place where magick is performed as well as doorways or entryways in a home. Objects of magick can be buried at crossroads after they have been used in a spell, or if the object is believed to harbor negative vibes. It is also believed that evil spirits will be confused by the multiple choices of the roads and not know where to go. This was a common reason why suicide victims, criminals, or supposed vampire and werewolves were buried at crossroads.

While crossroads are feared by more modern people, primate and ancient civilizations used crossroads as a place to set up altars, believing that there was great power to be tapped there. Where streams or bodies of water intersect is also a powerful crossroad because of the properties the element of water harbors. Cleansing objects or bathing in water from such spots will have a more powerful effect and enhance magick.

Elementals

The White Buffalo

Since the spirit is an incorporeal element there really is no elemental creature to coincide with it like undines, sylphs, salamanders or gnomes. The closest thing would perhaps by the Halloween and folkloric version of ghosts. However, in watching television one day with my daughters I was reminded of a Native American legend I had heard long ago about a white buffalo. I feel it is an appropriate creature to identify with the element of spirit because of its legend and meaning. The meaning behind the legend is indicative of the spirit of the earth and it is colored white, which is a color of spirit and corresponds with purity, angelic guidance, innocence, divine communication and protection. There is also legend of a white buffalo woman in Native American lore who taught the people how to live.

While most elementals are not considered "real" or at least of this plane, the white buffalo is real but is rare, perhaps one in every ten million births, and is still honored by Native Americans. In 1994 in Jainesville, Wisconsin on the farm of the Heider family one such buffalo was born. Given the name 'Miracle', she was seen as a sign and the Heider family allowed visitors to the farm and many Native American peoples felt it was their duty to protect and honor Miracle.

However, since there really isn't an elemental to work with in spirit magick, the ancestors or spirit can be invoked or honored and used by burning sweet grass (an ancestral herb) or by know our selves. We are of the spirit and therefore we only need to acknowledge and accept our inner selves and utilize the gifts or talents we have.

Gods and Goddesses

Unlike the other elements there really isn't one God that is just "of spirit." There are Gods that are depicted as just being an ethereal and incorporeal form such as the monotheistic god of Christianity, or Allah of Islam and Yahweh of Judaism but in polytheistic beliefs the gods are viewed more like physical beings and there isn't one that can be said to be of the spirit element.

In general paganism based on mainly on Wiccan practices, there is a concept a God and Goddess. This is an acknowledgement that there is both a male and female deity (ditheism) or even acknowledges many male and female deities (polytheism). It is impossible to identify every God and Goddess known to polytheistic faiths in one single book, but it is typical that pagan cultures have both genders. Eclectic pagans (those not on a set path) can take their God and Goddess inspiration from any one of the pre-Christian religions, from Christianity or from the Saints in Catholicism. Often a practitioner has a patron god or goddess, which means they have one main deity they acknowledge more than the others. However, there is a general belief in what God or Goddess means in generic terms and not as per a specific deity .

The Goddess

The Goddess is sometimes known in general terms as the Great Mother, Mother Nature, Universal Mother, Mother of Gods or Queen of Heaven. She gives the gift of life, but with life she promises that death will soon follow. Quite often she is represented by the Triple Goddess or Triple Moon imagery. The triple moon is a symbol of a full moon nestled in between two crescent moons. These moons represent the three phases of womanhood. Ritual tools for the Goddess are a cauldron, bell, cup, chalice, or a crystal ball. Basically anything that is cup-shaped since it represents the womb, which is (obviously) of only the female anatomy. On an altar the Goddess is represented on the left side, usually with a silver candle, and her correspondences are the colors silver or purple, the moon, pearls, and emeralds. In a ritual she is represented by the High Priestess and to dream of the Goddess means female strength.

The God

He is known as God, the Father, the Horned One, the Father of the Gods and sometimes as "the all-seeing eye". The sun is seen as male, so it or its personification of Sol is applied to the God as is the concepts of fatherhood, sexuality, vitality and power. His symbol is the full moon with the crescent moon resting on top (points up) which resembles a head with horns. Because of this, and his association with horned deities such as Pan, Cernunnos, or Ogham, we get the term "the Horned One." This as erroneously been applied to beliefs in Satan due to his depiction of also having horns and the inverted pentagram is seen as an angular face with the two points on top as horns. He is also known as the "Green Man" which is a concept similar to that of Mother Nature, but in the male sense. The correspondences for the God are the right side of the altar, bladed instruments, the wand or staff, the metal brass and the color of gold or green. In ritual, he is represented by the High Priest.

The God and Goddess are equal and complement each other. Both of them can be called upon in a spell or ritual in general invoking to represent universal deities or a specific deity can be called upon for a specific need. In this case, there is often not a second God called upon. For example, if looking for a job or needing extra money, a person might call upon goddess Fortuna but it is not necessary to call upon a male equivalent. However, in general worship or for the Sabbats both male and female are called upon and represented, which is exceptionally good as oven gatherings are of mixed genders. Usually their union is symbolized by placing the athame into the cup, but there is also an act known as the "Great Rite" in which male and female partners (usually the Priest and Priestess) simulate the joining of the God and Goddess.

Jesus Christ/God/Holy Spirit

The Christian concept of "the father, the son and the holy spirit" is a trinity that is slightly comparable to a Wiccan trinity of the Triple Moon or Triple Goddess. Jesus was a real person believed to have ascended into Heaven in his physical body and God is seen as an incorporeal entity.

Jesus Christ is his son who was born by Immaculate Conception to the Virgin Mary. Most people are familiar with the scene of Mary and her husband Joseph staying in a manger on Christmas Eve (despite arguments that he was actually born in the spring) because there is no room at the inns. He is at sometimes thought of as Jesus, the son of God and sometimes as the Lord himself. He is a messenger between God and mankind and viewed as the savior of man, he was crucified for the sins of man and was the last sacrifice to be made to the Christian God. Prior to that, animal sacrifices were quite common and are mentioned in the Old Testament

Triple Moon or Triple Goddess

While this concept actually has a variety of Goddess attributed to it, it deserves to be in the spirit section because it is an embodiment of the spirit of the female gender.

This aspect is a depiction the three phases of woman: maiden, mother and crone. Each phase is represented by a phase of the moon: maiden is the waxing crescent because the woman is growing into a mother like the moon is growing to full. When a woman becomes a mother she is like the full moon, complete and whole. Then she wanes (grows older) from mother to crone like the full moon wanes into a crescent. Traditionally, these phases of womanhood were said to start with the onset of the menstrual cycle and menopause. However, since girls are getting their cycles at earlier ages and are little more than children when they do, today the mother is typically thought to either start at having children or when a woman sets up her own housekeeping.

Triple God

There doesn't appear to be any solid basis for a male concept that is as concrete as the Triple Goddess, but some theories are starting to form about the Triple God being either a "young lord, warrior, and sage" persona or "lad, hero and sage." Similar to the Triple Goddess aspect, a male would call upon or honor any number of Gods that fit with his beliefs. The Christian trinity could also be seen as the phases of mankind with the "son, the father, and the holy spirit (old age or death?)

Regardless of the culture, the religion, or the gods associated with it, many areas tend to have a similar concept of a trinity in which the phases always are in this order: "youth, procreator, death." Try experimenting and coming up with a personal and unique trinity that is meaningful based on cultural or religious influences.

the author

Deanna, her husband, and their two daughters currently reside in South Carolina. She works as a Day Plan Coordinator for the Disabilities Board of her county. Deanna is certified in Occupational Child Care (1994), a freelance writer with a career diploma from Penn Foster (2010), a published author and this year she was also initiated by "Gaia's Wisdom Coven" as a 3rd Degree pagan. She currently holds a seat of Family Council with the Council of Rights in "Gaia's Wisdom" and will work towards an ordination for Priestess later this year. In her spare time she and her family enjoy camping, local or cultural festivals, and just spending time together.

"Magick for the Elemental Witch" is her 3rd book and the 2nd in the Copper Cauldron series. Her previous works include "Imagica: The Boy Who Had No Imagination" (Publish America 2006) and "Magick for the Kitchen Witch" (New Gaia Press 2009). She also writes key-word articles for Associated Content.com and Helium.com.

More about Deanna and her books or articles can be read at her website: www.thecoppercauldron.com.

bibliography

Books

Abraham, Sylvia. (1997). How to Use Tarot Spreads. Minnesota: Llewellyn Publications

Andrews, Ted. (1996). Animal Speak. Minnesota: Llewellyn Publications

Bartel, Pauline. (2000). Spellcasters: Witches and Witchcraft in History, Folklore and Popular Culture. Maryland: Taylor and Trade Publishing.

Brown, Dan. (2009). The Da Vinci Code. New York: Doubleday

Buckland, Raymond. (2002). The Witch Book: The Encyclopedia of Witchcraft, Wicca, and Neo-Paganism. Michigan: Visible Ink Press.

Conway, DJ (1995). Celtic Magick. Minnesota: Llewellyn Publications.

Cunningham, Scott. (2000). Cunningham's Encyclopedia of Magical Herbs. Minnesota: Llewellyn Publications.

Cunningham, Scott. (2002). The Magickal Household: Spells and Rituals For the Home. Minnesota: Llewellyn Publications.

Cunningham, Scott (2002) The Complete Book of Incense, Oils, and Brews. Minnestoa: Llewellyn Publications.

Daniel, Marilyn F. (2002). Kitchen Witchery: A Compendium of Oils, Unguents, Incense, Tinctures and Comestiles. San Francisco: Red Wheel/Weiser, Inc.

Dugan, Ellen (2003) Garden Witchery: Magick from the Ground Up. Minnesota: Llewellyn Publications.

Higginbotham, Joyce and River. (2009). Cristo-Paganism: An Inclusive Path. Minnesota: Llewellyn Publications.

Kemp, Gillian. (1999). The Good Spell Book. New York: Little, Brown and Company

Liao, Sabrina. (2000). Chinese Astrology: Ancient Secrets for Modern Life. New York: Warner Books, Inc.

Mother Goose. (1916) The Real Mother Goose. USA: Rand McNally & Co.

Pickering, David. (1996). Dictionary of Superstitions. London: Cassell

Roderick, Timothy. (1994). The Once Unknown Familiar. Minnesota: Llewellyn Publications

Stacy, Barbara; Theitic, Andrew; and Walsh, Jean Marie, editors. (2006). The Witches' Almanac. Rhode Island: The Witches' Almanac. Ltd.

Various Authors. (2007, 2009). Llewellyn's Magickal Almanac. Minnesota: Llewellyn Publications

Warring, Phillipa. (1978). A Dictionary of Omens and Superstitions. USA: Souvenir Press, Ltd.

Webster, Richard. (2002). Dowsing for Beginners. New Delhi (India): B. Jain Publishers.

Zell-Ravenheart, Oberon. (2004). Grimoire for the Apprentice Wizard. New Jersey: Career Press, Inc.

Web Sites

Advertising Mascots: People. (2009 November 30). In TvAvres.Com. Retrieved on November 30, 2009 from http://www.tvacres.com/admascots_mothernature.htm

American Indian Totem Poles. (2010 January 16). In Native Languages of the Americas. Retrieved January 16, 2010 from http://www.native-languages.org/totem.htm

Anderson, Deanna. The Role of the Augur in Ancient Rome. (2007 May 3). In Helium.Com. Retrieved on March 4 2010 from http://www.helium.com/items/365274-the-role-of-the-augur-in-ancient-rome

Atsma, Aaron J. Sky Gods (2009 November 30). In Theoi Greek Mythology. Retrieved on November 30, 2009 from http://www.theoi.com/greek-mythology/sky-gods.html

Aztec and Mayan Mythology. (2003 January 23). In Aztec and Mayan Mythology. Retrieved on November 30, 2009 from http://webpages.charter.net/sn9/religion/myth/aztecencyclopaedia.html

Bimini: The Road to Atlantis. (2010 January 1). In Subversive Element. Retrieved on January 13, 2010 from http://www.subversiveelement.com/biminiroad.html

Campfire Ashes. (2002 October 26). In BSA Troop 1393. Retrieved on December 11, 2009 from http://www.troop1393.com/campfire_ashes.html

Catholic Encyclopedia is maintained by Kevin Knight and is host to a variety of articles and definitions regarding all aspects of Catholicism. (http://www.newadvent.org/cathen/)

Celtic Mythology. (2003 January 23). In Celtic Mythology. Retrieved on November 30, 2009 from http://webpages.charter.net/sn9/religion/myth/celticencyclopaedia.html

Chinook Blessing. (2009 December 12). In High On Life1. Retrieved on December 12, 2009 from www.highonlife1.com/chinookblessing.htm

Chinook Nation. (2010 March 5). In Chinook Nation.org. Retrieved on March 5, 2010 from http://www.chinooknation.org/

Cline, Austin. Mictecacihuatl, Goddess of Death in Aztec Religion, Mythology. (2009 November 23). In Aztec Gods, Goddesses. Retrieved on November 23, 2009 from http://atheism.about.com/od/aztecgodsgoddesses/p/Mictecacihuatl.htm

Crystal, Ellie. Edgar Cayce: The Sleeping Prophet. (2010 February 17). In Crystalinks. Retrieved on February 17, 2010 from http://www.crystalinks.com/edgar_cayce.html

DragonFyre, Elswet. Dragon Spells (1995 August 3). In Elements of the Dragon. Retrieved on March 17th, 2010 from http://elswet.50megs.com/dragons/spells.html

Forlag, Maicar & Parada, Carlos. Scythia. (1997). In Greek Mythology Link. Retrieved on November 12, 2009 from http://homepage.mac.com/cparada/GML/Scythia.html

Gallagher, Phaedra. Dragon Magick. (2007 July 7). In Fox Moon. Retrieved on January 26, 2010 from http://www.fox-moon.com/dragon.html

Green, Araidne. Animal-Tribe Totem Pole (2009 December 3). In Animal Tribe. Retrieved on December 3rd, 2009 from http://www.

animaltribe.com/totem-pole.html.

Goibhniu. (2010). In Encyclopædia Britannica. Retrieved February 10, 2010 from http://www.britannica.com/EBchecked/topic/237171/Goibhniu

Hunt, J.M. The Titans. (2010 January 12). In Greek Mythology Gods. Retrieved on January 12, 2010 from http://edweb.sdsu.edu/people/bdodge/scaffold/GG/titan.html

Legend of the Sand Dollar. (2009 October 21). In Quality Shells. Retrieved on October 21, 2009 from http://www.qualityshells.com/legend-of-the-sand-dollar.html.

Lindemans, Micha F. Aegir. (1997 March 3). In Encyclopedia Mythica. Retrieved on November 10, 2009 from http://www.pantheon.org/articles/a/aegir.html

Lynxspirit. The Elements. (1999, January 1). In The Wiccan Garden. Retrieved on October 23, 2009 from http://www.angelfire.com/on/wicca/Elements.html.

Magick Sprite. Elemental Cauldrons. (2009 December 12). In The Inner Sanctum. Retrieved on December 12, 2009 from http://www.witchway.net/ritual/cauldron.html

Miller, Peter W. The Reality of Evil. (2002 November 27). In The Seattle Catholic: A Journal of Catholic News and Views. Retrieved on October 25, 2009 from http://www.seattlecatholic.com /article_20021127_The_Reality_of_Evil.html

Other Mythology. (2003 January 23). In Other Mythology. Retrieved on November 30, 2009 from http://webpages.charter.net/sn9/religion/myth/otherencyclopaedia.html

Rhymer, Eric. The Underworld. (2009 December 22) In Introduction to Greek Mythology. Retrieved on December 22, 2009 from http://historylink102.com/greece2/underworld.htm

Robber's Grave, The. (2007 August 8). In Mid-Wales Montogomery. Retrieved on December 11, 2009 from http://www.bbc.co.uk/wales/mid/sites/montgomery/pages/robbers_grave.shtml

Robinson, J.Dennis. The Lucky Horseshoe. (2004) In Poems and Ballads. Retrieved on 2009 September 12 from http://seacoastnh.com/poems/theluckyhorseshoe.html

Seawright, Caroline. Shu, Holder of the Sky, God of the Air, Wind, Sunlight and Protection. (2009 January 12). In Tour Egypt, Retrieved on January 12, 2009 from http://www.touregypt.net/featurestories/shu.htm

Sedna, Inuit Goddess of the Deep Sea. (2009 October 13). In Goddess Gift. Retrieved on October 13, 2009 from http://www.goddessgift.com/goddess-myths/inuit-goddess-Sedna.htm

Schumacher, Mark. Four Guardians of the Four Compass Directions. (2009 December 15). In Japanese Buddhist Statuary. Retrieved on December 15, 2009 from http://www.onmarkproductions.com/html/ssu-ling.shtml

Schwartz, Stephanie M. Miracle, the Sacred White Buffalo. (2009 March 31). In White Buffalo Miracle. Retrieved on November 25, 2009 from http://whitebuffalomiracle.homestead.com

Superstition Bash: Horseshoes (2009 October 25). In CSI: The Committee for Skeptical Inquiry. Retrieved on October 25, 2009 from http://www.csicop.org/superstition/library/horseshoes/.

Supreme Invoking Ritual of the Pentagram. (2009 October 23) In Living with Magick. Retrieved on October 23, 2009 from http://www.livingwithmagick.com/magick/sirp.php

Titans, The. (2010 January 12). In Greek Mythology.Com. Retrieved on January 12, 2010 from http://www.greekmythology.com/Titans/titans.html.

Tooth Fairy. (2010 March 4). In Tooth Fairy.Org. Retrieved on March 4, 2010 from http://www.toothfairy.org

Turretin, Dr. Francis. Creationism or Traducianism? (2010 January 19). In A Puritan's Mind. Retrieved on January 19, 2010 from http://www.apuritansmind.com/FrancisTurretin/ francisturretincrerationismtraducianism.htm

Unicorns. (2009 January 21). In Elemental Beings. Retrieved on January 21, 2009 from http://www.elementalbeings.co.uk/unicorns/

Vedder-Shults, Nancy Ph.D. Egg Divinations. (2009 November 28). In Matrifocus: Cross-Quarterly for the Goddess Woman. Retrieved on November 28, 2009 from http://www.matrifocus.com/BEL07/divination.htm

Waterman, Lynn. The Age of Fire. (2009 October 9). In Great Moments in Science. Retrieved on October 9, 2009 from http://www.usgennet.org/usa/topic/preservation/science/moments/ chpt1.htm

What is the Tarot? (2009 December 17). In Weejee's Magick. Retrieved on December 17, 2009 from http://www.wejees.net/whatistarot.html

White Buffalo Woman. (2009 December 17). In Native American, The White Buffalo. Retrieved on December 17, 2009 from http://www.merceronline.com/Native/native05.htm

Wikipedia a free encyclopedia that is host to a wide variety of articles that are written by anonymous authors. Various articles were used for reference in this book. (http://www.wikipedia.org/)

Yrondwode, Catherine. Graveyard Dirt. (2009 October 9). In Lucky Mojo.Com. Retreived on October 9, 2009 from http://www.luckymojo.com/graveyarddirt.html

Zaratyst. Elements of Magic, The. (2003 July 30). In The Cave of the Word Witch. Retrieved on February 3, 2008 from http://wuzzle.org/cave/elmagick.html

Zulu Superstitions. (2009 December 17). In Zulu Culture. Retrieved on December 17, 2009 from http://www.zulu-culture.co.za/superstitions_zulu_culture.php

LaVergne, TN USA
24 September 2010
198359LV00007B/1/P